Differentiating for Success

How to Build Literacy Instruction for All Students

By Nancy Witherell and Mary C. McMackin

MAUPIN HOUSE BY
CAPSTONE PROFESSIONAL
a capstone imprint

Differentiating for Success: How to Build Literacy Instruction for All Students
By Nancy Witherell and Mary C. McMackin

Cover Design: Richard Parker
Book Design: Peggie Carley

Library of Congress Cataloging-in-Publication Data
Names: Witherell, Nancy L., author. | McMackin, Mary C., author.
Title: Differentiating for success : how to build literacy instruction for
  all students / by Nancy L. Witherell and Mary C. McMackin.
Description: North Mankato, Minnesota : Capstone Professional, an imprint of
  Capstone Press, [2017] | Series: Capstone professional. Maupin House |
  Includes bibliographical references and index.
Identifiers: LCCN 2016008952 | ISBN 9781496606532 (pbk.) | ISBN
9781496606549 (ebook pdf)
Subjects: LCSH: Reading (Elementary) | Reading comprehension—Study
and teaching (Elementary)
Classification: LCC LB1573.7 .W57 2017 | DDC 372.4—dc23
LC record available at https://lccn.loc.gov/2016008952

Image Credits: Capstone Press: 14; Library of Congress: Created
by Education Team/URL (http://www.loc.gov/teachers/
usingprimarysources/guides.html), 13; Shutterstock: locrifa, Cover, Design
Element, PavelShynkarou, Design Element

Capstone Professional publishes professional resources for K-12 educators.
Contact us for tailored, in-school training or to schedule an author for a
workshop or conference. Visit www.capstonepd.com for free lesson plan
downloads.

This book includes websites that were operational at the time
this book went to press.

Maupin House Publishing, Inc. by Capstone Professional
1710 Roe Crest Drive
North Mankato, MN 56003
www.capstonepd.com
888-262-6135
info@capstonepd.com

Dedication

For Peter,
with me from the beginning…
Love always,
NW

To Declan, with love
MCM

Table of Contents

Introduction

Is differentiated instruction simply high-quality teaching? In an interview with reporters from the *North American Journal of Psychology* (Wells & Shaughnessy, 2009), Carol Ann Tomlinson, world-renowned expert on differentiated instruction, concluded by saying, "It's hard to make a case that you wouldn't want teachers to have clear learning outcomes, know where kids are in regard to those outcomes, and adjust the ways they teach and the ways kids can learn when they see the kids need something else to flourish. That's what we're talking about with differentiation. It's not an extra; it's just high-quality teaching" (p. 648). We agree. This thought was the catalyst for writing this book. It is a book containing differentiated lessons designed to meet the needs of all students: students who need a great deal of support, students who need minimal support, and students who need to be challenged.

It is with joy that we welcome you to our book, *Differentiating for Success: How to Build Literacy Instruction for All Students*. As alluded to earlier, we know that teachers are expected to provide support within their high-quality instruction so students can perform at their optimum level. We also know this is no easy task. The Common Core State Standards (2010) explain that scaffolding is often necessary and advisable. Yet, we must remember that the goal is to gradually diminish the amount of scaffolding students need and increase independence (National Governors Association Center for Best Practices & Council of Chief State School Officers, 2010, Appendix A, p. 9). This book offers the tools to help you make that happen.

Our work on differentiation in the classroom stems from our wish to meet the needs of all students. We all know that struggling readers need help, solid readers need challenge, and advanced students need a chance to learn at a more complex level. So the questions are: How do we make this possible? How do we make it realistic? Sustainable? How do we ensure that our students are actually thinking as they accomplish their work? As we visit and work in classrooms, we notice all kinds of wonderful differentiation taking place. Many times it is with other educators in the classroom. But what if there's nobody else to help? The lessons we offer here simplify differentiating instructional activities for your class and foster your students' thinking whether you are teaching solo or are lucky enough to have classroom help. We guide you through directed lessons and help you with the tools and materials needed to more easily differentiate content (skills and concepts), process (activities), and product (how students demonstrate understanding) (Tomlinson & Allan, 2000).

We begin with the reading skills that are evident throughout the CCSS. We unpack these skills, revealing exactly what readers of fiction and nonfiction in grades three through five need to be able to do to construct meaning from written texts. We offer you easy-to-follow lessons that you can adjust to your own students. These lessons stem from one objective that can be met at three different learning levels. In the lessons, we first base our discussion on what the literature has to say about each skill. We also give a brief explanation of how each skill increases as it is followed through the three grades. We then provide two easy-to-follow sample lessons; in most chapters, we offer a model lesson on narrative and informational texts. All lessons give you the choice of using the material we highlight or a similar type of text that you may have in your own resource collection. We offer two sets of three tiered, differentiated follow-up activities that align with the teacher modeling and guided practice instruction. In the follow-up activities, all students will be working on the same skill (e.g., identifying a theme or central idea) that was the focus of the sample lesson, but they will be reinforcing the skill by engaging in a follow-up activity that is "just right" for them on that particular day. Finally, in addition to the mentor texts we use in each lesson, we recommend at least three additional texts for each model lesson. These texts can be used to reinforce the targeted skill.

It is important to note that in our work with tiered instruction, we have found that a built-in assessment system is contained within the tiers. Teachers have told us that struggling students, with scaffolding, soon become successful with the lowest tier. Then teachers automatically take the next step with these students and begin to process the next level of instruction with these readers. A natural progression of assessment guiding instruction ensues, along with a decrease in scaffolding.

To summarize, each chapter contains:

- an explanation of the skill to be taught;
- a review of literature about the skill;
- an explanation of the complexity of the skill as explained in the CCSS;
- two lessons (narration and informational) that follow the Gradual Release of Responsibility Model: one lesson that provides explicit modeling from the teacher and a lesson for guided practice on the same skill;
- student application at three levels (Initial, Transitional, and Accomplished) for differentiation to help you meet the needs of all of your students; and
- additional recommended books for use with your students.

In some cases, we have selected picture books that your students may have seen in an earlier grade. These books clearly model the skill or strategy in the targeted lesson, contain universal concepts, and take only a few minutes to read. However, when matching up students to the appropriate level for the follow-up lesson, it will be important to consider which level will provide students with the most success. This may be fluid from lesson to lesson and will be based on your own observations.

The following section gives a short overview of each chapter's content. The chapters are not expected to be followed in order but to be chosen by the needs of your students and your school's curriculum, although we do recommend that you teach students theme **(Chapter 9: Identifying Themes)** prior to tackling comparing and contrasting two themes **(Chapter 10: Comparing and Contrasting Themes or Topics in Two Texts).** In addition, the websites offered in this book were available when it went to press. We can only hope they are still available for your use.

How the Book Is Organized

In **Chapter 1: Primary Source Photographs: Analyzing Visuals,** we turn our attention first to primary source photographs and help students analyze them. Then we explore how primary and secondary sources work in tandem to enhance comprehension and content knowledge.

In **Chapter 2: Investigating Texts and Visual Representations,** we look closely at visuals, explore the author's purpose in using them, and consider what we can learn from them. Next, we send students on a scavenger hunt to find and analyze photographs/illustrations. In our second lesson, we examine the jobs captions serve (summaries, examples or explanations, or unique new details).

In **Chapter 3: Working with Abstract Words and Derivatives,** we focus on abstract words as opposed to concrete words. Abstract words are words that represent something that cannot be touched or seen visibly, like the word *perseverance*. In addition, we introduce the concepts of root words and affixes and their role in aiding students to determine meaning from context.

In **Chapter 4: Comprehending Appositives and Relative Clauses,** we look at comprehension at the sentence level. Scott (2009) reports that sentence-level comprehension may be a major stumbling block for children and adolescents who struggle to comprehend texts; yet, instruction at the sentence level is an often-overlooked consideration for improving comprehension (p. 184).

In **Chapter 5: Distinguishing Main Ideas and Details**, we explain that the main idea can be stated explicitly or can be implicit. Then we get students to think of what the important ideas are in the text and what the author uses to support those ideas.

In **Chapter 6: Supporting Story Elements with Details,** we stretch students to think beyond the story map and to focus on supporting details from the text that tell about the element. We also challenge students to make inferences that stem from the stated evidence.

In **Chapter 7: Making Inferences**, we invite students to think beyond the literal and use both evidence from the text and their own knowledge to grasp deeper meanings. For the narrative text, we have students infer by first identifying characters' actions or thoughts and determining what these actions or thoughts tell us about the character. For informational texts, we investigate inferences at the sentence level, the multiple-sentence level, and at the multiple-page level.

In **Chapter 8: Summarizing,** we use trickster tales to introduce the concept of summarization. We also teach students how to identify Very Important Points (VIPs) (Bluestein, 2010), pull out or restate main ideas, and eliminate extra or repeated words to create effective summaries.

In **Chapter 9: Identifying Themes**, we begin to help students think abstractly about messages they can infer from texts (narrative and informational) and apply them to their own lives.

In **Chapter 10: Comparing and Contrasting Themes or Topics in Two Texts,** we ask students to investigate how a theme or topic is discussed when it appears in two different texts. We have students examine the interactions of characters, study what happened in the text, and determine the theme of each text prior to comparing and contrasting the messages given by the authors.

In **Chapter 11: Determining Point of View,** we help students reading narratives see how characters view their situations and, when reading informational texts, consider an author's purpose and beliefs.

In **Chapter 12: Getting Started with Arguments: Claims, Reasons, and Evidence,** we bolster students' skills in finding evidence to support a claim. Using our own Valuemeter, students rate the evidence they find and justify their ratings. In our second lesson, we shift focus slightly and investigate whether or not authors include enough evidence to support their claims.

In **Chapter 13: Examining Text Structure: Sequence**, we use text structure as a vehicle to improve comprehension. We have students work with the order of story events as they think logically about the sequence of these events.

In **Chapter 14: Demystifying Cause and Effect,** we investigate the causal relationships within a text and explore the continuum of these relationships within a text. The cause is defined as *the action that causes something else to happen* and the effect is *the result*. We use arrows and boxes to give a visual representation of these relationships.

In **Chapter 15: Reading Within and Across Texts,** we first delve into the narrative subgenre of mystery, identifying its elements and how writers integrate them to create engaging cases for readers to solve. For informational texts, we focus on how students integrate ideas from two texts on the same topic.

In **Chapter 16: Understanding Structural Elements of Drama,** we introduce basic components of dramas (e.g., setting, cast of characters, scenes, and stage directions) and then investigate how scenes are written so they move the story line forward.

Chapter 1

Primary Source Photographs: Analyzing Visuals

What Are Primary Sources?

A primary source, according to the Smithsonian National Museum of American History (n.d.), is "[A] firsthand, original account, record, or evidence about a person, place, object, or an event. Oral histories, objects, photographs, and documents such as newspapers, ledgers, census records, diaries, journals, and inventories are primary sources" (p. 5). The Library of Congress (n.d.) makes the following distinction between primary and secondary sources, noting that "primary sources are the raw materials of history—original documents and objects which were created at the time under study. They are different from secondary sources, accounts or interpretations of events created by someone without firsthand experience."

What Does the Literature Say?

Teachers have increasingly integrated primary source documents into instruction over the past several years. The *Reading Framework for the 2009 National Assessment of Educational Progress* (NAEP) (National Assessment Governing Board, 2008) demonstrated a shift in student reading materials from a heavy focus of reading literary (fiction) texts to a greater emphasis on reading informational texts. NAEP reading passages are distributed in the following way: 50 percent literary and 50 percent informational in grade four; 45 percent literary and 55 percent informational in grade eight; and 30 percent literary and 70 percent informational in grade 12. The Common Core State Standards currently use the same guidelines for text distribution as NAEP included in its 2009 *Reading Framework*.

Primary source documents provide us with insights into the lives and times of people who came before us. The use of primary source materials can evoke "aesthetic and emotional responses" (Morgan & Rasinski, 2014, p. 585) and may enhance critical thinking skills, especially when multiple perspectives are presented and a historical context accompanies the documents (Caskey, 2007).

In order for students to develop what Nelson (1994) defines as *historical literacy*—"the ability to understand and interpret the stories of the past" (p. 552)—they need to look closely at details. The Smithsonian (n.d.) emphasizes the need for researchers and students to look beyond the obvious, to detect biases and to consider alternative intentions for primary source materials, and photographs in particular. *Engaging Students with Primary Sources* (n.d.), an online resource from the Smithsonian National Museum of American History, points out, "Photographers have the ability to manipulate, intentionally or unintentionally, the record of the event. It is the photographer—and the camera's frame—that defines the picture's content. Thus, the photographer chooses what will be in the picture, what will be left out, and what the emphasis will be" (p. 24). When teachers begin to help students think critically about primary source materials, they can introduce an array of higher-order thinking skills that cut across genres and disciplines. Bates (2014–2015) suggests, for instance, that a photograph might contain "an argument or thesis ..., a point of view or bias ...." (p. 35). Looking at a photograph may seem like a simple task, but students can learn a great deal about history and themselves when they are guided to analyze what a photograph shows; who the intended audience is; what the author's purpose, possible antecedents, and consequences of the event depicted in the image are; and what they learned by examining the photograph.

In addition, Fertig (2005) reports that elementary students seldom make causal connections when studying historical events. When they do think about antecedents and consequences that "establish cause and effect relationships, they tend to attribute a single cause to an event rather than multiple causes acting in combination ...." (p. 5). The study of primary source and secondary materials can underscore that events in history don't occur in isolation.

Morgan and Rasinski (2012) encourage teachers to incorporate primary source materials into their instruction, noting, "The past we explore with our students is not about neutral events; rather it is about people living in a particular time with particular issues and challenges. By including more primary sources in classroom instruction, students have the opportunity to connect on both a factual and emotional level with people and events in our history" (p. 594).

Increasing Complexity through the Grades

In this chapter, we integrate several of the Common Core State Standards when using primary sources, particularly photographs. For instance, we explore details and main ideas when we analyze what photos show and tell. We address point of view when we consider a photo's purpose and possible biases, and we investigate how illustrations and texts help readers comprehend an author's intended message.

At grade three, students are expected "to use information gained from illustrations (e.g., maps, photographs) and the words in a text to demonstrate understanding of the text" (CCSS.ELA.RI.3.7). At this level, students may need specific guiding questions to analyze photographs and to grapple with what they see and what it means.

At grade four, students build on what they learned in third grade. Fourth graders are expected to "interpret information presented visually, orally, or quantitatively (e.g., in charts, graphs, diagrams, timelines, animations, or interactive elements on web pages) and explain how the information contributes to an understanding of the text in which it appears" (CCSS.ELA.RI.4.7). At this level, students may still need specific guiding questions to analyze photographs and to grapple with the information they see and read.

At grade five, students are expected to "draw on information from multiple print or digital sources, demonstrating the ability to locate an answer to a question quickly or to solve a problem efficiently" (CCSS.ELA.RI.5.7). At this level, students learn how to use multiple resources to gather and interpret information.

Model Lesson 1: Analyzing Primary Source Photographs

In this lesson, we use the *Primary Source Analysis Tool* from the Library of Congress. We supply a hard copy of the tool (Figure 1-1 on p. 13), but we encourage teachers to make use of the free online version available by searching for "primary source analysis" on the Library of Congress website. This version allows students to print, save, and share their work electronically.

Lesson Objective:
Students will be able to analytically observe, reflect upon, and pose questions about a primary source photograph.

Teacher Modeling
Have the following two sentences available for students to read.

> *"As people live their lives, they leave a trail of items they create or use as they go about their days that represents who they are and what they did. They leave evidence"*
> *(Morgan & Rasinski, p. 584).*

Talk about the kind of "evidence" we might leave that represents who you and your students are and what life is like today. Guide students to think about different types of sources: photos and videos, newspapers and magazines, video games, fast food wrappers, DVDs of TV shows and movies, song lyrics, etc. What would they show or tell about us? Why is it important for people who live in the future to know about how we live, how we communicate, how we travel, what we read and eat, and so on? Explain that historians call this type of firsthand evidence primary sources. Jot down this term on a whiteboard, along with a definition for primary sources and secondary sources. (Use the definitions found at the beginning of this chapter or your own.)

Share some primary source materials from books, magazines, and websites that show what life was like in the past, and share what you know about the materials. Introduce *Ernest Shackleton: Antarctic Explorer* (Dowdeswell, Dowdeswell & Seddon, 2015) or a text of your choosing that contains firsthand photos, and explain that you chose this book to read because it contains many primary source photos. If reading *Ernest Shackleton: Antarctic Explorer,* read the text aloud through page 8, stopping periodically to discuss the text and the photos. This reading should be for enjoyment and so students can get the gist. Setting a rich context for the photos will enable you and your students to interpret the images more fully, so it's important to take time to set the stage.

Display a copy of the Library of Congress *Primary Source Analysis Tool* and a list of the prompts that accompany the tool (Figure 1-1 on p. 13), or use the interactive tool available by searching for "primary sources" on the Library of Congress website. Next, if you are using *Ernest Shackleton: Antarctic Explorer,* display page 8 of the book and page 14 here (Figure 1-2 on p. 14). Think aloud as you ask and answer the questions that appear across the top of Figure 1-1. Use only the questions that are relevant to your photograph. In this model lesson, we use the following questions: Observe: Describe what you see. What do you notice first? What objects are shown? What is the physical setting? Reflect: Why do you think this image was made? Who do you think was the audience for this image? What can you learn by examining it? Questions: What do you wonder about who, what, when, where, why, how?

Record your summary notes. Your Shackleton Photo Analysis chart might look like this:

Shackleton Photo Analysis		
Observe	**Reflect**	**Question**
I observed one man, a team of dogs on a rope, a large wooden sailboat but no sails, a boat on snow-covered land or ice (not in water), and a man dressed in warm clothes. There are other people in the background and perhaps someone taking the photograph.	I think the image was made so the explorers could record what it was like trying to sail to Antarctica. Perhaps the photographer wanted to prove they were near the South Pole.	I wonder (1) what supplies they had and how long the supplies were expected to last, (2) how many people were on the ship, (3) how they got the boat out of the ice, and (4) who they shared the photos with when they returned to Britain.

Think aloud as you display and model your answers for the following open-ended questions: (1) Imagine you were with Shackleton and his team when this photo was taken. What do you think the men were doing shortly after it was taken? Why? (2) Look at the photo again. What do you think the photographer is trying to emphasize (stress, highlight, or call attention to) in this photo? Explain.

After you analyze the photo on page 8, continue to read aloud the remainder of the book so students understand the complete story.

Guided Practice

Display a blank copy of the *Primary Source Analysis Tool* (Figure 1-1 on p. 13) or use the digital version and select a second primary source photo to analyze with your students. Elicit student responses this time as you use the appropriate prompt questions to analyze the primary source photograph. Jot down summary notes on the graphic organizer. Before concluding this part of the lesson, ask students the two open-ended questions you asked above and have them engage in a conversation.

Student Application: Tiered Activities for Differentiation

Each student should receive a copy of the *Primary Source Analysis Tool* (Figure 1-1 on p. 13) (or have access to the online version) and a primary source photograph to analyze. Provide a context for the photo and then select and display appropriate prompt questions. In addition, display the following open-ended questions: (1) Imagine you were with the photographer when this photo was taken. What do you think happened shortly after it was taken? Why? (2) Look at the photo again. What do you think the photographer is trying to emphasize (stress, highlight, or call attention to) in this photo? Explain.

Initial Level

Students at this level analyze the photo, answer the preselected prompt questions, and jot down their responses in the "Observe," "Reflect," and "Question" boxes.

Teacher action: Select an appropriate photo for students to analyze, set a context for the photo, select appropriate prompt questions, and distribute the *Primary Source Analysis Tool* (Figure 1-1 on p. 13) or make available the electronic version of the tool.

Figure 1-1: Primary Source Analysis Tool (Library of Congress)

TEACHER'S GUIDE
ANALYZING PHOTOGRAPHS & PRINTS

Guide students with the sample questions as they respond to the primary source. Encourage them to go back and forth between the columns; there is no correct order.

OBSERVE

Ask students to identify and note details.

Sample Questions:

Describe what you see. • What do you notice first? • What people and objects are shown? • How are they arranged? • What is the physical setting? • What, if any, words do you see? • What other details can you see?

REFLECT

Encourage students to generate and test hypotheses about the source.

Why do you think this image was made? • What's happening in the image? • When do you think it was made? • Who do you think was the audience for this image? • What tools were used to create this?• What can you learn from examining this image? • If someone made this today, what would be different? • What would be the same?

QUESTION

Invite students to ask questions that lead to more observations and reflections.

What do you wonder about...

who? • what? • when? • where? • why? • how?

FURTHER INVESTIGATION

Help students to identify questions appropriate for further investigation, and to develop a research strategy for finding answers.

Sample Question: What more do you want to know, and how can you find out?

A few follow-up activity ideas:

Beginning
Write a caption for the image.

Intermediate
Select an image. Predict what will happen one minute after the scene shown in the image. One hour after? Explain the reasoning behind your predictions.

Advanced
Have students expand or alter textbook or other printed explanations of history based on images they study.

For more tips on using primary sources, go to

http://www.loc.gov.teachers

Figure 1-2: Shackleton's First Trip to Antarctica

Shackleton's first trip to Antarctica

In 1901, Shackleton joined Captain Robert Falcon Scott on the ship *Discovery*. Scott was another famous polar explorer. They wanted to be the first people in the world to reach the **South Pole**, near the middle of **Antarctica**.

Discovery carried the men, dogs and supplies needed to live in Antarctica.

8

Transitional Level

Students at this level analyze the photo, answer the preselected prompt questions, and jot down their responses for "Observe," "Reflect," and "Question." In addition, students select one of the following two open-ended questions to answer on the back of their graphic organizer and provide support for their responses: (1) Imagine you were with the photographer when this photo was taken. What do you think happened shortly after it was taken? Why? (2) Look at the photo again. What do you think the photographer is trying to emphasize (stress, highlight, or call attention to) in this photo? Explain.

Teacher action: Select an appropriate photo for students to analyze, set a context for the photo, select appropriate prompt questions, provide access to the *Primary Source Analysis Tool* (Figure 1-1 on p. 13) or the online version, and make available the open-ended questions students will answer.

Accomplished Level

Students at this level analyze the photo, answer the preselected prompt questions, and jot down their responses in the "Observe," "Reflect," and "Question" boxes of the *Primary Source Analysis Tool*. In addition, students at this level answer the following questions and provide support for their responses: (1) Imagine you were with the photographer when this photo was taken. What do you think happened shortly after it was taken? Why? (2) Look at the photo again. What do you think the photographer is trying to emphasize (stress, highlight, or call attention to) in this photo? Explain.

Teacher action: Select an appropriate photo for students to analyze, set a context for the photo, select appropriate prompt questions, provide access to the *Primary Source Analysis Tool* (Figure 1-1 on p. 13) or the online version, and make available the open-ended questions students will answer.

Additional Recommended Books

When selecting books, we suggest you check the authenticity of the photographs. Some informational books contain images from providers of stock photos rather than primary source photos from historic societies, libraries, private collections, etc. Photo credits are often found in the front or back of informational books.

Fitzgerald, S. (2014). *A Civil War timeline.* War Timelines. North Mankato, MN: Capstone.

Mara, W. (2002). *Amelia Earhart.* Rookie Biographies. New York: Children's Press.

Rhatigan, J. (2012). *White House kids: The perks, pleasures, problems, and pratfalls of the presidents' children.* Watertown, MA: Charlesbridge Publishing.

Urbigkit, C. (2005). *Brave dogs, gentle dogs: How they guard sheep.* Honesdale, PA: Boyds Mills Press.

Model Lesson 2: Combining Primary Source Photographs and Secondary Sources

Every text is written for a particular purpose. Authors write to inform, instruct, persuade, or entertain. In order to achieve their purposes for writing, authors of informational texts often include both art (e.g., photographs, illustrations, diagrams, charts) and written words. In this lesson, we investigate how authors present information by integrating photographs and texts.

Lesson Objective:
Students will be able to use the primary source photographs and a secondary source to comprehend a text and learn more about a topic.

Teacher Modeling

Reread *Ernest Shackleton: Antarctic Explorer* or a book of your choosing. During this second reading, help students dig deeply into the text to discover new understandings and to enhance comprehension. You may want to think aloud as you ask and answer the following questions: How did the authors describe Shackleton? What challenges did Shackleton face? Why did Shackleton risk his life to achieve his goal? What motivated him to do this? Explain that the authors' purpose is to inform and that their point of view is reflected in the first sentence: "Ernest Shackleton was one of the greatest British polar explorers that ever lived" (p. 4). Point out the cause-effect relationship between Shackleton's individual actions and outcomes. Talk about how all the actions combined to create this historically significant story. Finally, talk about primary source materials (photos that were taken by someone on Ernest Shackleton's expeditions) vs. information from the text (a secondary source that presents the authors' interpretation of historical events).

Next, display a blank copy of the *PAWS* graphic organizer (Figure 1-3 on p. 18). In this lesson, PAWS is an acronym for:

P = Purpose and Point of view (What was the author's purpose for writing this text and what is the author's point of view?)

A = Art [What did you learn from the art (the photographs)?]

W = Writing (What did you learn from what was written?)

S = Story (What did you learn from this story? Why is it an important piece of history?)

Think aloud as you model how you would fill in each section using information from the secondary source (text) and primary sources (photos). Show how you support your thinking with evidence as you record notes on the graphic organizer. Your completed organizer may look something like Figure 1-4 on page 19.

Guided Practice

Use a second text so students can draw on information from two different sources. If you used *Ernest Shackleton: Antarctic Explorer* as your primary text, you may want to use *Escape from the Ice* (Roop & Roop, 2001). Primary source photos appear on pp. 4, 8, 16, 24, 30, 36, 42, and 46 of this book for second and third graders.

Have four pieces of chart paper. Post one at each of the four corners of your classroom (or spread them out along a hallway) so students can engage in a carousel brainstorming activity. Write "Purpose and Point of View" on one piece of paper, "Art" (photograph) on the second, "Writing" on the third, and "Story" on the fourth. Divide your students into four groups. Send one group and one of four different colored markers to each chart. When everyone is in place, students should brainstorm as many ideas as possible for their chart and jot them down on the paper. After a few minutes, signal students to move to the chart on their right. They should take their marker with them so you'll be able to see which group contributed which ideas to each chart. Repeat this process two more times so everyone has an opportunity to contribute to every chart. As students brainstorm, walk around, providing guidance and assessing students' understandings so you'll be able to match them with the appropriate leveled follow-up activity. Finally, take a few minutes to debrief with students. Ask a few students to answer the following question: Which part of the PAWS provided you with the most interesting (or important) information? Explain.

Student Application: Tiered Activities for Differentiation

In this lesson, we differentiate the environment in which students complete the *PAWS* graphic organizer. Students who work with you are more supported than students who are working with a partner or working independently.

Initial Level

Provide students with a text that contains primary source photographs. The text should be at their instructional reading level. Introduce the text and then have students work with you to complete the *PAWS* graphic organizer (Figure 1-3 on p. 18). You may want to serve as the scribe. As students provide information, have them show you where they found the evidence to support their responses.

Teacher action: Select a text that contains primary source photos. The text should be written at the students' instructional reading level. Provide students with copies of the text and the *PAWS* graphic organizer (Figure 1-3).

Transitional Level

Provide students with a text that contains primary source photographs. The text should be at their instructional reading level. Introduce the text and then have students work with a partner to complete the *PAWS* graphic organizer (Figure 1-3 on p. 18). Students should jot down page numbers to indicate where they found evidence to support the notes they recorded.

Teacher action: Select a text that contains primary source photos. The text should be written at the students' instructional reading level. Provide students with copies of the text and the *PAWS* graphic organizer (Figure 1-3).

Accomplished Level

Provide students with a text that contains primary source photographs. The text should be at their instructional reading level. Introduce the text and then have students work independently to complete the *PAWS* graphic organizer (Figure 1-3 on p. 18). Students should include page numbers to indicate where they found evidence for their thinking.

Teacher action: Select a text that contains primary source photos. The text should be written at the students' instructional reading level. Provide students with copies of the text and the *PAWS* graphic organizer (Figure 1-3).

Figure 1-3: PAWS

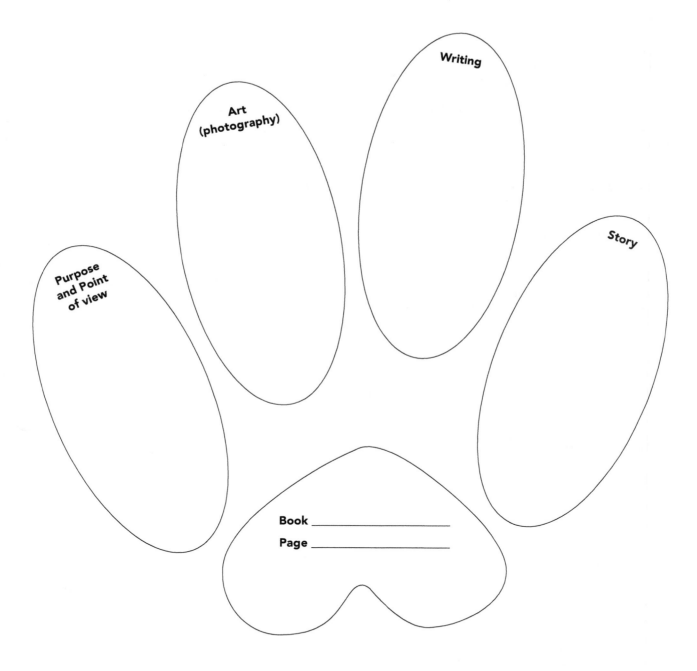

Writing

Art
(photography)

Story

Purpose
and Point
of view

Book _____

Page _____

Figure 1-4: PAWS for *Ernest Shackleton: Antarctic Explorer*

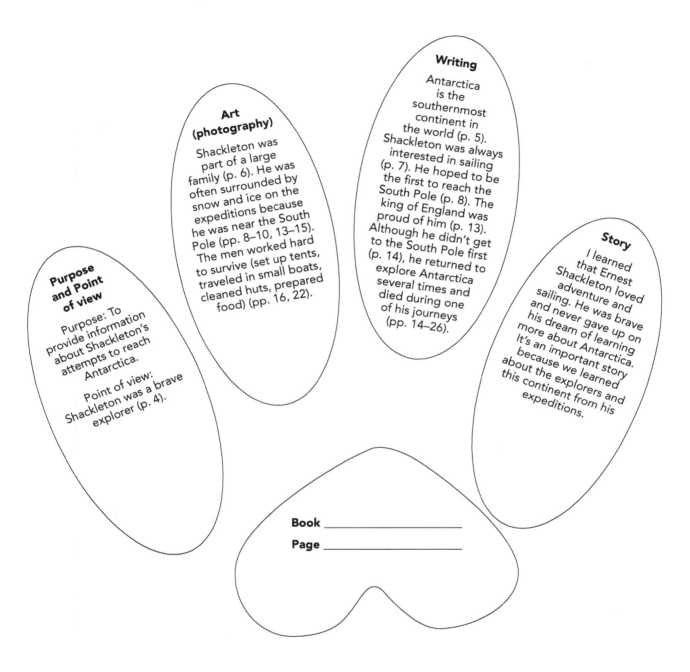

Art (photography)

Shackleton was part of a large family (p. 6). He was often surrounded by snow and ice on the expeditions because he was near the South Pole (pp. 8–10, 13–15). The men worked hard to survive (set up tents, traveled in small boats, cleaned huts, prepared food) (pp. 16, 22).

Writing

Antarctica is the southernmost continent in the world (p. 5). Shackleton was always interested in sailing (p. 7). He hoped to be the first to reach the South Pole (p. 8). The king of England was proud of him (p. 13). Although he didn't get to the South Pole first (p. 14), he returned to explore Antarctica several times and died during one of his journeys (pp. 14–26).

Story

I learned that Ernest Shackleton loved adventure and sailing. He was brave and never gave up on his dream of learning more about Antarctica. It's an important story because we learned about the explorers and this continent from his expeditions.

Purpose and Point of view

Purpose: To provide information about Shackleton's attempts to reach Antarctica.

Point of view: Shackleton was a brave explorer (p. 4).

Book _____

Page _____

Additional Recommended Books

When selecting books, we suggest you check the authenticity of the photographs. Some informational books contain images from providers of stock photos rather than primary source photos from historic societies, libraries, private collections, etc. Photo credits are often found in the front or back of informational books.

Powling, C. (1997). *Roald Dahl.* Tell Me About. Minneapolis, MN: Carolrhoda Books.

Venezia, M. (2006). *Grover Cleveland: twenty-second and twenty-fourth president, 1885–1889, 1893–1897.* Getting to Know the U.S. Presidents. New York: Scholastic.

Article: Carty, D. (2000). Cold sweat. *Boys' Life, 90(*10), 6.

Chapter 2

Investigating Texts and Visual Representations

What Are Texts and Visual Representations?

Most people would define a *text* as a written or printed work and a *visual representation* as a nonlinguistic image, such as a photograph, illustration, diagram, graph, flowchart, and map.

What Does the Literature Say?

Many of today's nonfiction texts include a range of visual representations. Moline (cited in Coleman, Bradley, and Donovan, 2012) makes a distinction between pictorial information and graphical information, which includes diagrams, maps, graphs, tables, and timelines. In this chapter, we look at pictorial and graphic information as well as what we refer to as ancillary texts that may appear as text boxes to support the main text. These may include sidebars, vocabulary words, fun facts, and so forth.

Pictorial and graphical information allows writers to visually represent ideas they write about in a text, compare and contrast ideas, and explain a sequence or process (Coleman, et al, 2012). They also help writers condense information, "distill and display complex relational information" (Moore-Russo & Shanahan, 2014, p. 529), present unique information that is not included in the text, and help organize content (e.g., flowchart) (McTigue & Flowers, 2011). Moore-Russo and Shanahan (2014) say, "color, placement of text and images, inclusion of illustrations, and font selection and size are all clues that readers can and should use to help make meaning of visual representations" (p. 528).

Since technology now allows publishers to infuse science textbooks and trade books with a broad array of visual information, students need to learn how to read, write, and interpret this diverse visual information (Coleman, et al, 2012). According to Yeh and McTigue (cited in McTigue & Flowers, 2011), "In an analysis of U.S. state science tests from grades 4–8, more than half of the questions included graphical representations, and 80 percent of those graphics contained essential information" (p. 579). It's reported that teachers commonly point out pictorial and graphic information in texts (Coleman, et al, 2012). A more effective practice, however, would be for teachers to model how they interpret the information provided in the visuals (McTigue & Flowers, 2011). McTigue and Flowers (2011), in their study with 30 children—10 each in grades two, four, and sixth through eighth—found, among other things:

1. Students lacked the vocabulary to name the features used in diagrams (e.g., text boxes, captions);
2. Students demonstrated a limited understanding of why illustrations were included in texts, stating that illustrations were used primarily to explain what's in the text;
3. Students seldom looked at the graphics in texts; and
4. Students used very few comprehension strategies while reading diagrams (p. 584).

Increasing Complexity through the Grades

Recognizing and accurately interpreting information from visual and quantitative sources is specifically addressed in Anchor Standard 7 of the Common Core State Standards for Reading, which states that students should be able to "integrate and evaluate content presented in diverse media and formats, including visually and quantitatively, as well as in words" (CCSS.CCRA.R.7).

Look how closely Reading Anchor Standard 7 mirrors Anchor Standard 2 of the Speaking and Listening strand, which says that students should be able to "integrate and evaluate information presented in diverse media and formats, including visually, quantitatively, and orally" (CCSS.CCRA.SL.2). The major difference comes at the end of each standard, with the reading standard focusing on written words and the speaking and listening standard focusing on oral language.

At grade three, students are expected to know how to "use information gained from illustrations (e.g., maps, photographs) and the words in a text to demonstrate understanding of the text (e.g., where, when, why, and how key events occur)" (CCSS.RI.3.7). This standard builds on second-grade expectations in which students should be able to "explain how specific images (e.g., a diagram showing how a machine works) contribute to and clarify a text" (CCSS.RI.2.7). In order to be successful, students need be taught explicitly how to gain knowledge from visuals. As Coleman, et al (2012) noted, pointing out visuals while reading aloud doesn't provide students with the skills they need to decipher complex visuals. Explicit instruction is necessary to teach and reinforce how to read, interpret, and integrate illustrations and words.

At grade four, students are expected to "interpret information presented visually, orally, or quantitatively (e.g., in charts, graphs, diagrams, timelines, animations, or interactive elements on web pages) and explain how the information contributes to an understanding of the text in which it appears" (CCSS.RI.4.7). Students must understand that information presented visually is an integral component of the text. They also must know how to comprehend and interpret the information.

At grade five, the expectation is that students can "draw on information from multiple print or digital sources, demonstrating the ability to locate an answer to a question quickly or to solve a problem efficiently" (CCSS.RI.5.7). At this level, students must be able to use a variety of visual and quantitative resources and formats to pinpoint information and to problem solve.

Model Lesson 1:
Comprehending Pictures and Graphic Information

Although students see many different types of pictures, illustrations, and graphics in the texts they are reading, they may not fully appreciate the role these visuals play in helping them construct meaning from the pages. This lesson is designed to build awareness of the types of visuals students may see in texts, the purposes these visuals serve, and the various text features (e.g., labels) that accompany visuals.

Lesson Objective:
Students will be able to closely read and reflect on what they learned from pictures/illustrations and graphic information.

Teacher Modeling
Have the following saying written on a whiteboard or chart paper: "A picture is worth a thousand words." Ask students to explain what this statement means and whether or not they agree with it.

Next, have available texts that include pictures depicting different types of images (e.g., pictures/photos or illustrations with labels and captions, an illustration with arrows that depict a sequence, a map that has a legend, a cutout or cross-section of something or someone that shows what is inside the object or body). You might also show a primary source photograph from a social studies text and a graph from a children's magazine such as *Time for Kids, National Geographic Kids,* or *Ranger Rick.*

If possible, provide examples of features we're calling *ancillary texts,* such as sidebars, vocabulary words with definitions, fun facts, tips, and so forth. Explain their purposes.

Read aloud the section of each text that introduces your visual. Talk about what you learned from each image and why you think the author included it (author's purpose). Begin to record notes on a blank *Types of Visuals* chart (see an example of a completed chart in Figure 2-1). Point out that the author may have included labels, captions, different fonts, arrows, and other text features to enhance the visuals. Use the correct terminology when talking about the visuals so students can become familiar with the vocabulary writers use in informational texts.

As you model how you identify and accurately interpret the visuals, demonstrate how you go back and forth between the text and the visuals, so students understand the processes good readers use to comprehend informational writing.

Figure 2-1: Types of Visuals

Type of visual	Purpose/main idea of visual	Text features in visual (caption, etc.)	What did the visual add to what you learned about the topic from the writing? (5 Ws and H)
Illustration cross-section or cutout	To show skeletal system—inside human body	Labels and lines	I could see exactly **where** the rib cage is in a body.
Primary source photo	To show young boys working in a textile factory	Caption written in the top left corner of the photo	Without the photo, I wouldn't know **how** young the boys were or **how** dangerous it was to stand on the big machines to fix them.
Diagram life cycle of butterfly	To show the four stages in a butterfly's life cycle	Arrows to show sequence of stages	The illustrations and arrows let me see **what** each stage was like.
Map	To show where coatis live in the world	Legend with colors that match up to areas of the map	The colored map let me see **where** the coatis live and that they live in large sections of the world.
Pie chart	To display the diversity in the state's population	Different colored pieces of the pie, lines, words in bold	The pie chart shows **who** lives in the state (by ethnicity).
Timeline	To show dates and significance of U.S. missions to Venus	Dates, photos, arrows, facts	Shows **when** the United States sent missions to Venus.

Guided Practice

Once you've modeled how you read, interpret, and evaluate different types of visuals, prepare for a scavenger hunt. Students will be in teams of three or four. You can either preselect four or five texts for each team to use or have students select their own texts from those you make available. You will also need a copy of the following *Scavenger Hunt* sheet (Figure 2-2 on p. 25) for each team. Explain that the purpose of the scavenger hunt is to see how many items students can find, interpret, and evaluate. Display the graphic organizer.

As students work collaboratively to complete the scavenger hunt, circulate to help and assess students' understanding. You will be using "kid-watching" information you gather to match students with the appropriate level graphic organizer when they complete the follow-up activity independently.

Student Application: Tiered Activities for Differentiation

The goal of the graphic organizer is to help students (a) attend to pictorial and graphic information in texts and (b) know how to read visuals and reflect on what they learned from them.

Initial Level

At this level, students are asked to go on paired scavenger hunts, locating as many items on the list as possible from books you provide for them. They should identify where they located each item. In addition, they select two visuals and prepare to explain orally what they learned from them (who, what, where, when, why, or how).

Teacher action: Provide students texts that contain a range of pictorial and graphic information. Distribute a copy of the *Scavenger Hunt* sheet (Figure 2-2 on p. 25) to each pair of students.

Transitional Level

At this level, students are asked to go on individual scavenger hunts, locating as many items on the list as possible from books you provide for them. They should identify where they located each item. In addition, they select two visuals and prepare to explain orally what they learned from them (who, what, where, when, why, or how).

Teacher action: Have available a selection of texts that contain different types of pictorial and graphic information. Distribute a copy of the *Scavenger Hunt* sheet (Figure 2-2 on p. 25) to each student.

Accomplished Level

At this level, students are asked to go on individual scavenger hunts, locating as many items on the list as possible from books they select. Students should identify where they located each item. In addition, they select two visuals and prepare to explain orally what they learned from them (who, what, where, when, why, or how).

Teacher action: Ensure that students have texts available to them that contain a range of pictorial and graphic information. Distribute a copy of the *Scavenger Hunt* sheet (Figure 2-2 on p. 25) to each student.

When students complete their scavenger hunts, provide a few minutes for them to share some of their findings. Conclude the lesson by revisiting the statement "A picture is worth a thousand words." See if your students' opinions have changed or if they have any additional insights to share.

Figure 2-2: Scavenger Hunt: Hunting for Pictures, Illustrations, and Graphics

---

Scavenger Hunt: Hunting for Pictures, Illustrations, and Graphics

Who is on your team? _____

Find as many items on the list as you can. Write where you found it (author's last name) and the page number. The team that finds the most visuals in the time allotted wins.

Good luck!

☐ A picture or an illustration with a label

Author's name: _____ page number: _____

☐ A picture or an illustration with a caption covering part of the picture

Author's name: _____ page number: _____

☐ A picture or an illustration with a caption under it

Author's name: _____ page number: _____

☐ A picture or an illustration without a caption or label

Author's name: _____ page number: _____

☐ A picture or an illustration with arrows

Author's name: _____ page number: _____

☐ A map with a legend or caption that tells about the map

Author's name: _____ page number: _____

☐ A diagram or flowchart with a caption or label

Author's name: _____ page number: _____

☐ A cutout or cross-section that shows what's inside something or someone

Author's name: _____ page number: _____

Put a check in front of the item on this list that you think is the most useful for you as a reader. Be prepared to tell us why this one is most useful for you.

BONUS: Can you find ...

☐ A sidebar

☐ A box or shape with vocabulary words and definitions

☐ A box or shape with fun facts

Additional Recommended Books

Brett, F. (2015). *Your skeletal system works!* Your Body Systems. North Mankato, MN: Capstone.

Fitzgerald, S. (2010). *Wind power.* Energy Today. New York: Chelsea Clubhouse.

Hicks, T. A. & McGeveran, W. (2012). *New Hampshire.* It's My State! Tarrytown, NY: Marshall Cavendish.

Model Lesson 2: Captions and Their Jobs

This lesson extends what we introduced in the prior lesson. Now, we look specifically at captions that accompany visuals. Captions have different "jobs." In this lesson, we focus on three of the jobs captions may have: The captions can summarize, clarify, or extend what's written in the text. By drawing students' attention to visuals and their supporting captions, we provide students with opportunities to investigate the relationships between texts and visual representations.

Lesson Objective:

Students will be able to identify the role captions play in informational texts.

Teacher Modeling

Preparation: Have available three texts with captions that serve different purposes (see below).

If possible, this lesson should follow the previous lesson on visual representations. If you have not yet taught the previous lesson, introduce the concept of *visual representation* by following the suggestions in the "Teacher Modeling" section of the prior lesson. If you taught the prior lesson, review *visual representations* by having students take out and share with each other the visuals they selected. Students should be able to tell one another what they learned from the visuals and why they were included in the texts.

After you introduce or review the concept, explain that good readers pay close attention to the graphics and captions authors include so they can fully understand texts. Explain that captions serve different roles—or have different jobs—in informational texts. Have available three preselected texts that illustrate the following roles captions can play: One caption should:

1. **Summarize what's written on the page.** The author retells the important points but in a shorter, easier-to-understand way. For example, the text on page 21 of *Ernest Shackleton: Antarctic Explorer* (Dowdeswell, et al, 2015) describes how Shackleton and his fellow explorers lived inside overturned boats to survive. The visual is a primary source photo of the men and a boat. The caption reads, "Life was hard in the cramped, dark boats" (p. 21).

2. **Give an example to explain or clarify what is written on the page.** For example, the main idea on page 5 in *Endangered Rain Forests: Investigating Rain Forests in Crisis* (Iyer, 2015) is that rain forests are important habitats for plants and animals. These habitats, however, are "in danger of disappearing. People are cutting and burning down rain forest trees at a rapid rate." The photo depicts this destruction. The caption reads, "a damaged part of a rain forest in Brazil" (p. 5). The visual and caption provide a *for instance*, a clear example of what was written in the text.

3. **Add unique new details that go beyond what is written on the page.** For example, on page 22 of *Blue Whales* (2014), author Ruth Bjorklund describes how blue whales eat, using their tongues to get food (krill) and swallowing the fish. The caption provides an amazing fact about a whale's tongue that cannot be found or inferred in the written text.

Display the *Jobs of Captions* chart (Figure 2-3). Read aloud the section of the text that is related to each visual you'll share. Show each visual and read the caption that goes with it. Think aloud the "job" that each caption serves. Fill in column 1 of Figure 2-3, putting a check in the correct box as you introduce each job. You'll continue to fill in the chart during the guided practice section of this lesson.

Figure 2-3: Jobs of Captions

Jobs of the Captions	1	2	3	4
Summarize what is written in the text				
Give an **example** to explain or **clarify** what is written in the text				
Add **new details** that go beyond what is written				

Guided Practice

Briefly remove the chart so students can't see it, and ask them to recall the three "jobs" captions can have (summarize, explain or clarify, supply additional information that goes beyond the text). If they struggle to come up with the jobs, show the texts, images, and captions again. Before moving to the next part of the lesson, display the *Jobs of Captions* chart (Figure 2-3) so all students can see it.

Pass out preselected texts with captions. The captions should represent the three categories you introduced above. Pair up students. Have each pair receive a text with a visual and a caption as well as a sticky note. Each pair should read the text, the visual, and the caption. They should be able to determine the caption's "job." If the caption summarized what was written in the text in a shorter, easier-to-understand way, students should write "summarize" on the sticky note and attach the note to the caption. If the caption gives an example ("for instance") to explain or clarify what was written in the text, students should write "explain" or "clarify" on the sticky note and attach it to the caption. Finally, if the caption gives unique new details that go beyond what's written in the text, students should write "new details" on the sticky note and attach it to the caption.

Some captions may fall into more than one of the three categories. Don't worry if there isn't consensus. The purpose of this activity is to provide opportunities for students to read texts, interpret the visuals, and analyze the captions. As long as students' reasoning is logical, accept their answers. When students have determined the jobs of their captions, have them briefly explain to their classmates what their text said, show the image, and read the caption. As students report the captions' jobs, tally the number of each type by putting a check in the appropriate box on the chart (Figure 2-3 on p. 27) in the "Teacher Modeling" section of the lesson. Spend a few minutes having students draw some conclusions about what they found when they tallied the jobs captions can do.

What If …

Before concluding this lesson, encourage students to think about why authors intentionally choose the visuals and captions they do to accompany specific texts. Select a page that you haven't yet used from an informational text. The page should contain a visual and a caption. Before showing the page to students, cover the caption so students can't see it. Display the page, read it aloud, and talk about the visual. Ask, "What if you were asked to write the caption?" Talk about the job the caption might serve, and have a student volunteer to write a caption to accompany it. Reveal the original caption and compare/contrast the information presented in the two captions. Repeat this process with two or three other texts and visuals.

Student Application: Tiered Activities for Differentiation

To prepare for this lesson, you'll need to find six to eight text excerpts that will be easy for your students to read and that contain visuals with captions that (1) summarize, (2) clarify, or (3) expand upon the information in each text. We want the texts to be easy for students to read because all your students will be using the same materials; you will differentiate the process and student products at the three levels. Use a documentation camera, if possible.

For these follow-up activities, group students so they can work as teams. Assign each student to one of the three levels: Initial, Transitional, or Accomplished. Work first with students at the Accomplished Level since we don't want them to see the authors' captions until after they have written their own captions to accompany the visuals. Then work with students at the Initial Level and, finally, with students at the Transitional Level.

Accomplished Level

Students will write their own captions and label them as "summarize," "example or clarify," or "new idea."

Teacher action: Have available six to eight text excerpts that include visuals and captions. Using a documentation camera, if possible, display the excerpts one at a time. As you did above, for each excerpt reveal the text and visual but cover the caption. Have students in this group read one of the excerpts silently and then talk about the job the caption might serve. Have students individually write a caption and label it as "summarize," "example or clarify," or "new idea." Have one or two students share their captions and then uncover the original caption. Compare and contrast captions. Repeat this process for the other excerpts you selected.

Initial Level

Use the same excerpts you used for students in the Accomplished Level group, but this time reveal the captions that accompany the visuals. Students will read the excerpts one at a time and, as a group, discuss the job each caption might serve (summarize, explain or clarify a text, or provide unique information). After the discussion, have one student write the caption's job on a sticky note and attach the note to the caption.

Teacher action: Have sticky notes available to pass out.

Transitional Level

Use the same excerpts you used with the Initial Level group. Students will read the excerpts one at a time. After reading each excerpt and thinking about the visual, each student will write either "summarize," "example or clarify," or "new idea" on a sticky note to indicate the job of the caption. Students should write their answer without allowing others in the group to see what they've written. Once everyone has had a chance to record his or her choice, students uncover their responses and justify their decisions.

Teacher action: Have sticky notes available for students.

Additional Recommended Books

Berne, E. C. (2014). *Summiting Everest: how a photograph celebrates teamwork at the top of the world.* Captured World History. North Mankato, MN: Capstone. (summary, p. 35)

Covert, K. (2012). *Ancient Greece: birthplace of democracy.* Great Civilizations. Mankato, MN: Capstone. (details that go beyond the text, p. 25)

Stewart, M. (2001). *Reptiles.* True Books: Animals. New York: Children's Press. (clarify/examples to support what is written in the text, pp. 18, 19, and several other pages)

Chapter 3

Working with Abstract Words and Derivatives

What Are Abstract Words and Derivatives?

Word work in the upper elementary grades should emphasize instruction on word parts and their meanings. Once students have broken the code, we bring word attack into the structure of the word, such as in teaching compound words, root words, and affixes. Students are taught to chunk words into recognizable pieces. In addition to using structural analysis in this chapter, we want to also focus on abstract words. According to Roe and Ross (2006), a concrete noun or term is something that you can see or touch, that which is accessible to our senses. Some examples are *table, trumpet, rose,* or *bird.* On the other hand, Roe and Ross (2006) describe an abstract noun as something that generally cannot be touched. It refers to concepts, ideas, or quality. Terms such as *trustworthiness, jealousy,* and *embarrassment* are not directly related to anything physical but are intangible and therefore harder to teach. These words are not only more difficult because they are abstract, they are also polysyllabic. This chapter focuses on the derivatives of abstract words. Often the derivative is a different part of speech than the original word.

What Does the Literature Say?

A few years back, when teaching a second-grade group of English language learners during my spring sabbatical, I (Nancy) was stumped by one student, Ntalty, who could not seem to use prediction skills. The regular "draw and write what you think will happen" became either scenes from the book or imagined scenes at home with his brother and toys. Ntalty had started with my group late and had less command of English than the others. It dawned on me, too late, that Ntalty did not understand the abstract term of "predictions." Reflecting on this, I realized I should have started with the concrete for this young man. I should have picked up a pencil and asked, "What will happen if I let go?" Then I should have taken a milk carton (I was teaching in the cafeteria, anyway), opened it, and asked, "What will happen if I turn this over?" When teaching abstract words, beginning with the concrete, when possible, is a recommended approach.

To help you understand how difficult it can be to not only learn, but teach, certain terms, let's discuss the term *run.* A search of the definition describes the word as to move at a speed faster than walking. We have seen the word *run* used in different contexts, such as running for office or to go back and forth, such as by train. These are all good definitions for *run*; nonetheless, it does illustrate the difficulty of teaching terms, and even more difficult with abstract terms.

In addition, to go beyond teaching meaning and nuances of abstract words, we also want to look at how the words are structured. According to Fox (2008), word parts themselves give children insight into word meaning, which makes adding new words to a reader's vocabulary much more efficient. This, in turn, enhances comprehension as vocabulary development positively impacts comprehension (Kieffer & Lesaux, 2008). Wagner, Muse, and Tannenbaum (2007) also found that teaching word structure potentially enables students to increase both vocabulary knowledge and comprehension.

Learning how to use a word part to figure out word meaning aids readers in deciphering meanings of unknown words. Carlisle (2010) concluded that using morphological awareness (word parts) increases the ability of students to infer meanings of unfamiliar words. According to Carlisle (2010), over time, children gain awareness that "words might be made up of familiar morphemes and that analysis of these help one understand unfamiliar words" (p. 476). For instance, if a child knows that the suffix -er means one who does, then worker, sanitizer, and shoemaker are nouns representing the person who does what the verb implies.

In this chapter, our goal is to model how to teach abstract words that are semantically related. Just think about the word relate. Relate is an abstract word that means to connect one thing to another but has multiple derivatives: related, relating, relation, relationship, relatedness, unrelated, relatives, just to name a few. When reading these derivatives, if a student knows that relate means connect, then the student will be able to grasp the concept of the word meaning and perhaps of the text. In the case of unrelated, if the student knows that un- means not, the student will be able to glean the meaning as not being connected.

Increasing Complexity through the Grades

When looking at expectations for word learning, it is important to take into consideration what is expected in literature, informational texts, and foundational skills. Although standard expectations show connections to the next level, some aspects of the standard are not necessarily built upon in the next level; however, all are important introductions to the skill.

At grade three, students are expected to be able determine words and phrases as used in the text (CCSS.RL.3.4), including grade-level domain-specific words and phrases (CCSS.RI.3.4). In this instance, students need to know how to use context to figure out word meanings. Chunking multi-syllable words to identify known root words and common affixes will aid in this process.

At grade four, students are expected to determine meaning of words and phrases, including those that allude to mythology, such as herculean, which stems from the muscular abilities of the Greek god, Hercules, son of Zeus (CCSS.RL.4.4). Students should also be able to determine the meaning of domain-specific words and use root words and affixes to determine word meaning (CCSS.RI.4.4).

At grade five, the expectation is that students can describe how words and phrases bring meaning into various genres, such as stories, poems, or songs (CCSS.RL.5.4). They should also be able to determine the meaning of domain-specific words and use root words and affixes to determine word meaning (CCSS.RI.5.4).

Model Lesson 1: Abstract Words and Derivatives

We use direct instruction to teach the root word of abstract terms. Students will then pick up more information on the word meaning over time as derivatives are found in different contexts. The overarching goal is to have students understand that, although a word may look unfamiliar, they may be able to recognize the root word or an affix and therefore get an idea of what the word means.

Lesson Objective:

Students will be able to use the meaning of preselected abstract root words and recognize that affixes can change word meaning, aiding in determining the word meaning in context. The words studied will be used to build a word bank for each student.

Teacher Modeling

When teaching structural analysis in the classroom, the modeling and practice should be explicit and then brought into literature as students need to know that chunking and analyzing word parts helps them in understanding what they are reading. We recommend students be told explicitly that using this strategy while reading can aid them in unlocking meanings of unknown words. Since we are specifically talking about abstract words in this chapter, we must first explain to students that words representing something that can't be seen, felt, or heard are sometimes harder to understand. The word chosen for this lesson is from the National Book Award winner, *Inside Out & Back Again* (Lai, 2011) and is a very common root word. This book, written in free verse, is about Hà, a young Vietnamese girl who survives the fall of Saigon and relocates to Alabama with her family. To model, begin with the abstract word *thought*. *Thought* is a word known to our students, but we are using this as our model as we want to focus on teaching the strategy, and we want students to recognize that this strategy can help them learn words they do not know. The verse from the book talks of feeling guilty because of not thinking of a father (p. 90). To explicitly teach abstract words, we will use three steps. Once students have a handle on what the abstract word means, we then go into derivatives.

Procedure for Teaching Abstract Words

- Write the word on the board or a word card and give the meaning.

  (*thought:* an idea or opinion in your mind, what you are thinking)

- Show examples as concretely as possible.

  (for thought, we would point to our heads and say that we are thinking. Then show an action of thinking. For example, write a word on the board, shake your head and say, "No, I can think of a better way to say this." Then put on a thinking face with your hand on your cheek and say, "I just thought of a better word.")

- Next show images from the web. A quick search brought up: Winnie the Pooh in his "thotful spot," a pensive woman in the woods, a gorilla in thought, a thought balloon, and images of men, women, boys, and girls thinking.

- Finally, model for students by drawing your own image of the word and writing a definition in your own words.

Teaching Derivatives

- Explain to students that sometimes a lot of different words can be made from one word. Tell students that the word *thought* is one of those.

- Explain that the suffix *-ful*, means "full of something," so *thoughtful* would be "full of thought," *sorrowful* would be "full of sorrow," etc.

- Then list the following words on the board: *thought, thoughts, thoughtful, thoughtfully, thoughtless, thoughtlessly, afterthought,* and *forethought.*

- Go through each derivative and tell students how you can figure out what the word means (*less* means "none," *-ly* means "in a way that is," etc.). Tell students that by looking at word parts, instead of just knowing the word thought, they have learned eight different words.

Now go back to the original verse. Show students how you can replace the word with the definition.

If you feel students need more modeling on this technique, go back to Lai's sentence from the book and work in the same fashion by going through the four steps with the word *guilty*. Some derivatives from the word *guilty*: *guilt, guiltier, guiltiest, guiltless, guiltlessly*. Again, discuss each derivative and explain how you can understand the meaning. In *guiltier*, *-er* means "more," like in *longer*.

Guided Practice

In teaching derivatives, the teacher takes the lead role. The student then discusses the meaning of the derivative in the text. For guided practice, we will continue on with *Inside Out & Back Again* (Lai, 2011) and use the word *compose* as we discuss a verse on page 95 about feeling grateful for a rocking boat. The word to focus on in this lesson is *composure*. In this verse, the mother is unable to scold her child because of the boat, which is rocking.

Begin with the first step using the word *compose*.

- Give the meaning or have students look up the meaning of *compose* (in this context, to have an attitude or stance others see, usually calm).
- Show some concrete examples of *compose*. For example, look nervous and pace back and forth a bit. Say, "I must compose myself." Take a deep breath and look calm. Show some images of calm and relaxed people, stating that they are composed. (We looked up images of compose but found composers and people writing, so be careful when looking up images as they should portray the book meaning.)

On an index card, have students write the following:

- The word *compose* (not *composure*)
- The verse from the book (or sentence the word was in)
- The meaning in their own words
- A drawing to help them remember the meaning

Derivatives

Explain to students that *composure* is a derivative of *compose*. This means that it is derived from the root word. *Composure* actually begins with the root word *pose*. (Since *compose* often has a musical meaning, it is important to keep to the meaning in the text.) Explain the following: The root word *pose* means "the attitude or stance of a person"; the prefix *com* means "with"; the suffix *ure* means "an action." So someone who has composure is acting with pose. Then ask what *compose* means? Guide students to say that someone with composure is one who acts calm. Next, ask students if they know any words that have *compose* in them. If needed, share some derivatives of *compose*: *composed, composes, composures, composition*.

Have students write the meaning of the affixes on the back of the index card and the list of derivatives. Have student begin or place these cards in a word bank.

Read the sentence with students once more, especially as the genre of this book (prose) makes it a bit more difficult to figure out the word's meaning. Ask your students if they can say this part of the sentence in a different way. Some ideas:

… so mother is feeling calmer and won't scold me.

… so mother doesn't want to scold me, not just yet.

… so mother hasn't the attitude to scold me, just yet.

Student Application: Structural Analysis with Abstract Words

Students will need your help in this activity as they begin to figure out word meaning by learning more affixes and root words. You will select the targeted abstract word. The word can contain an affix (as in *composure*) or not (as in *thought*). Before reading, make sure students have the correct definition of the root word.

Initial Level

At this level, students will fill out the following on an index card:

- The word
- The sentence from the book
- The meaning in their own words
- A drawing to help them remember the meaning

Teacher action: Preteach the definition of the word. After students are finished with the index card, go over possible derivatives.

Transitional Level

At this level, students fill out the index card as described above. After making the index card, students look up the meaning of the affix and write the meaning on back of the card. Students write a sentence on the bottom of the index card, replacing the word with a synonym, or words with like meaning.

Teacher action: Check to see that students have the correct meaning for the affixes. Discuss the list of derivatives with students.

Accomplished Level

At this level, do not provide additional support. Students fill out the index card as described above. On the back of the card, they write the affix and meaning. They then look up on the computer or in a dictionary derivatives of the word and write those on the back. Students write a sentence on the bottom of the index card replacing the word with a term of comparable meaning.

Teacher action: Check that students have the correct meanings of the suffixes. Give students more derivatives if needed.

Additional Recommended Books

Frasier, D. (2007). *Miss Alaineus: a vocabulary disaster*. New York: Scholastic.

McMullan, K. (2012). *Get to work, Hercules!* Myth-O-Mania. North Mankato, MN: Capstone.

Snicket, Lemony (1999-2006). A Series of Unfortunate Events (any book). New York: HarperCollins.

Model Lesson 2: Abstract Words and Derivatives

Many informational texts, such as autobiographies and biographies, contain abstract words that can be taught as shown in the previous lesson using fictional text. It is the domain-specific words, the content words, that are abstract and will be focused on here. In addition, a lot of academic words needed by students are also abstract words, such as *conclude, investigate, persuade, explore,* and *defend.* Any of these words can also be taught through structural analysis by using their derivatives. The more students know about academic or domain-specific vocabulary, the better their comprehension will be, whether reading or completing a task.

Lesson Objective:

Students will be able to use the meaning of preselected, domain-specific abstract words and recognize that affixes can change word meaning, aiding them in determining the word meaning in context. The words studied will be used to build a word bank for each student.

Teacher Modeling

As mentioned earlier, to begin teaching abstract words, when possible, start with the concrete. First explain to students that you can't see what all words represent because some words name an idea, a concept, or even a theory. To teach domain-specific words, we want to keep students focused on the content. Explain that content words, although many times used as common words, can have a different meaning depending on the context. When reading content material, learning a familiar word's definition can be almost like learning a brand new word because the meaning used in the content is so specific to the topic or subject. Ask students what is meant when someone uses the term *force*, as in "She used force to push the cart." Content-wise, *force* would be defined as "a push or a pull." Ask students what it means if someone says, "The man was forced to stop running because of a knee injury." In this sentence, the word *forced* means *made out of necessity*.

To model with the word *density*, we will use the book *How to Make a Liquid Rainbow* (Shores, 2011). This book explains—and has visuals showing—how to make a liquid rainbow. As some liquids are denser than others, and therefore heavier, a visual and concrete display shows the denser materials at the bottom of a clear jar. This book and activity provide an absolute perfect concrete example to use when teaching *density*.

Procedure for Teaching a Domain-specific Abstract Word

- Write the word on the board or show on a word card, and give the meaning, as stated in the text. For the word *density*, the glossary states "how closely packed particles are in a liquid or object" (p. 22).

- Show examples as concretely as possible.

- First read the book, which tells how to make a liquid rainbow. It begins with placing purple corn syrup in the jar and then blue dish soap. Layering of different liquids continues until the top layer, red rubbing alcohol. When making the rainbow jar, talk about the density of the liquids and why one would float on top of the other. Then show images of density. Some images show dense particles grouped in a package as opposed to less dense ones, and other images show layered liquids as in the experiment just completed.

- Then draw your own image of density, explaining to students that this will help you remember the meaning.

- Then use the word in a sentence. (We do not want to change the meaning from the content meaning, so use a sentence here instead of writing the definition in your own words.) Write on the board something like: "The corn syrup had a lot more density than the rubbing alcohol."

Derivatives

Tell students that other words can be identified because they have the word *dense* in them, just like the word *density*. Write the following on the board and explain each meaning as it relates to *dense*: *dense, denser, densest, density, densely, denseness*. For fun, you might consider sharing the word *densitometer*, an instrument that measures denseness.

Pick two of the derivatives and show students how you can write two possible sentences using the words.

> Your sentences could be:
> The olive oil was **denser** than the water.
> The corn syrup was the **densest** liquid.

Guided Practice

For guided practice, the same structure will be used, but the vocabulary word must first be explicitly taught. Then students can use this knowledge to create a word card. Although this procedure can be used to teach all words, again, we are focusing on abstract terms. In the book, *Daring Play: How a Courageous Jackie Robinson Tranformed Baseball* (Burgan, 2016), the author discusses Jackie, the first black Major League Baseball player, and his courage as a risk-taker. We are choosing the abstract word *courageous* as it is the theme of the book and life of Jackie Robinson.

Procedure for Teaching a Domain-specific Abstract Word

- Write the word on the board or show on a word card, and give the meaning, as used in the text. *Courageous* means "possessing or characterized by courage"; "brave"; "facing difficulty or danger without fear."

- Show examples as concretely as possible. Begin by talking about *The Wizard of Oz* movie and how the lion wanted courage because he didn't think he was courageous. Yet in the end, he did something very brave when he saved Dorothy. Explain that doing something you fear is courageous. Talk about recent events where someone has been brave, perhaps a firefighter or police officer. You can also talk about people in history who have shown courage. These people may include Harriet Tubman, Dr. Martin Luther King Jr., Anne Frank, and Charles Lindbergh, to name a few. Discuss that courage doesn't mean just physically being brave, but sometimes standing up for what is right. Ask students what a courageous person would do if he or she saw someone making fun of a small child in the cafeteria. Ask students to share times they have seen others act courageously.

On an index card, have students write the following:

- The word *courageous*
- The meaning of the word
- A sentence from the book (or title in this case)
- A drawing to help them remember the meaning

Derivatives

- Tell students that other words can be identified because they have the word *courage* or *courageous* in them. See if students can come up with derivatives such as: *courageously, courageousness, uncourageous, encourage* (loosely meaning "to give someone courage"; more exact, "to give hope"), *discourage* (loosely meaning "to not have the courage"; more exact, "to diminish hope").

- Have students write the derivatives on the back of their index card. Discuss the prefixes *un-* and *dis-* as meaning "not," and have students explain how these prefixes change the meaning of words.

Explain that as long as students remember the word *courage* is brave, they can figure out new derivative words.

- Have students help you write two possible sentences about Jackie using the derivatives.

> Some ideas might be:
> It took **courage** for Jackie to become the first black baseball player, and he led the way for others.
> Jackie acted **courageously** during the 1955 World Series game. He took a risk by stealing home and getting a run for the team.

Student Application: Structural Analysis with Abstract Words

At this point, you need to continue to choose abstract words for your students to learn. You should teach explicitly the definition and show images or teach the meaning as concretely as possible. Then have students independently add to their word bank.

Initial Level

At this level, students will fill out the following on an index card:

- The word
- The meaning of the word
- A sentence from the book that contains the word
- A drawing to help them remember the meaning

Teacher action: Preteach the definition of the word. After students are finished with the index card, the teacher goes over possible derivatives.

Transitional Level

At this level, students fill out the index card as described above. After making index cards, students make a list (looking up if necessary) of at least three derivatives of the word.

Teacher action: Check to see that students have the correct meanings and derivatives.

Accomplished Level

At this level, do not provide additional support. Students fill out the index card as described above. They list on their own or look up on the computer or in a dictionary for derivatives of the word and write those on the back of the card. Students write one possible sentence about the topic using a derivative.

Teacher action: Check that students have used the derivative correctly in the sentence.

Additional Recommended Books

Fern, T. (2014). *Dare the wind: the record-breaking voyage of Eleanor Prentiss and the Flying Cloud.* New York: Farrar Straus Giroux Books for Young Readers.

Gibbons, Gail. (2010). *Tornadoes!* New York: Holiday House, Inc.

Warren, A. (2001). *We rode the orphan trains.* New York: Houghton Mifflin Books.

Chapter 4

Comprehending Appositives and Relative Clauses

What Are Appositives and Relative Clauses?

Writers often add phrases or clauses to the main part of sentences to add information, convey complex ideas, and vary the length of sentences. Although writers can create sentences in many ways, we'll explore two similar constructions in this chapter: appositives and relative clauses.

An *appositive* is a word or phrase that follows another noun and explains or defines it. For example: *Dalmatians, white dogs with black spots, are smart and energetic.* In this example, *white dogs with black spots,* is the appositive that tells readers more about Dalmatians. Appositives are always nouns, noun phrases, or pronouns that "give more information about someone or something that we have already named" (O'Brien, n.d.). Simply put, the appositive "renames" the noun it follows (O'Brien, n.d.).

Relative clauses contain a subject and predicate. They begin with a relative pronoun *(who, whom, whose, that,* or *which)*, which serves as the subject of the clause. The following sentence contains a relative clause: *My best friend, who lives around the corner from me, has three sisters.* Relative clauses function as adjectives and provide specifics about the noun that appears before the clause.

Appositives and relative clauses can appear at the beginning of sentences, can interrupt the middle of sentences, or can be attached to the end of sentences. Good readers know that writers often use commas, dashes, and parentheses to signal additional information. Comprehension is enhanced when students understand how sentences are constructed.

What Does the Literature Say?

Scott (2009) suggests that sentence-level comprehension may be a major stumbling block for children and adolescents who struggle to comprehend texts; yet, instruction at the sentence level is an often-overlooked consideration for improving comprehension (p. 184). When children read sentences that contain embedded words, phrases, or clauses, they often have to hold some information in their short-term memory while they read the embedded texts and then continue with the main part of the sentence (Fluck, 1978; Gibson, Desmet, Groder, Watson, and Ko, 2005). Take, for instance, the appositive in the following sentence from *Hocus Pocus Hotel: The Return of Abracadabra* (Dahl, 2013):

"I had this one specially made," Brack said, "just so my two watches—the real antique one and the fake, practical-joke one—would look almost exactly alike" (p. 55).

There are nine words in the appositive that separates the noun phrase (*my two watches*) from the verb phrase (*would look almost exactly alike*).

Appositives are not the only type of embedded texts that can cause difficulties for readers. Relative clauses can be even more confusing than appositives. Relative clauses are designed to allow writers to shorten two longer sentences into one sentence with two "shared" parts.

For instance, we could say:
1. Jimmy Carter was the 39th president of the United States.
2. Jimmy Carter grew up on a peanut farm in Georgia.

Since *Jimmy Carter* is the same subject in both sentences, we can combine the sentences to read:

> Jimmy Carter, who was the 39th president of the United States, grew up on a peanut farm in Georgia.

Combining the sentences makes the writing less repetitive, but it places greater demands on the reader's "storage" capacity (Gibson, et al, 2005). Readers need to be able to understand the relationship between the relative clause and the noun to which it refers. Relative clauses serve as adjectives that modify nouns; they place restrictions on or add precision to the noun. In the example above, we weren't talking about any Jimmy Carter; we're talking specifically about the 39th president of the United States.

In the previous example, there is only one person for readers to think about throughout the sentence: Jimmy Carter. In many texts that children, adolescents, and adults read, however, nouns and pronouns within one sentence can refer to different people, making the sentences more complicated to understand. Let's take a look at the following sentence from *Hocus Pocus Hotel: The Return of Abracadabra* (Dahl, 2013). It's a short sentence, but the relative clause may present challenges, especially for struggling readers.

> Charlie glanced at Brack, who had a twinkle in his eye (p. 122).

Readers may wonder: Who had a twinkle in his eye? Charlie or Brack? The first part of the sentence refers to Charlie (*Charlie glanced at Brack*), but the second part of the sentence describes Brack (*who had a twinkle in his eye*). Less accomplished readers may make an inaccurate inference and think that both parts of the sentence refer to Charlie.

Finally, let's consider the following sentences from *Outfield Outcast* (Maddox, 2015). In order to understand these three short sentences, readers need to know that "It" refers back to the curveball and that "who," the first word in the relative clause, refers back to the unnamed batter.

> "Dalton delivered a decent curveball. It fooled the batter, who swung and missed. Strike one" (p. 66).

As the previous example shows, the construction of sentences can be complex and may require sentence-level skills to comprehend. We focus on sentence complexity in this chapter because sentence-level comprehension is critical to understanding texts. As Scott (2009) notes, "If a reader cannot parse the types of complex sentences that are often encountered in academic texts, no amount of comprehension strategy instruction will help" (p. 189).

Increasing Complexity through the Grades

Unfortunately, the Common Core State Standards say very little about reading or comprehending at the sentence level. However, when students read sentences that contain appositives and relative clauses, as well as other types of embedded texts, they do need to "read closely to determine what the text says explicitly and to make logical inferences from it," which is what is expected in Anchor Standard 1 for Reading (CCRA.R1).

At grade three, the CCSS assert that students should be able to refer to the text to support their thinking (CCSS.RL.3.1). In this chapter, we encourage students to demonstrate their understanding of sentences that contain appositives and relative clauses. Students identify these elements and determine to whom or to what the appositives and relative clauses refer.

At grade four, students are expected to "refer to details and examples in a text when explaining what the text says" both explicitly and inferentially (CCSS.RL.4.1). When fourth graders understand that appositives "rename" the noun that has already been identified in the sentence and that relative pronouns modify (restrict or add specificity to) the nouns that precede them, they are better equipped to use these sentence details to comprehend texts.

At grade five, students are expected to be able to "quote accurately" from texts to support their explicit and inferential understandings of texts (CCSS.RL.5.1). To be successful, students need to be able to read closely and to interpret accurately the author's intended message at the sentence level, as well as more globally.

Model Lesson 1: Appositives

In this lesson, we offer some suggested sentences to use when introducing and reinforcing appositives. Feel free to use them or your own sentences. We hope students will be on the lookout for additional examples of sentences that contain appositives in the texts they are reading in and out of school.

Lesson Objective:
Students will be able to identify appositives and label the nouns or noun phrases the appositives rename.

Teacher Modeling
Have the following sentences available on your whiteboard or a chart:

1. Zebras, animals that look like horses with stripes, live in different parts of Africa.
2. Alex, Michael's oldest brother, helps athletes train for downhill skiing competitions.
3. Hugo Cabret, an author and illustrator of children's books, is coming to visit our school next week.
4. My neighbor's Dalmatian, a white dog with black spots, knows how to roll over.
5. The ray, a thin line of light, was enough to wake me up.

Explain to students that sometimes writers create sentences that have multiple parts. Each part serves a different purpose. Knowing how the parts relate to each other helps make it easier for readers to comprehend the sentences. Explain that you'll look at one type of sentence construction today. Read aloud each of the following sentences and then reread each one as you annotate it: Think aloud as you put a box around the noun or noun phrase in each sentence and underline the appositive. Explain that the underlined part of each sentence is called an *appositive*. The job of an appositive is to add details. It explains or defines the noun or noun phrase that comes before it. Let students know that the appositive "renames" the noun/noun phrase. Complete this process with each of the following sentences.

1. Zebras, **animals that look like horses with stripes**, live in different parts of Africa.
2. Alex, **Michael's oldest brother**, helps athletes train for downhill skiing competitions.
3. Hugo Cabret, **an author and illustrator of children's books**, is coming to visit our school next week.
4. My neighbor's Dalmatian, **a white dog with black spots**, knows how to roll over.
5. The ray, **a thin line of light**, was enough to wake me up.

Read aloud each sentence again, and then reread, leaving off the appositive in each one.

Original sentence: Zebras, animals that look like horses with stripes, live in different parts of Africa.

Sentence without the appositive: Zebras live in different parts of Africa.

Explain that appositives are not essential to the meaning of a sentence.
Test out this hypothesis with each sentence.

Remind students that appositives always come after the nouns they rename. This rule applies even when there are two nouns in a sentence. Model by annotating the following sentences:

1. Jamal hit the baseball directly back to John, **the pitcher**.
2. Did you know that Kaitlyn lived in Dallas, **a big city in Texas**?
3. Soccer fans always get excited about the World Cup, **the largest soccer match for 32 competing countries**.
4. Sarah told Marcella, **the lifeguard,** that she would one day be able to do the Twister, **supposedly the most difficult dive to master**.

Sometimes appositives can help define unfamiliar nouns, as in the following example:

The marionette, **a puppet with strings or wires that make it move,** danced across the stage.

Finally, display the following sentence from *Hocus Pocus Hotel: The Return of Abracadabra* (Dahl, 2013). In this example, the author uses dashes to signal the appositive. Think aloud as you use the sentence construction to assist in determining the meaning of this passage. Share what you learned from the appositive.

> "I had this one specially made," Brack said, "just so my two watches—the real antique one and the fake, practical-joke one—would look almost exactly alike" (p. 55).

Recap: Appositives give readers information about a person, place, or thing that has already been identified.

Guided Practice

Display the following sentences for the class to see and ask students to annotate them with your support. Students should box the nouns/noun phrases and underline the appositives.

1. The new third-grade teacher, Mrs. Jackson, never gives homework on the weekends.
2. Fluffy, the cat that lives in an apartment on the third floor, is gray and white.
3. Reena got sauce on her cuff, the part of her shirt near her wrist, when she reached for the butter.
4. My niece, Jennifer, just graduated from high school.
5. Kid's Kingdom isn't as big as Monster Mountain, the largest amusement park in the state.
6. We rode the elevator to the penthouse, the apartment on the top floor.
7. I love to ride my unicycle, a bike with one wheel.
8. Sandra's dad, a truck driver, tells the best stories about places he's been.
9. Hailstones, balls of ice, bounced off the parked cars.
10. Meteorologists, scientists who study the weather, can predict when hurricanes and tornadoes will develop.

Conclude by asking: Why do writers include appositives in sentences? How do appositives help readers?

Student Application: Tiered Activities for Differentiation

All students will be working on appositives. We differentiate the activities by increasing the complexity of the sentence construction at each level.

Initial Level

At this level, provide sentences that contain one noun (subject) and one appositive that renames the noun. Have students annotate the sentences as you did earlier in the lesson (i.e., box the noun and underline the appositive). Students should be ready to explain how the appositives enhanced comprehension. The following sentences, or sentences of your choosing, may be used in this activity:

1. Carnivores, animals that eat meat, can be found everywhere in the world.
2. Our landlady, the person who owns our apartment building, won't allow any pets.
3. Tyler's uncle, the photographer, took our school pictures this year.
4. The golden retriever, an intelligent dog, is known for its gentle manner.
5. Gio's Pizza, the best pizza place in town, makes more than 30 kinds of pizzas.
6. "Laughter—deep and dark and scary—filled the auditorium" [*Hocus Pocus Hotel: The Return of Abracadabra* (Dahl, 2013, p. 27)].

Teacher action: Have available for each student a sheet with several sentences on it. Each sentence should contain one noun and a clear appositive that renames it.

Transitional Level

At this level, the teacher provides sentences that contain multiple nouns/pronouns and one appositive that renames the noun/pronoun that precedes it. Students practice sentence-level comprehension by boxing the noun and underlining the corresponding appositive. The following sentences, or sentences of your choosing, may be used in this activity:

1. Sofia wanted to invite Karina, a friend from school, to her birthday party.
2. I used to love to go to the Tot Lot with my grandmother, my father's mother.
3. Armando had his birthday party at Jackson Park, a playground with slides and swings.
4. When he grows up, Ryan would like to be a carpenter, a person who builds things with wood.
5. The closest planet to the sun, Mercury, can get as hot as 800 degrees Fahrenheit (427 degrees Celsius).
6. The bus I take home from school goes along Thunder Hill Street, a long and bumpy road.

Teacher action: Have available for each student a sheet with several sentences on it. Each sentence should contain multiple nouns/pronouns and one appositive that renames the noun/pronoun that precedes it.

Accomplished Level

At this level, provide sentences that contain multiple phrases and clauses. Students practice analyzing sentence constructions by boxing the nouns/noun phrases and underlining the appositives. The following sentences, or sentences of your choosing, may be used in this activity:

1. At the baseball field, Pedro and Alec watched as two bystanders—both wearing baseball gloves—reached out to grab the foul ball.
2. Dad told Fred, his co-worker, that he's afraid ground ivy, a purple wildflower, will spread and take over our lawn.
3. In the movie, Anton was pretending to be Doug, the last person to see the shaggy dog.
4. Allan Brady, a local newscaster, reported that Ana, a strong Category 4 hurricane, would likely strike the coast by early morning.
5. The booths at Rosie's, the new restaurant on Langton Street, are made of vinyl, a durable plastic.
6. "Mr. Abracadabra!" Theopolis said in his deepest voice. "I—the Great and Powerful Theopolis, lord of the demon realm and the greatest sorcerer in the dimension—have come to offer a challenge." [*Hocus Pocus Hotel: The Return of Abracadabra* (Dahl, 2013, p. 144)].

Teacher action: Have available for each student a sheet with several sentences on it. Each sentence should contain multiple phrases and clauses.

Additional Recommended Books for Appositives

Dahl, M. (2013). *The return of Abracadabra: Volume 2*. Hocus Pocus Hotel. North Mankato, MN: Capstone. [see pp. 20, 26, 27, and 31]

Fletcher, R. (1995). *Fig pudding*. New York: Yearling. [see p. 45]

Lowry, L. (2002). *Gooney Bird Greene*. New York: Yearling Books. [see p. 25]

Model Lesson 2: Relative Pronouns: Who, Whom, Whose, That, and Which

If possible, this lesson should follow the prior lesson on appositives.

Lesson Objective:

Students will be able to identify relative pronouns in sentences and enhance comprehension by analyzing how the relative clauses provide additional information about the nouns or noun phrases to which they refer.

Teacher Modeling

Begin by reviewing what students know about appositives. They should be able to tell you that authors often include nonessential words and phrases in sentences to provide readers with additional information about nouns that precede them.

Have the words *who, whom, whose, which,* and *that* written in large print on your whiteboard or chart paper. Explain that these five pronouns are like children who are line leaders because they are important words that other words like to follow. These five words often signal the start of clauses, a group of words that writers use to give readers additional, precise information. Just like appositives, clauses are often set off with commas. If developmentally appropriate for your students, explain that clauses contain a subject and predicate, and that *who, whom, whose, which,* and *that* are relative pronouns that serve as the subject of the clauses.

Have the following sentence on a chart or whiteboard:

> Carla rides to school with Frank, who is Ava's dad.

Explain that, like appositives, the words after the comma refer to the noun/noun phrase or pronoun that comes before it. Point out that groups of words that begin with *who, whom, whose, which,* and *that* often serve as adjectives and give us precise information about the noun. To illustrate this, reread the main part of the sentence (*Carla rides to school with Frank*). Explain that if we didn't have the clause at the end of this sentence, we wouldn't know much about Frank. The relative clause, *who is Ava's dad,* tells us exactly which Frank we're talking about.

Next, model this same process with the following three sentences, focusing now on the relative pronoun *which*:

1. The website, which listed the store's hours, was confusing to follow.
2. Rob likes to shop at Food Stop, which is on the corner of Elm Road and Oak Street.
3. My favorite sneakers, which are purple with white laces, no longer fit me.

Display the *Two-column Relative Clause Chart* for all to see (Figure 4-1 on p. 45). Think aloud as you connect the relative clauses in column B with the appropriate noun/noun phrases in column A. Explain that you are looking for relative clauses that give you specific information about each noun/noun phrase. After you put together each sentence, stop to talk about what specific information the relative clause provides.

Figure 4-1: Two-column Relative Clause Chart

Two-column Relative Clause Chart	
A	**B**
Isabella always wears pink,	which she hides in an old cookbook.
My grandmother has a secret apple pie recipe,	who is three years older than he is.
Jose likes to play with his cousin,	which is her favorite color.

Guided Practice

Once students understand the role of relative clauses, have them practice identifying and analyzing relative clauses with you. Have three cards available and write one of the following lines on each card.

Jim,

who bought a new Corvette,

drives with his convertible roof down whenever it's sunny.

Call three students to the front of the room and randomly hand each one a card. Have students line up so they create a complete, logical sentence. With students' help, go through the process of analyzing the sentence: To which word does the relative pronoun refer? Why did the author insert the relative clause? What precise information does it provide?

Repeat this process, writing one line on each card:

Hatchet,

which is a story about a boy who learns how to survive in the wilderness,

was written by Gary Paulsen in 1999.

Next, display the following *Three-column Relative Clause Chart* (Figure 4-2 on p. 46) or a similar one, and guide students through the process of creating sentences by matching each relative clause in column B with the appropriate noun/noun phrase in column A. Draw a line to connect them. Complete the sentence by drawing another line to the appropriate phrase in column C. Repeat until you have four complete, coherent sentences.

Figure 4-2: Three-column Relative Clause Chart

Three-column Relative Clause Chart		
A	**B**	**C**
Michelle's favorite candy,	who always sings while he drives,	invited us to sail with him around the island.
With his new skateboard,	whose boat is docked near ours,	can melt if it's in the sun.
Our bus driver,	which she shares only with her sister,	is moving to New York.
Peter,	which is black, green, and neon pink,	Tony can get to the field in ten minutes.

Remind students: Writers can provide readers with additional information by using *who, whom, whose, which,* and *that* in relative clauses that are set off by commas. The relative clauses supply precise details about the nouns they describe. Good readers pay close attention to the details that come after *who, whom, whose, which,* and *that.*

Student Application: Tiered Activities for Differentiation

As in the previous lesson, we differentiate by increasing the complexity of the sentences. At every level, we want students to understand that the relative clauses provide readers with specific information about the noun, noun phrase, or pronoun to which it refers.

Initial Level

Display a chart that looks something like Figure 4-3 on page 47. Students at this level create sentences by finding the relative clause in column B that defines or adds specifics to a noun in column A. They should draw a line to connect each one. If need be, model the first one: Draw a line between *My dentist gave me a toothbrush,* and *which is blue and white.*

Figure 4-3: Initial Level

Initial Level	
A	**B**
My dentist gave me a toothbrush,	who owns the Adams' Inn on Snake Island.
Dylan spent all day Saturday with Connor,	which is the day my aunt arrives from London.
Justin gave the clock to Mr. Adams,	which is blue and white.
Every morning Mr. Rodriquez raises the American flag,	which has 13 stripes and 50 stars.
We're going to the street fair on Friday,	whose dog had a litter of four puppies.

Teacher action: Prepare a two-column chart. Column B should contain randomly placed relative clauses that define or add specificity to nouns in column A.

Transitional Level

Students at this level create sentences by finding the relative clause in column B (Figure 4-4 below) that defines or adds specifics to a noun in column A and then complete each sentence with a phrase from column C (e.g., *Yellowstone National Park, which is the largest national park in the United States, attracts almost four million visitors each year.*). Have students draw lines to connect the appropriate words in columns A, B, and C to create coherent sentences.

Figure 4-4: Transitional Level

Transitional Level		
A	**B**	**C**
Yellowstone National Park,	whose sister is in my dance class,	isn't painted gold.
The Golden Gate Bridge,	which has nuts and raisins,	likes to play video games.
Miguel,	which is the largest national park in the United States,	tastes good with bananas and milk.
My favorite breakfast cereal,	who was 6'4" tall,	attracts almost four million visitors each year.
Abraham Lincoln,	which took just over four years to build,	was the tallest person to ever be president of the USA.

Teacher action: Prepare a three-column chart that contains randomly placed beginnings, relative clauses, and ends of sentences.

Accomplished Level

Students at this level first create sentences by finding the relative clause in column B that belongs with the noun in column A (Figure 4-5 below). They complete each sentence with a phrase from column C. (e.g., *Venus, which is the brightest planet in the solar system, is the closest planet to Earth*). In addition, students write relative clauses to complete the final three rows in the chart, adding specific information about each noun.

Figure 4-5: Accomplished Level: My Relative Clauses

Accomplished Level: My Relative Clauses		
A	**B**	**C**
Venus,	which is the second longest river in the world,	helped friends and family flee from slavery.
The Amazon River,	who was born a slave,	hides his children's names in his chapter books.
Harriet Tubman,	which is the brightest planet in the solar system,	is about 4,000 miles (6,437 kilometers) long.
Marc Brown,	who wrote all the Arthur books,	is the closest planet to Earth.
Liz,	whose hair is long and curly,	often wears a baseball cap on bad hair days.
Nicole,		can swim faster than anyone else in her family.
Disneyland,		is a magical place.
The kangaroo,		is the national symbol of Australia.

Teacher action: Prepare a three-column chart, as you did for the Transitional Level. Include three or four additional rows. In each of these rows, include the beginnings and endings of sentences. Leave off the relative clauses so students can write their own relative clauses. Your students may be able to do this without any modeling from you, but if they need an example to get started, share the following example: *Nicole, who is only eight years old, can swim faster than anyone else in her family.*

Additional Recommended Books for Relative Clauses

Hicks, T. A. & McGeveran, W. (2012). *New Hampshire*. It's My State! Tarrytown, New York: Marshall Cavendish. [see pp. 26, 29, 31, 46, and many more]

Raum, E. (2012). *Surviving hurricanes*. Children's True Stories: Natural Disasters. North Mankato, MN: Capstone. [see p. 6]

Sachar, L. (1998). *Holes*. New York: Dell Yearling. [see pp. 33 and 42]

Chapter 5

Distinguishing Main Ideas and Details

What Are Main Ideas and Details?

The main idea of a selection can be defined as the overarching message or information in a text. It can be an abstract concept that serves as the central thought of a selection, or it can be as concrete as a topic sentence in a selection. In nonfiction, the main idea is usually written in a topic sentence or title; in fiction, the main idea may be connected to the theme and is not as apparent. Either way, it is the most important idea in a selection. It tells the reader what the selection is about.

What Does the Literature Say?

The main idea is a tool used by readers to connect information in the text. Since readers use the main idea to help organize thoughts about the information given, this becomes an important support for readers' comprehension (Jitendra, Hoppes & Xin, 2000). According to research by the National Reading Panel (2000), one of the main components of comprehension, being able to understand concepts within a text, involves the ability to identify and recall main ideas and supporting details. This finding emphasizes the importance of teaching students how to identify the main idea and being able to connect the supporting details to the main idea.

Main ideas are easiest for readers to identify when the topic sentence states what the paragraph is about, but that is not the case in most texts. The placement of the main idea is important because if the main idea is not initially there for struggling or striving readers, research indicates that this may interfere with comprehension (Hedin & Conderman, 2010). It is often difficult for students to recognize the main idea if the text does not directly state a topic sentence or, as in most narrative text, if the main idea must be discerned from the writing. According to Wilawan (2011), being able to identify the most important ideas in a text is complex and involves multiple cognitive activities, such as understanding text structure and grasping main concepts from information in the text.

When Walmsley (2006) discusses main ideas and details in his article "Getting the Big Idea: A Neglected Goal for Reading Comprehension," he indicates that the main idea of a book relies on the main idea of paragraphs but extends into the "big ideas," which actually aid students in understanding the text at the sentence and paragraph level. Walmsley suggests that when readers focus on the "big idea," this actually promotes better understanding of the smaller details.

Increasing Complexity through the Grades

In order to differentiate with tiered instruction focusing on the main idea and details, we need to think about how clearly or obtusely a main idea can be stated, the number of details given that support that idea, and existing details in the text that may confuse the reader. When the main idea is not directly stated or is a "big idea" that spins off the topic of the text, this makes it more difficult for students to identify the main idea. So, the goal for teachers would be to scaffold students when there is too much information or not enough explicit information.

At grade three, students are expected to be able to determine the main ideas and key details from both narrative and expository text (CCSS.RI.3.2). Students are expected to also state how key details support the main idea.

At grade four, students are expected to not only determine the main idea and identify supporting details, but to be able to summarize the text (CCSS.RI.4.2). This would involve students being able to differentiate between that which is important and that which is interesting.

At grade five, the expectation is that students can identify two or more main ideas and supporting details and summarize (CCSS.RI.5.2). In essence, this makes the task a bit more complex by adding another layer on to identifying the main idea, and text must be chosen carefully to ensure that two main ideas do coexist in the text. As teachers, we need to make sure that the supporting details are chosen accurately and align with the main idea.

Model Lesson 1: Main Idea and Key Details

In fiction texts, the main idea and theme are often intertwined. For that reason, we are focusing more on paragraph level and not book level. We will look for smaller ideas within paragraphs and not the complete message of the story.

Lesson Objective:
Students will be able to identify the main idea and details that support the message of the main idea.

Teacher Modeling
Explaining main idea is relatively easy when students are reading or writing a patterned five-sentence paragraph. In reading regular texts, it is not so easy. Since we assume the main idea may not always be visible, we will start with a concrete explanation and have students tell us what the topic is and eventually identify and state the main idea. In order to do this, you can do a sports bag activity. Bring in two sports bags. The first sports bag should contain a pair of soccer cleats, soccer shorts, and shin guards. (These can be pictures if preferred.) The second bag should contain baseball cleats, a baseball cap, and a baseball glove. (These can be pictures.) Hold up the two bags and ask, "What am I holding?" After students say sports bags, put them down on the table for a moment while you write the topic on the board as "sports." Tell students that, as they read, they may figure out a main idea but must also unpack what the author has said to support the main idea.

Take out the contents of the first sports bag, and ask if they can tell you what sport the bag is about. Explain that the main idea of the first bag is soccer. Ask how students determined that the first bag was about soccer. Students will identify the items needed for soccer. Explain that these are the details that support the main idea of "soccer." Put that bag aside and take out the contents of the second sports bag. Then ask, "What is the main idea of this bag?" Elicit the answer of "baseball." Then ask students to share the details in the bag that helped them state the main idea. Students will explain that the items in the bag relate to baseball. Tell students that reading for main ideas and supporting details is not much different. As they read books, they should look for the whole picture (soccer, baseball) and the details (contents of the sports bags) that support the main idea. Explain that in reading, there are often details that may not be easily identified as supporting the main idea, so students need to read between the lines.

To model this for students, we will use the following paragraph, although you could easily use excerpts from literature. (One example is from Patrick Catling's *The Chocolate Touch* (1952) on page 13, where he describes the main character's bad fault.)

My neighbor, Mrs. Gonsalves, loves to travel. She says she keeps her suitcase packed and ready to go. Last year she went to Colorado, New York, and Portugal. This year she is going to Puerto Rico, back to New York, and to Vermont to ski. I just wish Mrs. Gonsalves would go to Disney World and take me with her!

Show the above paragraph on a projector or chart. Read and explain that the main idea is that Mrs. Gonsalves loves to travel. Then explain that the paragraph has lots of supporting details as the author names where Mrs. Gonsalves has been and where she is going, and this all supports the main idea.

Show students how you would write down the main idea and supporting details by writing the following on the board:

Main idea

Mrs. Gonsalves loves to travel.

Supporting details

Says her suitcase is always packed

Went to Colorado, New York, and Portugal

Will be going to Puerto Rico, New York, and Vermont

Tell students they will write all the supporting details down when doing this and that usually there are a few supporting details. To model a more implicit main idea, we will continue with the next paragraph and show the following to students:

My mom says she wishes Mrs. Gonsalves would take her, too. Mom says she doesn't care where Mrs. Gonsalves is going. She says she'd always want to come back home to me! Mom and I live in Illinois and we have been to Missouri, but that's it. I would only want to go with Mrs. Gonsalves if she were going to Disney World.

Explain to students that the main idea is not stated in this paragraph, but the reader must decide what it is. Read the sentence and explain your thinking to students. You may say something like, "I think the author is telling us something important here. Look at what the author has written: The author says the main character's mom would go with Mrs. Gonsalves'. I think the author is telling us that the mom really wants to travel but doesn't have the money." Explain that this can be stated in different ways, although it really says the same thing. As long as what someone says is the correct main idea, it doesn't matter if it is said a bit differently. Model this on the board. Write down the main idea in a couple of different ways. Then list the supporting details.

Although there are many graphic organizers on main idea and supporting details, we prefer that students write down the terms. This allows them to write as much information as they want or need and gives practice with the terms themselves. When a state test requires main ideas or supporting details, it is important that students understand these academic terms.

Guided Practice

For guided practice, you first want to review main idea and supporting details with students by explaining that sometimes the main idea is stated and sometimes the reader has to figure it out. For example, we will use pages from *The Chocolate Touch* for guided practice and explain that sometimes it takes more than one paragraph to grasp the author's main idea. In the story, John, who is a "pig" about chocolate, found a magic coin that he spent at a fantasy chocolate shop. He has hidden his chocolate purchase upstairs under his bed and pretends (to his parents) he is tired. So on pages 31 to 34, John is convincing his parents he is tired and wants to go to bed, even though it is early. His mother puts him to bed and he pretends to immediately fall asleep. After his mother leaves his bedroom, John jumps out of bed and gets the chocolate. He is planning on devouring the whole chocolate purchase.

Begin by having students write on a piece of paper the term *main idea* in preparation for after reading. As you read or students read, tell them to think about what John's main purpose is on these pages, as that will lead them to the main idea. After finishing the reading, ask what the main idea of this selection was and what was going on in John's mind. Discuss the events and motivation for what took place. Although it is not stated, the author has John wanting to go to bed early, which leads readers to know that he wants to sneak and eat the chocolate under his bed. Students should identify the main idea. Have them write the main idea on their paper. When they do this, write down all the different ways students expressed the main idea on the board. The board may have something like this:

Main idea

John is going to bed early to eat his chocolate without his parents knowing. OR

John is being sneaky and pretending to go to bed. OR

John is not being honest. He just wants to eat the chocolate.

Now have students write down the term *supporting details*. Have them list what the author said that led them to this main idea. Supporting details should look like the following:

Supporting details

John usually took a long time to go to bed.

He yawned very early in the evening.

Said he was sleepy.

John hates his tonic, but he ran and got it and took it quickly.

In bed, John pretended he was sleepy and then pretended he was asleep.

A few seconds after his mother left the bedroom, he got the chocolate basket.

Discuss the supporting details with students and ask, "How do you know when something supports the main idea?" Make sure students point out those actions that were not part of John's usual behavior showed he was being sneaky. Then explain there is a pattern that aids us in identifying supporting ideas.

Student Application: Tiered Activities for Differentiation

When first trying this activity, we recommend that you choose a book or a chapter that has an easily identifiable main idea. The activity for the initial level has a strong scaffold as you give the students the main idea. If they continue struggling with this concept, try giving them the details and letting them identify the main idea from the text.

Initial Level

At this level, give students the main idea. Students should write down the term *main idea* on their paper and then state the main idea. Next, they are to write down *supporting details* and then list at least two supporting details from the text.

Teacher action: Give students the main idea. Make sure there are at least two supporting details students can identify.

Transitional Level

At this level, give a statement to students that will help them discover the main idea. For example: "The main idea on these two pages has something to do with John's behavior. It focuses on honesty." Or, "The main idea is stated in the text, but you need to read and figure it out." Then students must write the supporting details.

Teacher action: Give a hint about the main idea and tell students the total number of supporting details they should find.

Accomplished Level

At this level, do not supply additional support. Students are to discover the main idea on their own and state the main idea in two different ways. Then they are to write the supporting details as modeled.

Teacher action: You may supply the number of supporting details students should find.

Additional Recommended Books

DiCamillo, K. (2000). *Because of Winn-Dixie*. Somerville, MA: Candlewick Press.

Naylor, P. R. (1997). *Shiloh*. New York: Scholastic.

Steele, M. (2014). *On cue*. North Mankato, MN: Capstone.

Model Lesson 2: Main Idea and Supporting Details

When dealing with informational text, we often assume that the main ideas and supporting details are more explicit than in fiction. Although this is often the case, there are many biographies or books that describe events in which the main idea is not explicitly stated and must be gleaned from details and comments within the text. The book, *Mr. Ferris and His Wheel* (Davis, 2014), is a case of both. This book portrays the building of the Ferris wheel for the 1893 Chicago World's Fair. To summarize, the organizers wanted something built that would outshine the Eiffel Tower that had been showcased in the 1889 Paris World's Fair. People were skeptical that a big wheel, with room-sized compartments that cycle up and around high in the air, would be safe. This book alludes to the skepticism and events leading up to the success of what we now call the Ferris wheel.

Lesson Objective:

Students will be able to identify the main idea and supporting details in an informational text.

Teacher Modeling

As you begin your lesson on main ideas, explain to students that the main idea is the most important information from what you are reading, talking about, or doing. Teach or review the concept by beginning with some familiar scenarios and discussing the main idea of the actions. In partners, have students talk to each other about going to the toy aisles in a department store. What section of the toy aisles do they head for? What do they see? Some may go to the area with building blocks, others where the dolls are kept, and yet others to the games. All of the toys in these aisles support the main idea of *toys*. Let's continue "shopping" as we teach students the concept of what *main idea* means, along with how details aid us in identifying the main idea. Tell students to think about the signs they see in drugstores as you bring out a set of pictures. Use pictures of *details*, and explain to students how you figure out the main idea. Using either a presentation slide or pictures cut out from sales flyers, unpack your thinking as you identify the main idea. One group of pictures could be toothbrushes, toothpastes, dental floss, etc. As you show these pictures to students, explain that you can easily tell the items are used for cleaning our teeth, and the main idea that would most likely be seen on a store sign would be something like *dental hygiene* or *oral care products*. Some other ideas for modeling the concept of details supporting main ideas can be found in Figure 5-1 on page 55, *Working with Main Ideas*. The main idea of the set of pictures focusing on joy or happiness is a bit more abstract. As you model for students, emphasize the feeling of joy that each picture portrays.

Figure 5-1 Working with Main Ideas

Working with Main Ideas	
Suggested Picture Items (Details)	**Main Idea**
Paper, pencils, ruler, eraser, crayons	School supplies
Hiking boots, backpack, walking stick, bug repellent, poncho	Hiking equipment
Baseball, football, basketball, hockey stick, baseball bat and glove	Sports equipment
[more abstract] Someone jumping for joy, a person smiling, someone laughing, someone with the "yes!" smile, a giggling baby, victory sign with a smile	Happiness or joy

Talk about how activities and events in books can help the reader identify the main idea the author is trying to make. Sometimes the main idea is right there, but many times the reader has to figure it out.

Tell students the book you are going to read is about the 1893 Chicago World's Fair (or whatever book you chose to read and the topic), and that they will have to listen carefully to figure out the main idea. In the case of *Mr. Ferris and His Wheel*, read the first three pages. The book begins 10 months before the fair is to open and explains that the fair must have a star attraction that would impress the world and outshine the Eiffel Tower. A contest was announced for entries for the star attraction. Discuss what is happening with students and explain that the author is telling us that the Chicago World's Fair organizers wanted something better than the Eiffel Tower. Explain that the main idea can be stated a few ways and you will write these on the board (see finished example below). Explain to students that, in this text, the main idea is extremely clear—something needs to be built for the Chicago World's Fair that will outshine the Eiffel Tower, which was the star attraction at the last world's fair. After reading all three pages, we can state the main idea in different ways, but they all mean the same thing: America is in a challenge and must win by creating something better than the Eiffel Tower. Tell students, as in shopping for toys, we have to look for details in the text that support our identified main idea—that the author gives us facts that support the main idea. Reread the three pages, and write down the facts as you discuss the support with your students (see Figure 5-2: *Star Attraction* on p. 56).

Figure 5-2: Star Attraction

Main idea

Star attraction must impress the world. (stated explicitly) OR

Star attraction must be much better than the Eiffel Tower. OR

Star attraction must be the best ever.

Supporting details

It's America's turn to impress the world.

What could outshine the famous French tower?

A contest was announced because the organizers were looking for the best.

Judges said no to all because they were too much like the Eiffel Tower.

Guided Practice

Once you have modeled how students are to identify the main ideas and supporting details, it is time to give them more responsibility with this task. We will continue on with *Mr. Ferris and His Wheel* to explain the process. The next five pages of the book describe how George Washington Gale Ferris, Jr. convinces the organizers to let him build the "Monster Wheel." The organizers allowed this with just four months left before the fair was to start. They were desperate, although they did not firmly believe this could be done. After reading, ask students what this section of the book was about. Can they identify the main idea the author is stating in these pages? After discussing, have students write "main idea" on a piece of paper and jot down the main idea as they would like to state it. Answers may look like:

Main idea

Only George knew his idea of the Monster Wheel would work. OR

Most people doubted George could make the Monster Wheel. OR

George's pride in America made him determined to build the Monster Wheel.

Now have students go back into the text to find support for the main idea. Ask the following questions: "What things did the author tell you that made you decide the main idea? What in the book supports the main idea?" Tell students they are to write supporting details on their papers, as you had modeled previously. Then reread the text and guide students in writing down supporting details in their own words or using the sentences in the text. Possible answers:

Supporting details

George thought it was a matter of national pride.

George couldn't allow a French tower to overshadow America's World's Fair.

George, with his co-worker William Gronau, worked hard on his invention.

The construction chief of the fair frowned upon George's idea.

Judges were desperate and said George could build the wheel.

Banks laughed at his idea and would not lend him money.

George used his own savings and money from investors to build the wheel.

At this point, if you think students are ready, you can assign independent practice. If not, model one more time. If you are using the Ferris wheel book, the main idea of the next four pages focuses on the hard work necessary to get the wheel built during the Chicago winter, especially with only four months to build. This can be assigned for student application, which is similar to what was done in the previous fiction text application.

Student Application: Tiered Activities for Differentiation

Students will identify the main idea, whether it is explicitly stated in the text or needs to be figured out. The goal is get students to write as much as they can in their own words.

Initial Level

At this level, give students the main idea. Students should write down the term *main idea* on their paper with the stated main idea. Then they write down the term *supporting details*. Tell students they are to look for facts in the text that support the main idea and write down at least three of the important facts.

Teacher action: Give students the main idea. Make sure there are at least three facts that support the main idea. (If not, the main idea given may not be broad enough.)

Transitional Level

At this level, talk about the topic of the text and give students a hint as to what the main idea would be about. Then students must write the supporting details.

Teacher action: Make sure students know the topic and tell students the total number of supporting details.

Accomplished Level

At this level, do not supply additional support. Students are to discover the main idea on their own and state the main idea in two different ways. Then they are to write the supporting details as modeled.

Teacher action: You may supply the number of supporting details students should find.

Additional Recommended Books

Edwards, R. (2010). *Who is Barack Obama?* Who Was ...? New York: Penguin Group.

Forten, C. (2014). *Diary of Charlotte Forten: a free black girl before the Civil War*. First-Person Histories. North Mankato, MN: Capstone.

Mochizuki, K. (1993). *Baseball saved us*. New York: Lee & Low Books.

Chapter 6

Supporting Story Elements with Details

What Are Story Elements and Details?

Story elements are the fundamental construction of a narrative, and sometimes informational text, such as in a biography or a summary of a historical event. Basic story elements are comprised of the characters, setting, problem, attempts to solve the problem, and solution. Understanding story structure and being able to recall details within the story elements are important to reading comprehension.

What Does the Literature Say?

For decades, research has touted the positive impact of students understanding story structure and the elements within the story. The understanding and knowledge of story structure, often referred to as *story elements* or *story grammar*, give students a cognitive structure in which they can categorize events and details. The categorizing of story elements aids students in their retrieval of information as the events within the story are conceptualized. Morrow (1985) found that when students were able to identify the structure of a well-formed story, they were able to more clearly recall story events. Rumelhart (1980) stated that story grammar (elements) are useful in determining important events in a story for (1) summarization, (2) analyzing a wide range of stories, and (3) improving comprehension of stories. In addition, discussion on story structure has been shown to be an effective strategy to improve reading skills (Fagella-Luby, Schumaker & Deshler, 2007).

Story mapping belongs in any discussion on story structure and story elements as story maps are widely used in elementary classrooms in both analyzing and creating stories. These graphic organizers are said to enhance students' structural awareness of stories (Gardill & Jitendra, 1999). The story maps give a graphic representation that supports students in visualizing the structure of story events and aids readers in organizing information and knowledge (Liu, Chen, Shih, Huang, and Liu, 2011). A study done by Grünke, Wilbert, and Stegemann (2013) demonstrated that story mapping is particularly effective when used with struggling readers.

Story maps do help students focus on important story elements; this, in turn, increases comprehension and recall. Story map construction may be simple and contain just four elements: character, setting, problem, and solution. Or the story map design may be more challenging through the addition of more complex descriptors (Witherell & McMackin, 2002). As students complete story maps, they pay particular attention to the story elements and tend to be able to recall more details. Crabtree, Alber-Morgan, and Konrad (2010) also found that having students self-monitor their understanding of story elements increased comprehension.

Increasing Complexity through the Grades

Differentiating the instruction of story structure can be done in various ways. Since we are focusing on story elements and details, it is important to have students notice the surrounding information that supports or offers elaboration on the elements themselves. For instance, a child can determine that Cinderella is a main character, but when asking for details, we want to know character traits and the evidence that supports those identified character traits. Initially, we want students to be able to identify key details that offer evidence for the elements. The next goal, being able to make an inference about an element and its details, is a more challenging task. When looking at the Common Core, it should be noted that Standard 1 for grades three, four, and five are exactly the same in the Reading Standards for Literature and in the Reading Standards for Informational Text.

At grade three, students are expected to be able to answer questions to demonstrate understanding of a text (CCSS.RL.3.1). When identifying story elements, students are answering the questions of who, where, what, how, why, and what happened. They should be able to support their answers.

At grade four, students are expected to refer to details in the text as they explain what is happening in the text (CCSS.RL.4.1). In addition to literal information, students should be able to draw inferences from information given in the text.

At grade five, the expectation is that students can draw inferences from literal information in the text and be able to support their inference by quoting accurately from the text (CCSS.RL.5.1).

Model Lesson 1: Story Elements and Details

Lesson Objective:
Students will be able to identify the story elements and state details that elaborate on the elements.

Teacher Modeling
Depending on your school's curriculum, some students may be very familiar with story elements while others may not. If your students have not been introduced to the story elements of character, setting, problem, attempts to solve, and solution, explain that the story elements answer the following questions: (Characters) *Who is in the story?*; (Setting) *Where does the story take place?*; (Problem) *What does the character need to solve?*; (Attempts to solve) *What happened to solve the problem?*; (Solution) *How is the problem finally solved?*

Put the graphic organizer, *Story Elements, Details, and Inferences* (Figure 6-6, p. 69), on a documentation camera or outline the boxes on the board.

Read the short story *Choo-Choo* below. After reading, model for students exactly how you would fill out the graphic organizer (see Figure 6-1: *Story Elements, Details, and Inferences for Choo-Choo* on p. 60). At some point, be sure to write at least one quote in the evidence section and explain that you are quoting exactly from the text and must use quotation marks. Begin using the graphic organizer by completing the first column, as that includes story elements and will guide the answers to the rest of the chart. Then, complete the second column, as you want to gather the evidence in the story and have this visible prior to explaining your inferences. Finally, read over the evidence, tell students what you think the evidence is implying about the events in the story, and model this on the graphic organizer. Explain that as we infer, we should be thinking about what happened in the entire story, not just the element we are describing and what we already know about similar situations or events.

Choo-Choo
By Nancy L. Witherell and Mary C. McMackin

> Matt knew Choo-Choo was a funny name for a dog, and he felt kind of silly walking around his yard yelling "Choo-Choo." His parents had gotten the tiny dog long before Matt was born. They told Matt that the dog's barking sounded like a sneeze, so they named him

Ah-choo, but over the years the name Choo-Choo had stuck. So now Matt was walking around the yard yelling "Choo-Choo" without success because Choo-Choo was getting a little older and couldn't hear as well. Matt was worried and feeling a little queasy; he couldn't find Choo-Choo. His mom had run to the store to get milk and left Matt home alone with the dog and now he couldn't find him.

Matt walked around the backyard and the front yard, sounding like a train as he went. Maybe yelling "Choo-Choo" was cute when he was five, but now it was kind of embarrassing. He looked all over the front porch and back porch and still couldn't find Choo-Choo. Finally, Matt got another idea. Matt decided to walk around the edge of the whole yard. Luckily, he spotted little Choo-Choo wiggling frantically as he tried to untangle himself from an overgrown bush. Matt breathed a sigh of relief, lifted Choo-Choo out of his tangled trap, and carried him into the house. Matt gave Choo-Choo a treat and hugged him tightly as they cuddled together on the couch.

Figure 6-1: Story Elements, Details, and Inferences for *Choo-Choo*

Element	Supporting Details from Text That Tell Us about the Element	What Can Be Inferred?
Character(s): Matt Choo-Choo	Matt was worried and queasy because he couldn't find his dog. Choo-Choo was a little dog that couldn't hear as well. He was tangled and couldn't get loose.	Matt was sick with worry because he loves his dog. Choo-Choo couldn't figure out how to get out of the bush.
Setting(s): Yard, inside house	Matt walked all over the yard. Matt and Choo-Choo cuddled up on the couch.	Matt had thought Choo-Choo was somewhere in the yard. Matt was glad he found Choo-Choo.
Problem: Matt couldn't find Choo-Choo	The story said he was yelling and couldn't find Choo-Choo. The story said Choo-Choo couldn't hear. The story said Matt was worried.	Matt loves his little dog and was worried that he lost Choo-Choo forever.
Attempts to Solve: Walked around yard yelling "Choo-Choo" Looked on front porch and back porch	The text said he looked in the front and backyard and sounded like a train. The text said he looked all over the porches and couldn't find Choo-Choo.	Matt was looking everywhere he thought Choo-Choo might be. Choo-Choo could be sleeping on one of the porches.
Solution: Matt walked around the edge of the yard and found Choo-Choo tangled in a bush.	"Luckily, he spotted little Choo-Choo wiggling frantically as he tried to untangle himself from an overgrown bush."	Choo-Choo was too little and couldn't get himself loose. Matt was happy to spot Choo-Choo.

Review the filled-in graphic organizer and make sure students are clear as to why you chose to write particular information.

Guided Practice

Use a short story book that your students are familiar with. When choosing a book to use with the story elements, it is important that all elements be present in the book. Some books, such as *The Paperboy* (Pilkey, 1996), a lovely tale about morning paper delivery, are short reads but do not contain all story elements. *The Paperboy* could be used as a great study for setting but does not include a problem or rising action. For purposes of modeling guided practice, we chose the familiar and easy-to-read *Knuffle Bunny* by Mo Willems (2004). *Knuffle Bunny,* a well-loved book for younger children, should be familiar to your class. We chose *Knuffle Bunny* because it helps students understand that evidence from the book may be found in the surrounding graphics and not just in the text. In the case of this book, evidence can be found in the written text, in the pictures, and in the speech balloons. If preferred this activity can be easily adjusted to a grade-level text, such as the beloved multicultural book by Margaree King Mitchell, *Uncle Jed's Barbershop.*

The story of *Knuffle Bunny* involves a father and young daughter (Trixie) going to the Laundromat. Knuffle Bunny, Trixie's "security blanket," is accidently left in the machine as the father and daughter walk home. The walk home is dramatic as Trixie keeps babbling that she wants Knuffle Bunny, but her father doesn't understand. As soon as they arrive home, the mother knows exactly why Trixie is upset. The three of them return to the Laundromat to get Knuffle Bunny. After students read the book, guide them through deciding the story elements and write these on a large chart or projected graphic organizer (Figure 6-6 on p. 69). Once this is completed, look through the book together and talk about where evidence can be found. For instance, one page has Trixie's baby talk in speech balloons, the only text on the page. Readers have to infer that this is evidence of Trixie trying to tell her father she left Knuffle Bunny at the Laundromat. When Trixie is crying, the reader can tell by the pictures that the father is annoyed. For supporting details, have students work in partners, one section at a time. Begin by telling students to fill in the "Supporting Details from Text" (column 2) for characters and then discuss. (See Figure 6-2: *Story Elements, Details, and Inferences for* Knuffle Bunny on p. 62 for reference.)

Continue in this fashion for all elements. For the inference column, remind students that they have to look at what the supporting details from the text say and then think about the entire story and what they already know about the events or situations. The completed graphic organizer should look something like the chart on page 62.

Figure 6-2: Story Elements, Details, and Inferences for *Knuffle Bunny*

Element	Supporting Details from Text That Tell Us about the Element	What Can Be Inferred?
Characters: Trixie Dad Mom	Trixie is a toddler. Dad is doing the laundry. Mom was at home.	Trixie can't talk yet.
Setting: Outdoors, city Laundromat	Pictures of houses and park Picture of washers and dryers Book says they zoomed into the Laundromat.	It seems to be a pretty long walk to the Laundromat.
Problem: Trixie lost her Knuffle Bunny. It was left at the Laundromat.	And the end of the story when Trixie gets Knuffle Bunny back, she is happy.	Trixie loves her Knuffle Bunny.
Attempts to Solve: Trixie babbled. She waved her arms and pointed. Trixie cried. She went boneless.	The speech balloons show Trixie crying. The pictures show Trixie making all kinds of motions. The author says that she goes boneless.	Dad could not figure out what Trixie was trying to tell him.
Solution: Trixie's mom knew she wanted Knuffle Bunny and they found Knuffle Bunny in the dryer.	The first thing mom does is ask where Knuffle Bunny is. They all ran back to the Laundromat and found Knuffle Bunny.	Trixie was happy again.

Student Application: Tiered Activities for Differentiation

In order to tier instruction in analyzing story elements and details, two graphic organizers are offered. Students using the first one, *Story Elements and Details* (Figure 6-5 on p. 68), will fill in the story elements and supporting details. Students using the second level, *Story Elements, Details, and Inferences* (Figure 6-6 on p. 69), will additionally draw inferences from the stated details.

Initial Level

At this level, provide students with the *Story Elements and Details* graphic organizer (Figure 6-5 on p. 68). Students read the book and fill in the story elements. After that, they look back in the book for details on the story elements provided.

Teacher action: Check to make sure story elements have been identified correctly. If necessary, guide students in identifying the story elements.

Transitional Level

At this level, give students the *Story Elements, Details, and Inferences* graphic organizer (Figure 6-6 on p. 69). Students are to read the book, fill in the story elements first, and then go back and find supporting details. After both columns are completed, students think about the entire plot and write down what they can infer from the details.

Teacher action: If needed, use discussion to guide students through inferences.

Accomplished Level

At this level, do not provide additional supports. Give students the *Story Elements, Details, and Inferences* graphic organizer (Figure 6-6 on p. 69). Students are to read the book, fill in the story elements first, and then go back and find supporting details. At this level, students should be directed to include direct quotes from the text in the "Supporting Details from Text" column. After this column is completed, students think about the entire plot and write down what they can infer from the details.

Teacher action: It may be necessary to review using direct quotes as evidence from the text.

Additional Recommended Books

Howe, J. (2006). *Bunnicula: a rabbit-tale of mystery.* New York: Atheneum Books for Young Readers.

Dahl, R. (1983). *The witches.* New York: Scholastic.

Davies, J. (2007). *The lemonade war.* The Lemonade War Series. New York: Houghton Mifflin Harcourt Publishing Company.

Model Lesson 2: Story Elements and Factual Details

As stated previously, story elements are usually well known to students, but a review is recommended. Children often think of a story as something of a fictional nature. To help emphasize the difference between fictional accounts and factual accounts, we will discuss factual accounts as being comprised of story elements and supporting factual details.

Objective:

Students will be able to identify the story elements and state facts that offer details on the elements.

Teacher Modeling

This second lesson is similar to the first one, except instead of asking for supporting details, we have chosen to ask for supporting facts. To introduce story elements and supporting factual details, review with students that informational texts are real and contain facts. Facts are known to be true. To model this lesson, we will use a biographical sketch focusing on the young life story of Helen Keller (search "Helen Keller" on the Mr. Nussbaum Learning and Fun website). Show the graphic organizer, *Informational Text: Story Elements, Facts, and Inferences* (Figure 6-8 on p. 71), and explain that you will be thinking about the story elements as you read. Read Helen Keller's biographical sketch to your class and, if possible, project so all can see. After reviewing the true events in the biography, use the *Informational Text: Story Elements, Facts, and Inferences* graphic organizer to analyze the biographical sketch. Project the graphic organizer, enabling students to see what you are writing. Begin with the "Element" column and fill in each section as modeled in the chart on the next page.

As you model, ask yourself out loud: "Who is in the story? Where did the story take place? What was the problem? What was done to fix it? How was it fixed?" Then show students how you figure out supporting facts from the biographical sketch by using the "Supporting Facts from Text" column. Finally, talk about what can be inferred from the details with each element. Explain that you have to think about the whole incident when you infer because it helps to make a more correct inference. As you share your thinking with your students, write the inference in the correct box.

Figure 6-3: Informational Text: Story Elements, Facts, and Inferences for *Helen Keller Biography for Kids*

Element	Supporting Facts from Text	What Can Be Inferred?
Characters: Helen Keller, Annie Sullivan	Helen Keller was deaf and could not hear or speak. She did learn to speak and to read Braille. Annie had been legally blind. The text mentions she is loving, patient, and determined.	Helen was very smart. Annie could understand how it felt to Helen to be blind.
Setting: Helen's home, outside yard	Annie came to Helen's house to work with her. She worked with her for 49 years.	Annie and Helen must have gotten along very well.
Problem: Helen couldn't communicate, got very frustrated, and behaved very badly.	The text mentions she is unruly and spoiled and often had temper tantrums.	Helen got away with a lot of stuff and acted mean sometimes.
Attempts to Solve: Helen's parents spoiled her and just let her misbehave. They hired Annie Sullivan to teach Helen. Annie tried teaching Helen sign language.	First, Annie taught Helen to behave. She taught Helen to spell, but Helen didn't understand what the finger spelling was about.	Annie must have been very kind and worked really hard. Maybe Helen thought the finger spelling was a game.
Solution: Annie was able to get Helen to understand that sign language gave names to things.	Annie kept trying to teach Helen finger spelling. Helen learned the meaning of her first word, *water*, when she was outside at the pump. The text said that something clicked and she understood what Annie was doing.	Helen and Annie must have been so excited. Annie finally understood how to communicate.

Guided Practice

Once you are certain that students understand that they are looking for facts from the text to offer more details about the elements, guide students through this process. Your choice of text is very important. When using this graphic organizer with informational text, the text must include story elements, so this would most likely be an autobiography, a biography, or a historical event. In this guided practice, you want to co-construct the graphic organizer (Figure 6-8 on p. 71), *Informational Text: Story Elements, Supporting Facts, and Inferences*, with your students. It is important to walk students through each column as they supply information from the text. You may want to project this on the board to guide students with visual clues.

The book, *The Man Who Walked Between the Towers* by Mordicai Gerstein (2003), works well in analyzing story elements as it is a true story and contains all elements. This is a factual account about Philippe Petit, who broke the law and did a tightrope (wire) walk a quarter of a mile high between the two towers that once existed at the New York World Trade Center.

Explain that an informational text is a true story and that authors must research facts to make sure what they write is accurate. To write this book, Mordicai Gerstein states that he did not see Petit walk between the towers. For accurate sources of information, Gerstein used two factual books—one written by Petit himself—and newspaper articles.

Have students read the book and ask them to focus on the story elements within this factual account as they read. Hand out the *Informational Text: Story Elements, Supporting Facts, and Inferences* graphic organizer (Figure 6-8 on p. 71) to each student or have them work in partners. Discuss the story elements with students and have them fill in the first column. (Refer to the completed graphic organizer, Figure 6-4 on the next page, for input.) Next, have students go back in the book and find supporting facts. Discuss these before beginning the inferences column. Make sure to discuss citing quotes directly from the text. Finally, have students discuss in pairs what they might infer from the supporting facts and write down the inferences in the third column. The completed graphic organizer will look something like the chart on the next page.

Figure 6-4: Informational Text: Story Elements, Facts, and Inferences for
The Man Who Walked Between the Towers

Element	Supporting Facts from Text	What Can Be Inferred?
Characters: Philippe Petit, friends, police	Philippe was able to walk on a wire between two quarter-mile-high towers. Philippe's friends helped him set up the wire between the two towers even though they knew they could get in trouble.	He was very good at what he did. His friends were good friends.
Setting: The Twin Towers	They no longer exist. They were a quarter of a mile high. They were being built when Philippe did this.	It would be very scary to be up that high on a wire. Philippe could tie the wire because the towers were not done.
Problem: Philippe wanted to walk on a tightrope between the two towers, but it was not legal.	The text says that Philippe looked at the space between the towers. He made his plan in secret. He had done something like this in Paris and had gotten in trouble.	Philippe was a real daredevil and liked adventures. Philippe could be sneaky.
Attempts to Solve: He and a friend dressed like construction workers to get material up top. They hid out until nighttime. They stretched the wire across.	They took a 400-pound cable up to the top. It was 7/8-inch thick. Friends from the other tower shot a rope over and they tied the rope to the cable. They almost dropped the wire. It was heavy and it took hours, but they were able to stretch the wire.	The men that did this must have been very strong. Getting the wire ready must have made them tired.
Solution: Philippe did a show across the wires and was immediately arrested!	It was dawn when he began to walk. People saw him, and the police came. Philippe performed for an hour and then was arrested. For punishment, the judge made him perform for children of New York.	Philippe must not have slept all night. The police were there and he kept performing, although he knew he would be arrested. He liked his punishment.

As you finish the guided practice, remind students that you are looking for true facts that support and elaborate on the element. Explain that informational texts are not written from made-up or imagined events. The events are real, and in 1974, Philippe Petit really did walk between towers that were a quarter of a mile high in the sky!

Student Application: Tiered Activities for Differentiation

Using one of the two offered graphic organizers will allow you to differentiate for students. The first graphic organizer, *Informational Text: Story Elements and Supporting Facts* (Figure 6-7 on p. 70), has two columns. The second graphic organizer, *Informational Text: Story Elements, Supporting Facts, and Inferences* (Figure 6-8 on p. 71), makes the factual narration more challenging to analyze as it adds inferences.

Initial Level

At this level, provide students with the *Information Text: Story Elements and Supporting Facts* graphic organizer (Figure 6-7 on p. 70). Children read the book and fill in the story elements. After that, they look back in the book for facts on the narration elements provided.

Teacher action: Check to make sure story elements have been identified correctly. If necessary, guide students in identifying the narration elements.

Transitional Level

At this level, give students the *Informational Text: Story Elements, Supporting Facts, and Inferences* graphic organizer (Figure 6-8 on p. 71). Students are to read the book, fill in the story elements first, and then go back and find supporting facts. They are to think about the events in the entire factual account and how these events affect each other and influence the inferences that can be made.

Teacher action: If needed, use discussion to guide students through inferences.

Accomplished Level

At this level, do not provide additional supports. Give students the *Informational Text: Story Elements, Supporting Facts, and Inferences* graphic organizer (Figure 6-8 on p. 71). Students are to read the book, fill in the story elements first, and then go back and find supporting facts. They are to think about the events in the entire factual account and how these events affect each other and influence inferences that can be made. At this level, have students include direct quotes from the text in the "Supporting Facts from Text" column.

Teacher action: It may be necessary to review using direct quotes as evidence from the text.

Additional Recommended Books

McKissack, P. & McKissack, F. (2013). *Martin Luther King, Jr.: Civil Rights leader*. Famous African Americans. New York: Enslow Publishing.

Parker, M. B. (2012). *Colorful dreamer: the story of artist Henri Matisse*. New York: Dial Books.

Tonatiuh, D. (2014). *Separate is never equal: Sylvia Mendez & her family's fight for desegregation*. New York: Abrams.

Figure 6-5: Story Elements and Details

Name(s) _____

Element	Supporting Details from Text
Characters:	
Setting:	
Problem:	
Attempts to Solve:	
Solution:	

Figure 6-6: Story Elements, Details, and Inferences

Name(s) _____

Element	Supporting Details from Text	What Can Be Inferred?
Characters:		
Setting:		
Problem:		
Attempts to Solve:		
Solution:		

Figure 6-7: Informational Text: Story Elements and Supporting Facts

Name(s) _____

Element	Supporting Facts from Text
Characters:	
Setting:	
Problem:	
Attempts to Solve:	
Solution:	

Figure 6-8: Informational Text: Story Elements, Supporting Facts, and Inferences

Name(s) _____

Element	Supporting Facts from Text	What Can Be Inferred?
Characters:		
Setting:		
Problem:		
Attempts to Solve:		
Solution:		

Chapter 7

Making Inferences

What Are Inferences?

Making inferences, often called "reading between the lines," is one of the most complicated reading comprehension skills. When a reader infers, he or she must go beyond the literal message within the text and supply information that is implied.

What Does the Literature Say?

As humans, we make inferences all the time. We open our back door and see muddy footprints on the kitchen floor. We immediately infer that a family member arrived home before we did. We stand in line at the grocery store and because someone has a cart full of groceries, we infer that the line will probably move more slowly than some of the other lines. Readers also infer as they construct meaning. According to Kylene Beers (2003), "… an inference is the ability to connect what is in the text with what is in the mind to create an educated guess" (pp. 61–62).

More than 30 years ago, Louise Rosenblatt in her forward-thinking book, *The Reader, the Text, and the Poem* (1978), introduced many of us to the notion that meaning doesn't come solely from a piece of writing; rather, it is the "transaction" between the reader and the text that results in comprehension and an appreciation for a text. "For Rosenblatt, texts are never autonomous structures that can be viewed with objectivity. Rather, they are always read and interpreted differently by different readers. There can therefore never be a single valid interpretation but only multiple ones that are more or less responsive to the text" (Flynn, 2007, p. 68). In other words, readers construct different meanings from the same text in part because they bring to the text their unique knowledge and experiences. Keene and Zimmerman (1997) explain readers' interpretations in a slightly different way: "To infer as we read is to go beyond literal interpretation and to open a world of meaning deeply connected to our lives. We create an original meaning, a meaning born at the intersection of our background knowledge (schema), the words printed on a page, and our mind's capacity to merge that combination into something uniquely ours. We go beyond the literal and weave our own sense into the words we read. As we read further, that meaning is revised, enriched, sometimes abandoned, based on what we continue to read" (p. 149).

Not surprisingly, as children mature and experience new situations, most are able to make greater and more meaningful inferences and connections before, during, and after reading extended discourse (Kendeou, van den Broek, Helder, and Karlsson, 2014). Students, for example, recognize which antecedents are represented by pronouns in a passage, can determine implicit relationships among characters, understand what motivates a character to behave as he or she does, and, in general, are able to fill in gaps that authors leave in texts. Teaching students how to make these types of inferences is an important part of reading instruction. Kendeou, et al. (2014) report, "Readers who are weak in making inferences almost inevitably fail to comprehend all but the simplest texts because they are unable to identify important connections that lend coherence to their text representations" (p. 12). Furthermore, del Pino, et al, (2013) note, "text comprehension and therefore the memory of the reading depend largely on readers' inferences" (n.p.). The goal for teachers is to help readers use clues in the text to figure out what an author has not directly stated; in other words, to make logical, plausible "educated guesses." Doing so will enable readers to accurately understand and retain the author's intended message.

Increasing Complexity through the Grades

In order to differentiate using tiered activities, teachers need to understand how reading skills increase in complexity (i.e., the "staircase" effect of the CCSS) across the grades. This understanding serves as the basis for designing activities that increase or decrease in cognitive demand. Although the ability to make inferences is a skill that's necessary for many of the Common Core State Standards (e.g., point of view, theme), we focus here on Standard 1 of the Reading Literature and Reading Informational Texts standards, which explicitly mentions "inferences."

At grade three, students are expected to know how to "ask and answer questions to demonstrate understanding of a text" (CCSS.RL.3.1). Although the standard at this grade level does not specify whether the questions should be literal and/or inferential, the standard does state that students must be able to justify their answers with evidence from texts. In order to ask and answer text-dependent questions, students must be familiar with different types of questions, as found, for instance, in Raphael and Au's (2005) Question Answer Relationship (QAR): "Right There,"—literal questions; "Think and Search,"—literal or inference questions; "Author and You,"—inference questions; and "On My Own"—evidence does not come from the text.

At grade four, students are expected to "refer to details and examples in a text when explaining what the text says explicitly and when drawing inferences from the text" (CCSS.RL.4.1). To be successful, students must be able to determine when information is stated explicitly and when, for various reasons, authors leave gaps in their writing, expecting readers to be able to fill them in as they read. Finally, students must have sufficient background knowledge and experience to bring to the text to draw inferences.

At grade five, the expectation is that students can "quote accurately from a text when explaining what the text says explicitly and when drawing inferences from the text" (CCSS.RL.5.1). At this level, students must take responsibility for ensuring accuracy of the evidence they use to support their claims. They must take care not to alter the author's intended message.

Model Lesson 1: Inferring Character Traits

Although readers make myriad inferences within texts, this model lesson uses characters' actions or thoughts to teach inference skills. For this model lesson, we use the book *Kylie Jean, Cupcake Queen* by Marci Peschke (2013).

Lesson Objective:
Students will be able to infer character traits.

Teacher Modeling

Character traits are revealed through actions in this story. Begin the lesson by making sure students understand the concept of how actions can show what a person is like—the person's nature, the character's traits. Read the first example on the next page. Explain how you know that Tom is kind and thoughtful. Have students read aloud the remaining sentences one at a time, ask the following questions, and explain the traits that correspond with each character's actions.

When the lady fell, Tom helped her up.
Ask: What does this action imply about Tom? (Tom is kind and thoughtful.)

Danny looked for his birthday present when his mother was in another room.
Ask: What does this action imply about Danny? (Danny can be sneaky.)

Jerome's little brother was crying, so Jerome gave him his candy.
Ask: What does this action imply about Jerome? (Jerome is kind and loves his brother.)

Emily didn't understand the math problem, and Kara helped her solve it.
Ask: What does this action imply about Kara? (Kara is good at math and nice.)

Everyone likes to hang around with Joshua because he acts silly and tells jokes.
Ask: What does this action imply about Joshua? (Joshua is popular, funny, and likable.)

Once students understand the concept of identifying character traits from actions, begin your story by working with the *Character Traits* graphic organizer (Figure 7-3 on p. 77). Choose a book that you are working on in the class. For the purpose of this lesson, we have chosen *Kylie Jean, Cupcake Queen* because it is not difficult to read and we want students to concentrate on the skill. In this book, Kylie Jean goes to yard sales with her grandparents and mother and notices how other young children are selling water, soda, and lemonade to make money. This gives Kylie Jean the idea that she can start a business and make her own money. Chapter 1, "Saturday Sales," will be used to teach and reinforce how readers take clues from the text and combine them with their experiences to understand more about the characters' personalities. If this is a new book for students, prepare the graphic organizer by writing the characters' names in it prior to the activity, and then model for students how this graphic organizer should be completed. As you'll see below, we'll use this same graphic organizer in three different ways to differentiate the reinforcing activity your students will engage in after you complete this model lesson.

Modeling with the graphic organizer: In chapter one of *Kylie Jean, Cupcake Queen*, Kylie Jean sees her grandparents waiting out in the car for Kylie and her mother. Use the *Character Traits* graphic organizer (Figure 7-3 on p. 77) for this lesson.

On page 12, Kylie thinks, "I better hurry up! If I take too long, Pappy will honk the horn and wake up Miss Clarabelle, my neighbor." Explain what this action implies about Pappy. Fill in the action, page, and character trait on the graphic organizer. (For suggestions, refer to Figure 7-1: *Character Traits—Kylie Jean, Cupcake Queen, Chapter 1* on p. 75).

On page 15, Kylie Jean, sitting in a restaurant says, "We're peachy keen, and today I'm a garage sale queen. I would like a short stack and juice, please, ma'am." Share how you put together clues from the text and your experiences to figure out that Kylie Jean is happy, hungry, and polite. Write the information on the graphic organizer.

On page 18, "Granny digs through a box of junky jewelry and buys an old necklace for fifty cents. After she pays, Granny puts the necklace in the palm of my hand." Use a think-aloud to reveal what Granny's action shows about her. Write the information on the graphic organizer.

On page 20, Kylie asks Momma if she can borrow money to buy a stuffed cat. Momma replies, "No way, little lady. You have too many stuffed toys already!"

Figure 7-1: Character Traits—*Kylie Jean, Cupcake Queen*, Chapter 1

Character	Action or thought	Page action is found on	What this implies about the character
Pappy	Honks the horn if he waits too long	12	Impatient, in a hurry, not thinking of others
Kylie Jean	She's peachy keen, orders pancakes, and says "please, ma'am"	15	happy, hungry, and polite
Granny	Buys a cute necklace and gives it Kylie Jean	18	Nice, loves Kylie Jean
Momma	Momma does not let Kylie borrow money to get a stuffed cat	20	Doesn't give in, uses "little lady" instead of Kylie Jean's name

Guided Practice

Once you have modeled how to determine character traits by integrating information from the text with your own knowledge, prepare a copy of the graphic organizer that you can complete with students' help. Co-constructing this graphic organizer for Chapter 2, "Teatime Treats," will provide additional inference practice for your students and will allow opportunities to assess how much support your students will need to identify character traits independently.

In Chapter 2 of *Kylie Jean, Cupcake Queen*, Kylie and her cousin Lucy are going to a tea party. Kylie had promised to give Lucy a stuffed animal when Pappy lent her the money to buy the stuffed cat. Read the selection together and explain that you are searching for actions or thoughts that imply a character trait. (See Figure 7.2: *Character Traits*—Kylie Jean, Cupcake Queen, *Chapter 2* for suggestions.)

On page 26, Kylie Jean takes Lucy upstairs to her bedroom to pick out a stuffed animal. Discuss what this action implies about Kylie. In the next paragraph, Lucy looks at all the stuffed animals and says, "I sure do like this pony, but you probably want to keep it." Discuss what this says about Lucy and add the information to your graphic organizer.

Figure 7-2: Character Traits—*Kylie Jean, Cupcake Queen*, Chapter 2

Character	Action or thought	Page action is found on	What this implies about the character
Kylie Jean	Kylie tells Lucy to pick a stuffed animal	26	Keeps her promises, trustworthy
Lucy	Lucy says she likes the pony, but Kylie probably wants to keep it	26	Thoughtful, cares about her cousin, not greedy

When you have finished modeling and practicing the skill of inferring character traits, students should be ready to complete this independently. You may need to adjust the graphic organizer so students can be successful.

Student Application: Tiered Activities for Differentiation

In order to tier instruction with the graphic organizer (Figure 7-3 on p. 77), fill in information for the Initial and Transitional Levels (see details below). The goal of this graphic organizer is to support children as they begin to infer character traits and include supporting evidence for the identified character trait or traits.

Initial Level

At this level, provide a scaffold for students by filling in the characters' names, the page number where the action can be found, and the character trait this action implies. Children then look back into the text at the designated pages to find the character's action on that page and infer the identified character trait.

Teacher action: Fill in characters, page numbers, and character trait.

Transitional Level

At this level, fill in the characters' names and actions before distributing the graphic organizer to students. Also fill in the page numbers where the action is found to ensure that students do a "look back" into the text. Then the student must write the character trait this action implies.

Teacher action: Fill in characters and action in Figure 7-3 on page 77.

Accomplished Level

At this level, do not provide additional supports. Depending on the goal of the lesson, you can give students names of specific characters to focus on for this activity. Students read about the character, identify a character action or thought that demonstrates an implied meaning, record the page, and label the character trait or traits that can be inferred from the character's action.

Teacher action: May fill in characters' names in Figure 7-3 on page 77.

Additional Recommended Books

DiCamillo, K. (2000). *Because of Winn-Dixie*. Somerville, MA: Candlewick Press.

MacLachlan, P. (1985). *Sarah, plain and tall*. New York: HarperCollins Children's Books.

Norwich, G. (2013). *I am Harriet Tubman*. New York: Scholastic, Inc.

Figure 7-3: Character Traits

Character	Action or thought	Page action is found on	What this implies about the character

Model Lesson 2: Inferring Actions and Events

The fifth-grade-level book, *Zane and the Hurricane: A Story of Katrina* by Rodman Philbrick (Scholastic, 2014), is a about a young boy, Zane Dupree, who, along with his dog Brandi, survives Hurricane Katrina. This book is a great pick for this skill, as the main character often provides insights into his thinking by sharing his thoughts. For instance, in Chapter 8 "Something Big and Bad," which occurs during the middle of the hurricane, Zane begs for the wind to stop. In fact, he states that he kept asking for the wind to stop. Many texts would have the reader infer from the italics text feature that this is what the character is thinking. Sharing this with students would be beneficial, as similar instances occur throughout the book. In this situation, we never know to whom Zane is asking to stop the wind, but students can make an inference based on other facts about Zane. This model lesson focuses on helping students to infer from actions and events within plots.

Lesson Objective:
Students will be able to explain actions and events within plots.

Teacher Modeling

To introduce how to infer actions and events in plots, the following sentences should be discussed. Remind students as they give evidence that they are inferring from the evidence/facts in the text.

John came running into his home, and there were dirt stains all over his baseball uniform.

Ask: What do you think happened to John? (He slid into one of the bases.)

Ask: What evidence in the sentence made you think that? (dirt stains all over his uniform)

Samantha's mother frowned when she noticed the chocolate ice cream drips on Samantha's new dress.

Ask: What do you think just happened? (Samantha ate ice cream.)

Ask: What evidence made you think this? (Ice cream was on the dress.)

Ask: How does Samantha's mom feel about this? (not happy)

Ask: What evidence in the sentence made you think this? (She frowned.)

The pink "Welcome Baby" sign hung in the driveway. As we walked into the house, we could hear faint crying sounds from the back of the house. As we walked through, it was almost like walking in a garden.

Ask: What do you think happened? (Someone had a baby girl, the baby was crying, and this person had been given lots of flowers.)

Ask: What evidence in the sentences made you think this? (pink sign, faint sounds of crying, "like walking in a garden")

Next, we move back into a text students are reading to demonstrate how to make these same types of inferences while reading. Using a text, such as Chapter 8 in *Zane and the Hurricane: A Story of Katrina,* we can pull examples that demonstrate how we can make inferences from one sentence, multiple sentences, and multiple pages.

Sentence level: While in the midst of the hurricane, Zane talks about keeping away from the windows and staying near the middle of the house (p. 37). We read this sentence with students and explain what is happening and why the character is in this position. Through this sentence, students should be able to infer that Zane is worried the windows are going to be blown in, he could get hurt, and he is trying to protect himself. Explain that when we ask ourselves why something in the text is happening, we often make inferences that deepen our understanding of the text. Let students know that you asked yourself, "Why did Zane crouch in the middle of the house?"

Multiple-sentence level: In the book, Zane looks at a street sign that is moving back and forth from the wind and says that's how he feels inside (p. 38). When modeling with an example like this, we again ask ourselves questions that lead to deeper meaning. In this case, it's best to begin with the literal meaning. We think aloud: What does Zane see the sign doing? Explain what is implied in this sentence. We might return to the description of the sign moving back and forth and explain what this says about the sign (that it is bendable and strong). Then point out his comparison: "I wonder what Zane meant when he said that he was like the street sign. We might ponder: Can Zane be like this sign?"

Multiple-page level: As we continue with this lesson, we read a larger amount of text, and in this same chapter, the next three pages (pp. 39–41) describe the hurricane, snapping sounds, windows exploding, and the fear that makes Zane so tired he falls asleep. At the end of the chapter, Zane hears popping and sees manhole covers popping up. Water is spewing out and going all over the place. As we infer from this larger piece of text, it is best to concentrate on the message the author is sending. In this case, there is rising suspense and the inference would result in a prediction, as good predictions are based on inferential comprehension. At this level of the text, we simply ask "What do you think is going to happen?" Then go back to the evidence, "What evidence made you think that?" (The manhole covers are popping, water is coming out, and the author states that water is going all over the place.)

Guided Practice

For guided practice, the same structure will be used—going from sentences to larger chunks of the text. Now, however, students will help identify inferences that can be generated from texts.

Sentence level: As we go on to Chapter 9, "Trapped," suggest students look at the first page (page 42) for sentences that lead to inference, and guide them to the first sentence where the dog, Brandi is trying to pull Zane back into the house. Encouraging students to lead the discussion, ask what hidden messages are in this statement (Brandi, the dog, senses danger; Brandi is a smart dog; Brandi wants to keep Zane safe and thinks being inside the house will be safe). Continue through the first page in the same way, asking students to select a sentence that makes them infer.

Multiple-sentence level: Next, we take the guided practice to the paragraph level. In Chapter 10, "A Face in the Window," Zane and Brandi have climbed in the attic to be above the water level, but it is too hot and they can't get outside. Then the author explains that the house is beginning to shift and move comparing this to an old wrestler who can't stand against his opponent's strength. In this paragraph, we would point out to students that the author uses a simile to describe what is happening to the house. Can they describe the undercurrents of what is happening in this paragraph? What is this text implying? What might be predicted from this scene?

Multiple-page level: Finally, we work with students at the more challenging level as we finish the chapter, which has Brandi almost dying from the heat in the attic until Zane realizes he can kick open a vent. Zane falls asleep or passes out, and Brandi's barking results in the two of them being rescued.

When we go into the deeper meaning and inferences from this chapter, we need to ask the question, "How did Brandi and Zane help each other survive?" The author never states this, but these two living things are dependent upon each other at this very scary time. Can students infer that Zane saved Brandi's life when he kicked open the vent and brought cooler air into the attic? Can students infer that Zane and Brandi were rescued because Brandi barked for attention as Zane slept or remained passed out? As we bring children into inferring from larger pieces of text, we need to help them search for deeper meaning and messages from the author.

Student Application: Tiered Activities for Differentiation

To differentiate for inferential comprehension, as students infer meaning from actions and events, it is best to reinforce this skill in reading-level or skill groups. Each of the three differentiation levels for this lesson (sentence, multiple-sentence, and multiple-page level) needs to be discussed in groups to ensure that students are applying this skill accurately. If students can successfully make inferences independently at their current level, they are ready to apply the task without face-to-face teacher support. The goal is to have students gradually progress to the next level of instruction and application.

Initial (Sentence) Level

At this level, provide scaffolding as you guide students to analyze just one sentence. By analyzing one sentence, you can continue to build the concept of inference. Also, through discussion, you can bring students back to the evidence to help them make accurate inferences as they construct meaning.

Teacher action: Guide students to analyze a sentence, and have them explain the inference. See if students can select another sentence that leads to inferential thinking.

Transitional (Multiple-sentence) Level

At this level, scaffold the materials as you lead students to a paragraph that contains inferences. The group discusses the inferences and the evidence that led them to this thinking. Then encourage students to continue reading and identifying paragraphs or sections that lead to inferences.

Teacher action: Guide students to a paragraph that leads to inferential thinking and lead students in a discussion. See if students can find another paragraph that contains messages they need to figure out.

Accomplished (Multiple-page) Level

At this level, do not provide additional scaffolding. Students are told to read a section of the text and be prepared to discuss inferences throughout the section. They need to be reminded that they are to have evidence from the text that lead them to the inference.

Teacher action: Lead a discussion of the section after the reading to ensure that inferences were accurate and complete. We recommend that students orally read the sentences they use as evidence for their inference.

Additional Recommended Books

Curtis, C. P. (1999). *Bud, not Buddy*. New York: Delacorte Books for Young Readers.

Raum, E. (2013). *Abraham Lincoln*. American Biographies. North Mankato, MN: Heinemann-Raintree.

St. George, J. (2004). *So you want to be president?* New York: Philomel Books.

Chapter 8

Summarizing

What Is Summarizing?

When readers summarize, they provide a condensed version of a text in which the main points are captured but details and redundancies are omitted.

What Does the Literature Say?

According to Brown, Day, and Jones (1983), "the ability to summarize information is important for understanding and remembering texts, and therefore, the development of this ability in children should be of considerable pedagogical interest" (p. 968). Almost 20 years later, Burke (2000) echoes this statement by saying, "The ability to summarize varying amounts of information is crucial for adult success in most fields. Being able to take an entire article, poem, or book and sum it up in a sentence or a short paragraph helps readers to better understand what they read" (p. 262). Brown, Campione, and Day (1981) developed a four-step process for summarizing a text: First, delete any unimportant information. Second, delete any redundant information. Third, substitute general words for specific words. Fourth, select or create a topic sentence (p. 17). Although these four steps sound simple, for many readers, they aren't.

Good readers monitor comprehension before, during, and after reading. They pause at different points to see if they can summarize what they've read (Paris, Wasik, and Turner, 1991). Older and more experienced readers generally demonstrate more skill in summarizing than do younger or less expert readers (Paris, Wasik, and Turner, 1991). Brown, Day, and Jones (1983), for instance, found several differences between summaries created by fifth and seventh graders versus high school and college students: Fifth and seventh graders were likely to copy or slightly paraphrase ideas, retain the same order of ideas as in the original text, find it challenging to condense ideas, identify important information, and plan ahead when creating summaries. Older students, on the other hand, were more likely to go beyond copying and deleting ideas from the original text by paraphrasing, combining ideas, and using language to capture the ideas in the original text. They also typically spent more time planning summaries than did the younger students.

Since summarizing often involves both reading and writing, we look briefly at a meta-analysis conducted by Graham and Herbert (2011). The researchers studied the effect of writing on comprehension of skilled and struggling readers and writers in grades two through 12. They found that four types of writing about reading lead to enhanced comprehension: summary writing, extended writing, note taking, and answering/generating questions (p. 728). The results held true for narrative and expository texts and for texts that cut across content areas (p. 733).

In order for students to effectively summarize, however, they must be able to distinguish important information from details that are interesting yet not significant to the main idea or purpose of the writing. Bluestein (2010) explains that readers of informational texts use text features to help identify "very important points" (VIPs) (p. 600). The table of contents, font (e.g., bold), summary statements that may appear on the first page of an article or chapter, as well as headings and subheadings, can serve as signposts for key points. Bluestein (2010) suggests that students identify two to four VIPs in a section or text (depending on the length of the text) and create summaries from these VIPs.

Increasing Complexity through the Grades

Beginning in grade four of the CCSS, students are expected to be able to summarize texts. Summarizing appears at every grade level between four and 12. Beginning in grade six, the summaries must be "distinct from personal opinions or judgments" (CCSS 6.2), and beginning in grade eight, the summaries should be "objective" (CCSS 8.2).

At grade three, students are expected to "recount stories, including fables, folktales, and myths from diverse cultures; determine the central message, lesson, or moral and explain how it is conveyed through key details in the text" (CCSS.RL.3.2). In order to retell a story, students need to be able to determine the elements of narratives (characters, settings, problems, attempts at resolving the problems, and resolutions). When reading informational texts, students focus on the main ideas and supporting details (CCSS.RI.3.2). When reading narrative and informational texts, students need to be able to distinguish important from less significant details in texts.

At grade four, students are expected to "determine a theme of a story, drama, or poem from details in the text; summarize the text" (CCSS.RL.4.2). Building on what students learn in grade three, fourth graders must be able to focus on important information as they construct the gist of a story, drama, or poem, as well as the main idea in informational texts (CCSS.RI.4.2).

At grade five, students are expected to be able to summarize narrative texts (CCSS.RL.5.2). When reading informational texts, the expectation is that they will be able to "determine two or more main ideas of a text and explain how they are supported by key details; summarize the text" (CCSS.RI.5.2).

Model Lesson 1: Summarizing Trickster Tales

In this lesson, we want students to think about the essential parts of a story so they can use the information in a summary. In the "Teacher Modeling" section, we provide a three-column chart that provides students with the support they'll need to cull the important information for a summary. In the "Guided Practice" section, we peel back some of the support and provide only the clue words that signal the essential parts of a story. Our hope is that students will internalize these clue words and be able to recall them when asked to create summaries in the future.

Lesson Objective:
Students will be able to summarize a trickster tale.

Teacher Modeling

Begin by explaining that summarizing is something we do outside of school without even thinking about it. Imagine, for instance, that Jamal just watched a movie. A friend stopped by and asked what the movie was about. Jamal says, "It was about a girl named Riley who had to move to San Francisco because her dad got a new job." Jamal goes on to tell what happened. He summarized the movie. Or imagine that your cousin Sophia tweeted, "Met Meg for lunch @ Gio's—yum. Bought new jeans @ The Shed and ran into Aunt Jenn with her new son, Jackson—almost 6 weeks old. So cute." Your cousin summarized her afternoon.

Explain that when we summarize, we select the most important points to convey, as we keep in mind our purpose and audience. We want someone who hasn't seen a movie to know what it's about, or for a friend who wasn't able to join us for an afternoon to know the important things she missed, or for a classmate who's thinking about a book selection to know which one might be of interest to him.

In this lesson, we'll use trickster tales as the mentor texts because they are often short, clearly structured, engaging stories. Trickster tales are written with animal characters that have human characteristics. The stories provide lessons about human behaviors.

For this lesson, we'll use *Outfoxed* (Twohy, 2013), a humorous picture book with a surprise ending. The book begins with Fox grabbing a chicken from a henhouse. He's about to cook the chicken when he realizes it's a duck. Duck tries to convince Fox that he isn't a duck; he's a dog. As you set a purpose for listening, let students know that you'll be reading most of the story and then asking them to predict the ending. Note: Read aloud *Outfoxed* and stop reading after Fox says he should have kept Duck and wonders if he made a mistake. Ask for predictions and justifications. Return to the book. When you share the last few pages, students will see that Duck left an egg for Fox. Fox realizes that Duck outsmarted him. As you read, fill in the *Sum It Up* graphic organizer (Figure 8-1 on p. 84) to highlight the important parts of the story.

Figure 8-1: Sum It Up

Parts of the Story	Guiding Questions for Each Part of the Story	Your Answers
Who?	Who is/are the main character or characters?	
Wanted?	What did the main character(s) want?	
Worried? (What's wrong?)	Why can't the main character(s) get what she/he/they want(s)?	
Whoa (not so fast)!	What events took place?	
Well, it's like this …	How did the story end?	

Think aloud as you fill it out.

Your completed chart might look like this (Figure 8-2 below):

Figure 8-2: Sum It Up: *Outfoxed*

Parts of the Story	Guiding Questions for Each Part of the Story	Your Answers
Who?	Who is/are the main character or characters?	Fox
Wanted?	What did the main character(s) want?	To have a chicken for dinner
Worried? (What's wrong?)	Why can't the main character(s) get what she/he/they want(s)?	Instead of grabbing a chicken from the henhouse, he grabbed a duck.
Whoa (not so fast)!	What events took place?	Duck pretended to be a dog so Fox wouldn't eat him.
Well, it's like this …	How did the story end?	Fox didn't want a dog and returned Duck to the henhouse. When Fox got home, he found an egg Duck laid. Fox knew he had been tricked.

Talk through each part of the story, letting students know why you made the decisions you did. The main character is obvious and what he wanted is fairly explicitly revealed.

The problem—or what's wrong—is evident on the next page when Fox says that he felt like a chicken dinner but a duck would do.

Next, explain how you determined the "Whoa (not so fast)!" section. It's in this section that you'll show students how they can combine the details to generate one overarching main idea. Explain that often in trickster tales (and narratives, in general), the characters and problems come at the beginning of the stories. Readers can usually identify them without too much trouble. To complete the "Whoa (not so fast)!" section, however, readers need to make inferences. They can't simply copy something verbatim from the story. They need to think about all the events and condense them. Review the events in the picture book by identifying everything Duck did to make him appear to be a dog (e.g., barking, chewing up things). Explain that in a summary, we don't want to list all the separate details; rather, we want to try to combine them into one idea. In this case, the idea is that Duck behaved like a dog so Fox wouldn't eat him.

Read the end of the story again and explain how you decided what to write in the "Well, it's like this …" section. For several pages, Fox tells Duck why he needs to return Duck to the henhouse. Again, remind students that you don't need all the details. The author also explains what happened when Fox did return Duck to the henhouse. You need to boil everything down into a sentence or two. In a nutshell, you need to say what happened (e.g., *Fox returned Duck to the henhouse. When Fox got home, he found an egg Duck laid. Fox knew he had been tricked.*).

Read through what you have in the third column to create your summary. You may need to add or change some wording to make it read smoothly. (*Fox wanted to have a chicken for dinner. Instead of grabbing a chicken from the henhouse, he grabbed a duck. Duck pretended to be a dog so Fox wouldn't eat him. Fox didn't want a dog and returned Duck to the henhouse. When Fox got home, he found an egg Duck laid. Fox knew he had been tricked.*)

Spend a couple of minutes reviewing the summary to point out that you included all the major parts of the story. Point out too why you didn't need to add any of the details you left out.

Once you and your students are satisfied with your summary, explain that you are going to revise it to see if you can make it even more concise, while keeping all the important information intact. We're modeling this task now because you'll be asking students who complete the Accomplished Level activity to engage in this process. Begin by counting the words in your original summary (58 words). Demonstrate how you can determine the number of words you would need to eliminate if you were to shorten the summary by 10 percent (need to eliminate about six words). Talk through a revised summary [e.g., *Fox tried to catch a chicken for dinner but caught a duck instead. Duck behaved like a dog, knowing Fox wouldn't eat a dog. Fox didn't want a dog and returned him to the henhouse. When Fox got home, he found an egg Duck laid and knew he had been tricked* (51 words)]. Explain that in this version, you don't specify at first where Fox was when he grabbed the duck, but readers know he was in a henhouse because you mention it in the third sentence. In the original version, you mention the henhouse twice. In this version, you eliminate the redundancy and save some words. [Note: If students have experience with percentages, challenge them to calculate exactly what percentage of the summary they eliminated (12 percent).]

Guided Practice

Prepare to read aloud "Buzzard and Wren Have a Race" (from *A Ring of Tricksters: Animal Tales from America, the West Indies, and Africa*, Hamilton, 1997).

Display the *Summary Shortcut* graphic organizer (Figure 8-3 on p. 89). Since this graphic organizer contains only the clue words [Who?, Wanted?, Worried? (What's wrong?), etc.], it is a bit more challenging than the *Sum It Up* chart (Figure 8-1 on p. 84) you used when you modeled summarizing (above). Explain that you want students to internalize the steps in summarizing, so you're going to use a visual that contains only the clue words.

With students' help, complete the *Summary Shortcut* graphic organizer (Figure 8-3) after reading aloud "Buzzard and Wren Have a Race" (Hamilton, 1997). As you approach each "stop" along the shortcut, ask students what information they should include. If students aren't sure what the terms on the shortcut signify, refer to the guiding questions (middle column) of the *Sum It Up* chart (Figure 8-1).

With your guidance, students may include the following information on the graphic organizer:

Who? Bruh Buzzard and Bruh Wren

Wanted? Bruh Buzzard challenges Bruh Wren to a race to see which one could fly higher.

Worried? (What's wrong?) Bruh Wren knew he was too small to fly up into the clouds.

Whoa (not so fast)! Without Bruh Buzzard knowing it, tiny Bruh Wren hopped on Bruh Buzzard's huge wing and rode on it into the sky.

Sample summary: Well, it's like this … Bruh Buzzard began to worry that Bruh Wren might be getting too tired, so the birds flew back down. Great big Bruh Buzzard was puzzled. He never understood why small Bruh Wren always stayed close to the ground, even though he could fly as high as Bruh Buzzard.

Students often have to combine events in the "Whoa (not so fast)!" section of the graphic organizer. Remind students that, in this section, they can't copy something verbatim from the story. They need to take their time and think about how the events fit together. In this story, for instance, several details were conveyed in a conversation between Bruh Buzzard and Bruh Wren while they were flying. These details, although interesting, can be omitted without altering the main story line. The details that talk about how Bruh Wren carried out his trick are the details that are important.

After you complete the graphic organizer, go back to have a student read the summary you created. Your students may need to revise it to clarify ideas or to capture the essence of the story. When we first wrote the "Wanted?" section, for example, we wrote Bruh Wren wanted to be able to fly as high as Bruh Buzzard. When we read back the summary, we realized that although Bruh Wren did want to be able to fly high, this was not exactly the problem in the story. The problem stemmed from Bruh Buzzard's challenge to Bruh Wren.

Once you and your students are satisfied with the summary, invite students to calculate how many words they would have to eliminate to reduce the summary by 10 percent. With students, discuss ways in which the summary could be shortened without sacrificing any of the important ideas (e.g., the word *tiny* or *small* may be redundant; combine the last two lines. New: Still confused, Bruh Buzzard never understood why small Bruh Wren always stayed close to the ground, even though he could fly as high as Bruh Buzzard).

It might be tempting for students to substitute *he* for *Bruh Buzzard* or *Bruh Wren* to save some words. Substitutions are fine as long as readers know which character "he" refers to.

Student Application: Tiered Activities for Differentiation

Students at the Initial Level will use the three-column chart (Figure 8-1 on p. 84) because it provides guiding questions that may be useful for students who have not yet internalized the essential parts of a story. Students at the Transitional and Accomplished Levels are challenged to rely solely on the clue words to generate ideas for a summary (Figure 8-3 on p. 89).

Initial Level

Students at this level will summarize a story using the *Sum It Up* chart (Figure 8-1).

Teacher action: Select a short text for students to read. The text should have a well-defined narrative structure (characters, problem, attempts to solve, resolution). Distribute one copy of the *Sum It Up* chart (Figure 8-1 on p. 84) to each student.

Transitional Level

Students at this level will summarize a story using *Summary Shortcut* (Figure 8-3 on p. 89).

Teacher action: Select a short text for students to read. The text should have a well-defined narrative structure (characters, problem, attempts to solve, solution). Distribute one copy of *Summary Shortcut* (Figure 8-3 on p. 89) to each student.

Accomplished Level

Students at this level will summarize a story using the *Summary Shortcut* graphic organizer(Figure 8-3 on p. 89) graphic organizer. They will also reduce their summaries by 10 percent while retaining the main ideas of the story. To create a greater challenge, have each student trade his or her original summary with a classmate, and have each student reduce the classmate's original summary by 10 percent. The revised summary should follow the original one on the back of the *Summary Shortcut* sheet.

Teacher action: Select a short narrative text for students to read. Distribute one copy of the *Summary Shortcut* graphic organizer (Figure 8-3) to each student.

Additional Recommended Books

McKissack, P. & Isadora, R. (1986). *Flossie and the fox.* New York: Dial.

Van Allsburg, C. (1992). *The widow's broom.* Boston, MA: Houghton Mifflin Harcourt.

Wyllie, S. (1996). *A flea in the ear.* New York: Dutton.

Figure 8-3: Summary Shortcut

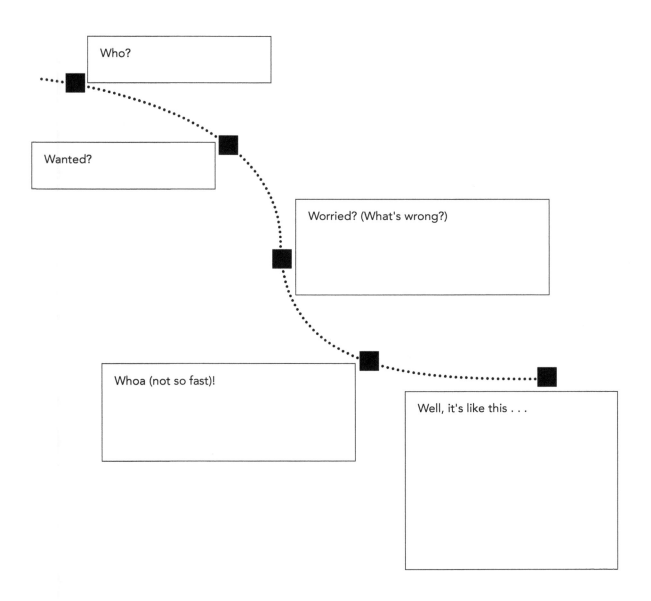

Summary Shortcut

Who?

Wanted?

Worried? (What's wrong?)

Whoa (not so fast)!

Well, it's like this . . .

On the back of this paper, write your summary.

Model Lesson 2: Summarizing Informational Texts

Writing summaries of informational texts can be challenging because expository writing tends to be dense and filled with important facts. It can be perplexing for students to determine what information to keep and how to condense ideas. In this lesson, we rely on Bluestein's (2010) idea of "Very Important Points" (VIPs) to help students create summaries.

Lesson Objective:

Students will be able to summarize an informational text.

Teacher Modeling

Begin by reviewing what students know about summarizing. Next, make a comparison between creating a summary and making a smoothie. If you were to make a smoothie, you might put the following ingredients into a blender: pineapple juice, celery, a frozen banana, and frozen pineapple chunks. The blender would be full of ingredients. You'd turn it on and watch all the ingredients blend together and shrink down in size. The ingredients you started with would still be there, but they would be combined and condensed. When writing a summary, the same thing happens. We take lots of important information, put it into our brain, combine, and paraphrase ideas. We leave only the gist of the text to pour back out onto a piece of paper.

Information writing can be dense and packed with disconnected lists of facts. When teaching students to write effective summaries, we suggest using short informational texts that are well developed rather than texts that present information in compact list forms. For this lesson, we'll use *Pony Express*, a Library of Congress text.

Begin by setting a purpose for listening. Let students know that today it costs 49 cents to send a letter from anywhere to anywhere in the United States. Ask them if they think it would have been more expensive or less expensive to send a letter in 1860. Have students listen as you read aloud the article to see if their predictions were correct.

Read aloud *Pony Express* (Figure 8-4 on p. 91). Tell students that *Pony Express* was written to let readers know why the Pony Express came into existence and why it is no longer needed. Write this purpose statement on the board or chart paper. You'll keep this purpose/main idea in mind as you create your summary.

Explain that you are going to try to find or create a few "very important points" (VIPs) (Bluestein, 2010) from the article to add into a summary. These VIPs can come from text features such as a summary statement or abstract if the article has one, words in bold font, subheadings, and so forth. Also, the topic sentence in paragraphs often contains VIPs. Explain that the title is the only text feature in *Pony Express*, so that will become a VIP. Write the title on a slip of paper and, if possible, attach it to the board by the purpose statement.

Go through each paragraph and look for VIPs—points that talk directly about the article's purpose/main idea. Highlight each VIP (see underlined sentences in Figure 8-5 on p. 92).

Figure 8-4: *Pony Express*

Pony Express
A Local Legacy

Nowadays, it takes only a few days for a letter to travel from coast to coast, and you can send an e-mail in seconds. But in the mid-19th century, it took six months for a letter to travel from Washington, D.C., to California!

As the United States expanded to the West Coast, communication became very important to the success of the nation and its Western pioneers. The country needed a speedy way to send messages. As a result, the Pony Express was born.

In April 1860, 75 young men were hired and 100 horses were purchased to carry mail on horseback from Pony Express headquarters in the Patee House hotel, in St. Joseph, Missouri, to California. The cost to have the Pony Express carry one letter, which took 10 days, from Missouri to California was $5. Today, that $5 is worth about $90! Can you imagine spending $90 to send a letter?

By October 1861, however, the Pony Express was extinct. The telegraph could send messages much cheaper and faster, and, by 1869, railroads stretched from coast to coast. Today, you can visit the Patee House, which is now a museum dedicated to the history of the Pony Express. The building is a National Historic Landmark.

Figure 8-5: *Pony Express* with Highlighted VIPs

Pony Express
A Local Legacy

Nowadays, it takes only a few days for a letter to travel from coast to coast, and you can send an e-mail in seconds. <u>But in the mid-19th century, it took six months for a letter to travel from Washington, D.C., to California!</u> (VIP 1)

<u>As the United States expanded to the West Coast, communication became very important to the success of the nation and its Western pioneers. The country needed a speedy way to send messages. As a result, the Pony Express was born.</u> (VIP 2)

In April 1860, 75 young men were hired and 100 horses were purchased to carry mail on horseback from Pony Express headquarters in the Patee House hotel, in St. Joseph, Missouri, to California. The cost to have the Pony Express carry one letter, which took 10 days, from Missouri to California was $5. Today, that $5 is worth about $90! Can you imagine spending $90 to send a letter?

<u>By October 1861, however, the Pony Express was extinct. The telegraph could send messages much cheaper and faster, and, by 1869, railroads stretched from coast to coast.</u> Today, you can visit the Patee House, which is now a museum dedicated to the history of the Pony Express. The building is a National Historic Landmark. (VIP 3)

Explain that the next step will be to look at what you underlined as VIPs and restate them. Let students know that sometimes you'll paraphrase a sentence—use your own words instead of the words the author used—and sometimes you'll combine sentences as you go along.

VIP 1—This sentence tells us specifically how long it took for a letter to travel from Washington, D.C., to California in the mid-19th century. We can tell from the detail that in the mid-19th century, mail delivery was very slow. On a slip of paper, write: *in the mid-19th century, mail delivery was very slow*, and place this paper on the board.

VIP 2—Explain that because these two sentences are long, you don't want to copy them as is. You'll figure out the gist—the idea the author was trying to express—and put the idea in your own words. Say that you're pretending each word is very expensive and you want to spend as little money as you can to convey the author's ideas: *When pioneers moved to the West Coast, they needed a speedy way to get messages, so the Pony Express was born*. Write this sentence on a slip of paper and put it on the board.

VIP 3—Explain that there are two key ideas in these two sentences: (1) the end of the Pony Express and (2) new, faster, cheaper ways of getting messages to people at a distance. The following two sentences capture these main points: *In 1861 the Pony Express ended because telegraphs were cheaper and faster. By 1869 trains took messages from coast to coast*. Write these sentences on a slip of paper, and attach it to the board.

Take the slips of paper in the order in which you posted them and read through the summary to see if you captured the essence of the *Pony Express* article. Make any revisions you think are needed.

Write the following steps on an anchor chart as you review the process you used to write the summary:

1. Read the article and think about its purpose—why the author wrote the article.
2. Look for and underline Very Important Points (VIPs)—information that reinforces and emphasizes the author's purpose. Remind students that sometimes these VIPs may be bold words, summary statements, headings, topic sentences, etc.
3. Pull out or restate the main idea of each VIP. What does the author want us to know?
4. Eliminate extra words or repeated information. Pretend each word you use is very expensive. You want to spend as little as possible to create an effective summary.
5. Reread your summary to be sure it captures the important ideas in the text.

Guided Practice

With your guidance, have students create a summary for a short, informative text or a section of a text. If students are just learning how summarize, select a text that has a narrative base rather than a text that reads more like a list of facts. For this guided practice, we'll use pages 16 and 17 of *Is My Dog a Wolf? How Your Pet Compares to Its Wild Cousin* (Bidner, 2006).

Have available some blank sentence strips on which to write VIPs.

Read aloud pages 16 and 17. Ask students why they think the author wrote this section of the book (purpose). They may respond with something like: *To show that wolves aren't good or bad; unless wolves are protected, there will be fewer of them*. Write these sentences on the board or chart paper.

Remind students that you'll keep this main idea or purpose in mind while thinking about a summary.

Draw students' attention to the text features on these pages (title, list of questions under the photograph, statement in text box). Ask if they could come up with a VIP for these related text features.

With your students' help, underline the VIPs in each paragraph. When complete, return to each VIP. See if students can restate the important idea for each one. What does the author want us to know? Write down students' responses. The VIPs your students generate may be something like these: *Real wolves aren't like the good or bad ones in picture books. Wolves are really good hunters that kill other animals for food—sometimes big animals—which helps the wildlife community but makes wolves seem scary. Wolves live in many countries. Many wolves are in danger because there is less food, fewer safe shelters, and people who get rid of them. Several countries, including the United States, have laws to protect wolves. Wolves have been reinstated in the Yellowstone National Park and other parts of the country.*

As you work through the summary, emphasize the strategies you used: looking for topic sentences; combining details to save words (e.g., Instead of listing all the countries, as the author does in the original text, you could say, "*several countries, including the United States*); combining sentences; and omitting smaller details to save words (e.g., *Many wolves are in danger because ...*).

When all the VIPs are recorded on slips of paper, take them off the board in the order in which you posted them and read through the summary to see if you captured the essence of the text. Make any revisions you think are needed.

Conclude by returning to the anchor chart you prepared earlier that listed the process you used to create a summary. Revise the chart to reflect any new processes you and your students used in the "Guided Practice" section of this lesson.

Initial Level

Students at this level work with you to create a summary of a short, informational text. Together, underline VIPs in the text and then combine, condense, and paraphrase the ideas from the text. Students write the new VIPs on slips of paper. When you finish recording the VIPs, have a student read them to be sure you captured the essence of the text.

Teacher action: Select a short, well-developed informational text that is written at students' instructional reading level. Have available slips of paper on which to write notes for the summary.

Transitional Level

Students at this level work independently to create a summary of a short, informational text. They underline the VIPs in the text, then combine and condense ideas, and paraphrase ideas from the text. They write their revised VIPs on slips of paper. When complete, they reread the VIPs to make sure they have an accurate, effective summary.

Teacher action: Select a short, well-developed informational text that is written at students' independent reading level. Have available slips of paper on which to write notes for the summary for each student.

Accomplished Level

Students at this level work independently to create a summary of a short, informational text, using the steps detailed in the description for the Transitional Level activity. In addition, challenge them to work in pairs or individually to think abstractly about the concept of summary writing. Have students work with a partner to produce an analogy for summary writing. They may say, for instance: *Summary writing is like the coin-counting machine at a grocery store or bank. People put lots of separate coins into it, the coins get sorted, and at the end, the person gets one small slip of paper, which can be converted into dollar bills. The important information (the amount of money) remains intact even though the original content was condensed in size.*

Teacher action: Select a short, well-developed informational text that is written at students' independent reading level. Have available slips of paper on which to write notes for the summary.

Additional Recommended Books

Allen, K. (2012). *Ancient Egyptian hieroglyphs*. Ancient Egyptian Civilization. North Mankato, MN: Capstone.

Krull, K. (2015). *Sonia Sotomayor*. Women Who Broke the Rules. New York: Bloomsbury.

Tonatiuh, D. (2014). *Separate Is never equal: Sylvia Mendez & her family's fight for desegregation*. New York: Abrams.

Chapter 9

Identifying Themes

What Is a Theme?

According to Brooks (2009), the "theme of a fable is the moral. The theme of a parable is its teaching. The theme of a novel is much broader because it includes a view of life and how people behave. It's the underlying philosophical idea that the story conveys. In other words, it answers the question, What is the story about?" (p. 113). Brooks (2009) goes on to say that "the message of the theme is what the reader takes away from the story" (p. 113). Theme applies to nonfiction, as well. When reading information texts, readers think about messages and what they'll take away from the text.

What Does the Literature Say?

Themes are all around us: A child's bedroom may be decorated in a sports theme or a jungle theme; children go to birthday parties that have superhero or princess themes; adults attend bridal showers with a "love is sweet" theme; many of us have spent time at theme parks—parks that are designed around a common setting or idea. Yet, when it comes to identifying underlying themes in literature, readers often struggle and teachers often find this concept difficult to teach (Peha, n.d.).

Cleverly, Bunyi (2011) lets her students know that theme is "THE MEessage. This helps students remember that a theme is a message that you can find and apply to your own life" (n.p.). Bunyi reminds upper elementary students that when determining the theme of a story, they may want to start by identifying a "key word," such as *friendship, courage,* or *perseverance*. Once students have a key word (or a short phrase) in mind, they ask themselves what the main character learned about the key word (Bunyi, n.p.). For example, if the key word is *changes*, students would ask themselves what the main character learned about *changes*. The theme may be: *Sometimes changes can be scary, but often they lead to rewarding new experiences.*

Peha (n.d.) explains the concept of *theme* by saying, "Things that happen in a story sometimes have two meanings: a literal meaning, where something that happens is just what it appears to be, and a figurative meaning where that same something is an example of an idea like loneliness, friendship, trust, courage, hope, honor, love, etc. When several different things that happen in a story share the same figurative meaning (different examples, same idea), we often say that the author is exploring a theme, especially if the figurative meaning deals with something important in life that could apply to many people" (n.p).

Most of us are probably more likely to consider themes in narration texts than informational texts; however, some experts in the field would go so far as to argue that all texts are fundamentally narration (Calkins, Ehrenworth & Lehman, 2012; Newkirk, 2012). Newkirk (2012) argues, "Narrative is the deep structure of all good writing" (p. 29). He suggests that instead of having students move away from narrative in the upper grades (as described in the Common Core State Standards), teachers should help readers look for the story that holds together all well-written texts— regardless of genre. He recalls his experiences reading a nonfiction book about cancer and concludes that he's lost the details of the text but still holds on to the "basic theme and the feeling the book created for me" (p. 32). Themes help readers elevate unique ideas in a text to universal truths that are shared by many humans. Perhaps we are doing our students a disservice if we don't encourage them to think about themes and life lessons while reading informational texts.

Increasing Complexity through the Grades

At grade three, when students read literature, they are expected, according to the CCSS.RL.3.2, to recount stories told in different genres (e.g., fables and myths), identify "the central message, lesson, or moral," and explain how the details support the central message of the text. Similarly, in informational texts, students are expected to determine the main idea of a text and explain how the details support it (CCSS.RI.3.2). Since the main idea or main message of a text is seldom stated explicitly, students must use the details provided to infer the author's intended meaning.

At grade four, when students read literature, they are expected to determine the text's theme, which is the message of a text—the universal truth of the piece of writing. Students are also expected to summarize texts (CCSS.RL.4.2). When reading informational texts, students are expected to focus on main idea and details, as well as summarize the text (CCSS.RI.4.2). Determining main idea requires readers to use details to identify the essence of the text. Theme is often more abstract than main idea. It requires readers to look closely at the details and language used in a text and then to elevate the main idea into a life lesson they can apply to their lives.

At grade five, when reading literature, students are expected to use details to determine theme in different literary genres. Students focus on how characters face challenges and, in poetry, the speaker's reflections (CCSS.RL.5.2). Students are also expected to summarize the text. Whether reading literature or informational texts, students should understand that complex texts often contain multiple themes and/or main ideas. When reading informational texts, students are expected to determine two main ideas of a text and identify the details that support each one. They are also expected to summarize the text (CCSS.RI.5.2).

Model Lesson 1: Determining Themes

In this lesson, we introduce the concepts of *key words* and *theme* (as defined by Bunyi, 2011) and provide instruction and practice in determining the theme of a text. Since key words are often abstract words, if you taught the lessons in **Chapter 3: Working with Abstract Words and Derivatives**, review what your students learned about abstract words.

Lesson Objective:
Students will be able to determine a key word and theme for a text and provide evidence to support their thinking.

Activating Prior Knowledge
Begin by asking students what they know about the word *theme*. Guide them to think about where they've experienced themes: birthday and family celebrations (using a movie theme for a party), sports events (based on a local team), amusement parks (Wild West), bedrooms (princess), lunch boxes (cartoon character), etc. As you think aloud, explain that stories too have themes.

Teacher Modeling
For this lesson, read aloud a short story or a picture book that your students know well. We'll use *Whistle for Willie* (Keats, 1965). After reading, let students know that you think Peter is very persistent; he continues to try to whistle even when he struggles to do so. Write the word *persistent* on the whiteboard. Provide examples of Peter being persistent (specific examples of when he tried to whistle). Next, say: "I think Peter learned that when people are persistent, they can accomplish what they set out to do." This is a theme—or a message—that runs through this book. Again, show evidence (the whistle came out, Peter showed his parents what he could do).

Take time to explain that themes are sentences that tell us what the author wants us to learn from the story. It's the message the writer wants us to think about when we're done reading. For example, if the key word is *loyalty*, the theme may be: *When fans are loyal, they don't give up on their team, even when the team is not doing well.* Let students know that one teacher describes the theme as "THE MEessage. This clever wording reminds students that theme is a message that applies to many people, including themselves" (Bunyi, 2011).

Display a chart that you've labeled *Key Words and Themes* (Figure 9-1 below). Explain that when determining the theme (or themes) of a text, it's often easier to decide on a key word and then use it to determine the theme, just as you did in the *Whistle for Willie* example. Next, point out possible themes that relate to the key words in Figure 9-1 so students can become comfortable with these terms and concepts.

Figure 9-1: Key Words and Themes

Key Words	Possible Themes
Curiosity	Being curious can be good or it can cause problems.
Determination	Success comes from those who don't give up.
Dishonesty	Dishonesty often leads to problems that are bigger than the ones you began with.
Imagination	There's no telling where our imagination will take us.
Teamwork	Everyone benefits when people learn to work together successfully.
Families	Family members connect with each other in their own unique ways.
Friendship	True friends watch out for each other.
Good vs. Evil	Good triumphs over evil.

Conclude by explaining why it's important for readers to think about key words and themes: Writers create stories to entertain, but stories also "teach us valuable lessons, often the kind that are not easy to learn unless we're wrapped up in a good yarn" (Peha, n.d., n.p.). When readers read critically and understand the underlying lessons authors are sharing, readers can make connections between themselves, the stories' characters or the information in the text, and the intended message of the text.

To conclude, if appropriate, talk about a time when you were persistent (like Peter) and how your persistence allowed you to accomplish something you didn't think you'd be able to do (theme). Invite two or three students to share a few examples of how this theme connects to their experiences. Talk also about other texts that contain this same theme (e.g., *Green Eggs and Ham*, Seuss, 1960).

Guided Practice

Read aloud a short, familiar book or story. Let students know that they should be listening to determine key words and a theme. You might use *Miss Rumphius* (Cooney, 1982). Display the *Key Words and Theme* graphic organizer (Figure 9-2 on p. 99) and have students help you fill it in:

Figure 9-2: Key Words and Theme

Key Words and Theme

Key Word:

_____

Theme:

_____

_____

_____

_____

_____

_____

Why I think this is the key word ...

_____

_____

_____

_____

_____

Why I think this is the theme ...

_____

_____

_____

_____

_____

Students may decide the key words are *giving back* and the theme is *The world would be better if everyone played a role in making it more beautiful.* Help students find examples from the text to support their thinking (e.g., conversation with grandfather, planting lupines).

If appropriate, give an example of a time when this theme was relevant in your life. Have students connect this theme to their own experiences and to examples in other texts they've read.

Student Application: Tiered Activities for Differentiation

If determining key words and themes is a new experience for your students, you may want to have available a running list of key words (e.g., *fear, survival, determination, power, nature, greed, danger, heroism, generosity*) to which students may refer while they complete these activities. To make the activities even easier, you should have on the list the key words that relate to the themes of the texts your students will be reading.

Initial Level

Students at this level will determine the key word and theme of a text. They will provide evidence from the text to explain why they decided on the key word and theme they identified.

Teacher action: Select a story that is written on students' instructional reading level. The story should have a clear key word and theme. Provide each student with a copy of the *Key Words and Theme* graphic organizer (Figure 9-2 on p. 99).

Transitional Level

Students at this level will complete the same activity as described for students at the Initial Level. In addition, they will make a connection between the theme they identified in the text they are reading and their own experiences. They should write this connection on the back of the *Key Words and Theme* graphic organizer (Figure 9-2 on p. 99).

Teacher action: Select a story that is written at students' instructional reading level. The story should have a clear key word and theme. Provide each student with a copy of the *Key Words and Theme* graphic organizer (Figure 9-2).

Accomplished Level

Students at this level will complete the same activity as described for students at the Initial Level. In addition, they will make a connection between the theme they identified in the text they are reading and a different text they have read. They should write this connection on the back of the *Key Words and Theme* graphic organizer (Figure 9-2 on p. 99).

Teacher action: Select a story that is written on students' instructional reading level. The story should have an identifiable key word and theme. Provide each student with a copy of the *Key Words and Theme* graphic organizer (Figure 9-2).

Additional Recommended Books

Barrett, J. (1978). *Cloudy with a chance of meatballs.* New York: Aladdin Books.

dePaola, T. (1993). *Tom.* New York: Penguin Putnam Books.

Howard, E. F. (1991). *Aunt Flossie's hats (and crab cakes later).* New York: Clarion Books.

Model Lesson 2: Theme in Informational Texts

This lesson should be taught after students are familiar with themes in narrative texts.

Lesson Objective:
Students will be able to identify key words in informational texts.

Teacher Modeling

Explain that, like stories, informational texts can have themes that run through them. Read aloud a short informational text such as "Jellyfish or Plastic Bag?" (*Scholastic News Edition 2,* April 2015). This article offers readers four different choices they could consider if they bought a toy and the store clerk put the purchase in a plastic bag. They could throw the bag on the ground, put it in the trash, recycle it, or decide that they shouldn't have the clerk give them a plastic bag for the toy. Set a purpose for listening: Have students listen to determine which of the four choices they think is best. After reading, talk briefly about the choices and how each choice impacts the environment.

Next, display the *Key Words and Themes in Informational Texts* graphic organizer (Figure 9-3 on p. 102). Let students know that you think a key word for this article is *choices.* Jot this word down in the first box. Think aloud how you determined the key word. Write down one piece of evidence in each of the boxes on the graphic organizer (e.g., The title offers readers a choice: jellyfish or plastic bag; the word *choice* appears in the second paragraph and in the headings of the four sections of the article; the article ends with a question to readers, asking how they will help planet Earth.) (p. 3).

Repeat this process to determine the theme. Explain that themes are messages readers can infer from the information in the text and apply to their own lives. Once readers determine key words, they can often establish a theme by asking themselves what they learned about this topic. You might suggest that *choice* is the key word and that the theme is *The choices people make can help or hurt our environment.* Add this sentence to the graphic organizer and continue to think aloud as you articulate the reasons you used as evidence for this theme (e.g., examples and implications of choices that are cited the text: throwing plastic bags on the ground, putting them in the trash, recycling the bags, using environmentally-friendly materials to carry things).

Guided Practice

Display a clean copy of the *Key Words and Themes in Informational Texts* (Figure 9-3 on p. 102). Have available another short informational text that has a clear theme and that your students can read—for example, "Lightning Chaser" (*Scholastic News Edition 2,* March 2013). With your guidance, students should be able to determine a key word for this article (e.g., *knowledge* or *learning*) and defend their decision with evidence from the article (e.g., The cover page and first paragraph says the lightning chaser is trying to learn more about dangerous weather; the photos the scientist takes will help him learn more about wild weather, and so forth). Record the information on the graphic organizer.

Help students move from the key word to a theme (e.g., *Learning something important takes time and effort*). Have students go back through the text to see if this theme is an important message about life that's evident throughout the text. Have them suggest places in the text that support this decision (e.g., text states that Tim Samaras, the lightning chaser, has been a storm chaser for years; he used to videotape tornadoes to gather information; now he takes photos with a "superfast camera").

Point out that complex texts sometimes have more than one theme. Make sure students realize that, when working on themes, they aren't trying to "guess the right theme"; rather, they are interpreting the text—trying to explain what they think the message is that the author wants readers to walk away with—based on information provided in the text.

Figure 9-3: Key Words and Themes in Informational Texts

Transitional and Accomplished Levels

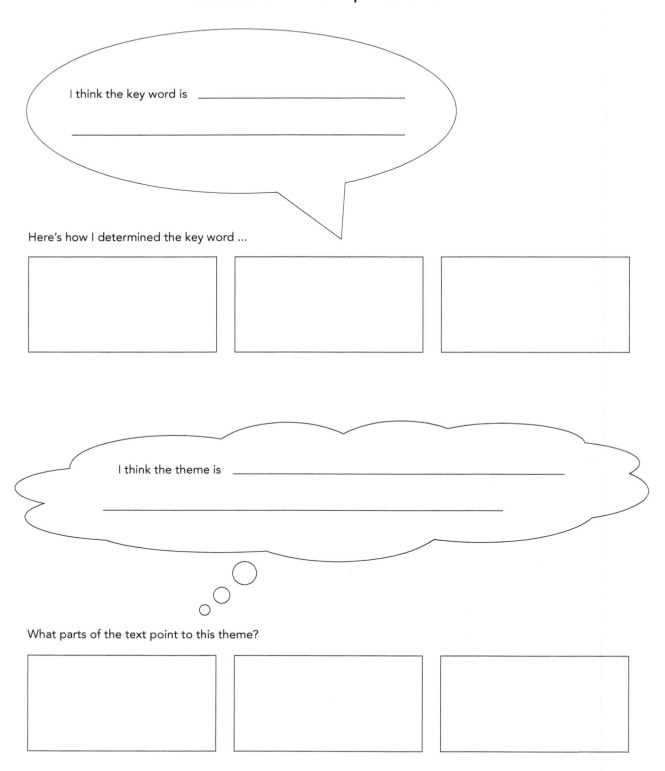

I think the key word is _____

_____

Here's how I determined the key word ...

I think the theme is _____

_____

What parts of the text point to this theme?

Figure 9-4: Key Words

Initial Level

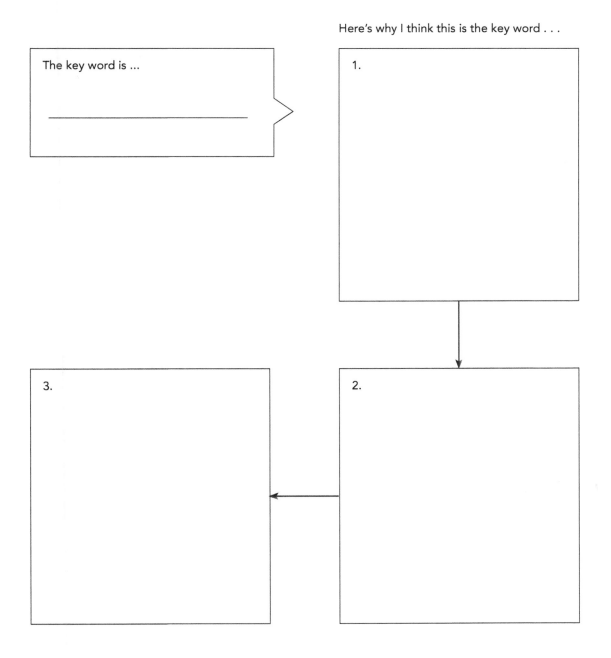

Here's why I think this is the key word . . .

The key word is ...

_____

1.

3.

2.

Before concluding this lesson, ask students if there might be another theme woven into "Lightning Chaser." Accept all appropriate responses and have students justify their claims. One possible key word might be *courage*. The theme might be *Courageous people often risk their lives so others can stay safe.* Help students read the text to gather support for this key word and theme.

Student Application: Tiered Activities for Differentiation

Since determining theme of an informational text may be new for students and more abstract than deciding on the theme of a story, we suggest you begin by having students identify just a key word or words in a text. When students are comfortable thinking abstractly and can identify key words, they can move on to determining themes.

Initial Level

Students at this level determine the key word of an article. They justify their decisions with evidence from the text.

Teacher action: Provide students with a text that is on their independent reading level and that has clear, consistent key words. Distribute the *Key Words* (Figure 9-4 on p. 103) graphic organizer.

Transitional Level

Students at this level determine a key word and theme of an article. They justify their decisions with evidence from the text.

Teacher action: Provide students with a text that is on their independent reading level and that has a clear, consistent theme. Distribute the *Key Words and Themes in Informational Texts* (Figure 9-3 on p. 102) graphic organizer.

Accomplished Level

Students at this level determine a key word and theme of an article. They justify their decisions with evidence from the text. In addition, after working independently on identifying a key word and theme, each student compares his or her key words and themes with another student working at this same level. If both students identify the same key word and theme, they work together to determine and justify a second key word and theme in the text.

Teacher action: Provide students with a text that is on their independent reading level and that may have more than one key word and theme. Distribute copies of the *Key Words and Themes in Informational Texts* graphic organizer (Figure 9-3 on p. 102).

Additional Recommended Books

Immigrant life in New York: A local legacy. (n.d.). Retrieved October 10, 2015, from http://www.americaslibrary.gov/es/ny/es_ny_museum_1.html.

Lyon, G. E. (2003). *Mother to tigers*. New York: Atheneum Books.

Van Steenwyk, E. (2008). *First dog Fala*. Atlanta, GA: Peachtree Publishers.

Chapter 10

Comparing and Contrasting Themes or Topics in Two Texts

Authors' Note

In this chapter, we investigate how a theme or topic is discussed when it appears in two different texts. We highly recommend that you first use the model lesson from **Chapter 9: Identifying Themes** to give students the underlying concept of theme.

What Is a Theme?

Theme is an interesting concept and a word with a broad meaning. The focus of this chapter is on comparing and contrasting a theme from one source to a second source. There are articles that refer to *theme* as something as simple as the theme of elevators in children's books (Zingher, 2011), but the spectrum shifts into much more serious themes such as bullying, forgiveness, hatred, love, and death. According to *The Literacy Dictionary* (Harris & Hodges, 1995), *theme*, as used in the context of this chapter, is defined as "a major idea or proposition broad enough to cover the entire scope of a literary or other work of art" (p. 256). The Literary Devices website defines *theme* as "the base that acts as a foundation for the entire literary piece." It goes on to say theme is basically the big idea of the story. Often a novel would have a major theme and subthemes, in which the author is sending multiple messages. A theme can be a hidden motive among characters, a moral of a story, a pattern of truths within a story, or statements about human nature or society. In any event, a theme is usually a hidden truth the reader needs to figure out.

Topic is the main idea or subject in an informational text. We tend to consider theme within fiction, such as the theme of *love is a powerful emotion* in *Romeo and Juliet*, and *topic* within nonfiction, such as the topic of *butterflies* in the young reader, *Caterpillar to Butterfly* (Marsh, 2012). Yet, books with themes also have topics, and the theme can be considered the point or "truths" about the topic. A topic is usually more easily identified than a theme, although both topics and themes cover the big ideas within a text.

In this chapter, we investigate how a theme or topic is discussed when it appears in two different texts. Readers must assimilate information from both texts and then compare and contrast the information. This is not an easy task; it can be simplified for students by identifying the theme or topic together prior to having students compare information from two texts.

What Does the Literature Say?

Theme can be either very apparent or difficult to discern in both stories and informational text. Themes often focus on characters' emotions and values and, consequently, their actions; "themes can be stated explicitly or implicitly (Tompkins, 2010, p. 300). Teachers probe students' thinking as they aid students in constructing a theme. Comparing and contrasting themes in literature goes beyond theme identification, as students must also be able to discuss how one book's theme relates to another. When students relate to books by theme, this helps them to make text-to-text connections and increases students' understanding as they discuss those connections (Smolen, Collins & Still, 2008).

It is through exploration and analysis of story content that students engage in theme and begin to think deeply about the author's message and the meaning of that message. When comparing and contrasting themes from two different books, students may be dealing with different views and varying information. They also need to identify similarities and differences within the information read. Walther and Fuhler (2008) state "As students compare and contrast the content and approaches used by different writers, they are engaged in critical thinking, both about the content and also about the craft of writing" (p. 23).

Yet, the challenge of using more than one text is worth the effort as the outcome is not only teaching students beginning research skills, but enlarging their knowledge base. Research done by Gelzheiser (2005) concluded that one of the causes of struggling readers' poor comprehension is because they have a limited knowledge base. Gelzheiser, Hallgren-Flynn, Connors, and Scanlon (2014) purport that using books organized into text sets by topics, along with direct instruction, increases students' knowledge base. They recommend pairing simpler texts with more complex texts, thereby exposing students to more experience with the concepts and vocabulary, along with providing contextual support to aid comprehension. In addition, Gelzheiser, Hallgren-Flynn, Connors and Scanlon (2014) found that using connecting mini-themes/topics was the fastest way to build a knowledge base.

Increasing Complexity through the Grades

When comparing and contrasting themes and topics, students need to know this entails identifying what is the same with two items and what is different. In essence, students are selecting information from two texts and placing the information into three categories: different for text one, different for text two, and the same for both.

At grade three, students are expected to be able to read books by the same author and compare and contrast the themes, settings, and plots (CCSS.RL.9.3). The books can be a series in which the characters remain pretty much the same. The themes, in this case, could be very different in nature or not. For instance, the theme in one book could be on how to make to new friends, and the theme in a second book could focus on forgiving friends. For informational text, they are to compare and contrast important points and key details in texts on the same topic (CCSS.RI.9.3).

At grade four, students are expected to compare and contrast the treatment of similar themes and topics (CCSS.RL.9.4). For instance, the theme of Cinderella—that being that a good and kindhearted person is eventually rewarded—could be compared and contrasted to *The Rough-Faced Girl* (Martin, 1992), a haunting Cinderella tale that stems from Algonquin Indian folklore, in which a young girl, scarred from working by the fire, is able to see a very handsome, powerful, and rich invisible man that her mean older sisters could not see … and you know the ending. In informational text, students are to integrate information from two texts on the same topic (CCSS.RI.9.4).

At grade five, the expectation is that students can "compare and contrast stories in the same genre" on their approaches to similar themes (CCSS.RL.9.5). In this case, students would be expected to read something, such as two survival stories, then compare and contrast what human qualities allowed the main characters to survive, such as overcoming or having the ability to accept loneliness, along with the differences in the authors' craft. For informational text, students are to integrate information from texts on the same topic (CCSS.RI.9.5).

Model Lesson 1: Comparing and Contrasting Theme

Students should understand how to identify theme (Chapter 9) prior to your teaching this lesson. This lesson expects students to be able to analyze theme as they compare one with another.

Lesson Objective:

Students will be able to compare and contrast the theme shared by two texts and write out the comparison on a Venn diagram.

Teacher Modeling

To begin, we will review what students learned in **Chapter 9: Identifying Themes** and the mnemonic device THE MEssage (Bunyi, 2011) that is meant to remind students that the theme of a book is the message the author is sending. Write *THE MEssage* on the board and ask students what they remember about the concept of *theme*. Tell students that just like books, movies have themes. Discuss the movie, *Finding Nemo*, and the events that take place in that movie. Let students who have seen the movie tell you the plot. Then ask: "What life lesson does Dory, one of the main characters, teach the audience?" (Don't give up, no matter the hardships.) Compare that to the movie, *How to Train Your Dragon*. Have students relate events that happened in that movie. Then ask: "What does Hiccup, the main character, teach us?" (Don't give up, you can succeed, just keep trying.) Ask if students can tell you the similarity in the theme of the two movies. (Don't give up!) Explain that many themes are used over and over again in books. Discuss some themes that you have talked about before, which stemmed from various key words. For instance, as mentioned in Chapter 9, Peter in *Whistle for Willie* is *persistent* (key word). The theme is that when people are persistent, they can accomplish whatever they set out to do. Another example is *King Midas and the Golden Touch*, in which the key word is *greed* and the theme is *having lots of money may not make you happy*.

To help students understand how to think about comparing and contrasting themes between two texts, put the following short poems up on the whiteboard or documentation camera:

Forever Friends! By Nancy L. Witherell & Mary C. McMackin	**Friends Forever?** By Nancy L. Witherell & Mary C. McMackin
"Friends forever," the two girls said, As they put matching bows upon their head. The first lost her bow, the second ran to her mother. Got another bow and gave it to the other.	"Friends forever," the two girls said, As they put matching bows upon their head. The first lost her bow, so she grabbed the other. The second one cried and ran to her mother.

Read each poem to the class, tell them you are thinking that both poems are similar, and explain that you see they are talking about friendship. Discuss how theme is an inference and that clues are given within the text. Read the poems again and show students how you would fill in the *Themes from Two Texts: Forever Friends! and Friends Forever?* chart (Figure 10-1 on the next page), explaining how you decided what to write in each of the columns. Explain to students that you are comparing the action of the characters from one poem to the other and what happened in each poem and also identifying a possible theme for each poem. Tell students that the actions or interactions of characters and a pattern of events in a story can help in identifying the theme.

Figure 10-1: Themes from Two Texts: *Forever Friends!* and *Friends Forever?*

Key Word: Friendship

Comparisons	Forever Friends!	Friends Forever?
Action of characters	Friends throughout the poem	Friends at the beginning
What happened?	One girl lost her bow and the other girl got her a new one	One girl lost her bow and took the bow from the other girl
What might the theme be?	Be kind to your friends	Not everyone is kind

Guided Practice

Tell students they are going to compare and contrast the theme of two different books. To simplify the lesson, picture books with the theme of friendship will be used. Each book is to be read to the class and the chart filled in together. You may use the two books we chose or choose two of your own. First read *Too Many Tamales* (Soto, 1993). In this book, Maria helps her mother make tamales as aunts, uncles, and cousins are about to arrive for a family gathering. At one point, Maria loses her mother's diamond ring and thinks it is in the cooked tamales. Her cousins, who are also her friends, eat all the tamales trying to find the diamond. Their tummies hurt, but they keep trying to help. Maria later saw the diamond was on her mother's finger—and more tamales had to be made.

The *Themes from Two Texts:* Too Many Tamales *and* My Friend Rabbit chart (Figure 10-2 on p. 109) would be filled out with students' help. Figure 10-2 is a model for you.

Next read *My Friend Rabbit* (Rohmann, 2002). In this tale, Rabbit is always in trouble and always assures his friend, Mouse, that he has an idea to fix the problem. A motorized toy plane gets stuck in a tree and Rabbit forces all the animals to make a tower to get the plane down. The tower crashes and the animals are not happy. At that time, Mouse is flying the tiny plane and Rabbit hangs on and covers Mouse's eyes. The plane, along with Mouse and Rabbit, gets stuck in the tree. The story ends with Rabbit saying he has another idea.

Now discuss the next column of the chart about *My Friend Rabbit*. Once you have discussed both columns, discuss the themes and how they are alike or different.

Figure 10-2: Themes from Two Texts: *Too Many Tamales* and *My Friend Rabbit*

Key Word: Friendship

Comparisons	Too Many Tamales	My Friend Rabbit
Action of characters	Friends help willingly.	Friends helped but not willingly. Rabbit had to carry them.
What happened?	Maria thought she lost her mother's diamond in the tamales. All her cousins (friends) helped her eat them to find the diamond.	Rabbit got the plane stuck up in the tree but forced the animals to help him. His friend Mouse was willing to help him. Then they both got stuck in the tree.
What might the theme be?	Friends stick by you when you're in trouble.	Friends stick by you when you're in trouble.

Student Application: Tiered Activities for Differentiation

Give each student a blank *Themes from Two Texts* graphic organizer (Figure 10-3 on p. 110 or create your own) as they read your selected texts. Tell students at the Initial and Intermediate Levels the topic. Remind students that the theme is the message of the text, and they can figure out the theme by using information from the text. You may consider doing this chart over a two-day span.

Initial Level

Using the *Themes from Two Texts* graphic organizer (Figure 10-3 on p. 110), guide students to fill in the name of the two texts and the key word. Have students read the first book and fill in the first column. Then fill in the second column after reading the second book. Tell students not to fill in the theme as they will fill in this box after they have met as a group.

Teacher action: Guide students to fill in the topic and the titles of book one and book two. After each book, gather these students together and discuss the theme. Once you have come to a consensus, students are to fill in the box.

Transitional Level

At this level, students are to do most of the chart, *Themes from Two Texts* (Figure 10-3 on p. 110), independently. They should be told the key word and be given a list of four possible themes. They are to choose the one or two that would fit in with the texts.

Teacher action: Tell students the topic. Write down four possible themes for the stories being read.

Accomplished Level

At this level, the teacher does not provide additional support. Students are to fill in the *Themes from Two Texts* graphic organizer (Figure 10-3 on p. 110) on their own.

Teacher action: Tell students to write in the key word after they have read both books. Check to see the key word is correct, as that will guide the theme.

Additional Recommended Books (Sets)

Key Word: Friendship

Gurtler, J. (2015). *Cora's decision*. Mermaid Kingdom. North Mankato, MN: Stone Arch Books.

Stead, R. (2009). *When you reach me*. New York: Random House.

Key Word: Survival During the Depression

Curtis, C. P. (1999). *Bud, not Buddy*. New York: Delacorte Books for Young Readers.

Moss, M. (2003). *Rose's journal: the story of a girl in the Great Depression*. New York: Harcourt.

Key Word: Homelessness

Bunting, E. (1991). *Fly away home*. New York: Clarion Books.

Williams, L. (2010). *The can man*. New York: Lee & Low Books.

Figure 10-3: Themes from Two Texts

Key Word:

Comparisons	Book 1	Book 2
Action of characters		
What happened?		
What might the theme be?		

Model Lesson 2: Comparing Topics from Two Informational Texts

Girls Research! Amazing Tales of Female Scientists (Phillips, 2014) showcases more than 50 women researchers. A biography of varying lengths is included for each researcher that highlights the challenges the women faced and each researcher's accomplishments. The topic of the book is obvious—girls do research—but within the book are subtopics—the various scientific areas women researched or still research. We chose this book as it contains about 50 short biographies and each woman researcher gets her own spotlight, along with others who have studied similar topics. The biographies in this book will be used for both the teacher model lesson and the guided practice. There is enough information in this book so that it could also be used for the independent student application. This informational text does have a theme, which, like many themes in informational text, is written near the end of the book. Speaking about the women highlighted in the book, the author states, "They prove that nothing is impossible for girls who rock."

Lesson Objective:
Students will compare and contrast important points from two texts on the same topic and write this information on a Venn diagram.

Teacher Modeling
Explain to students that you are going to focus on the topics of informational text and that you will be comparing information from one text with information from another. Because topics and information vary, the best graphic organizer to use for this exercise is a Venn diagram. The Venn diagram allows students to list various pieces of information, considering all attributes, such as nationality, education, and so forth. We will model by comparing two women who researched animals in the wild. Explain to students that you are going to compare and contrast Jane Goodall and Biruté Mary Galdikas's biographies as they are both woman researchers who studied animals in the wild. Using page 10 in *Girls Research!*, place Jane Goodall's biography on a projector or write the short passage on the board. Read this with students and discuss.

Next, do the same with Biruté Mary Galdikas, whose short biography is on the same page. Tell students that as you read, you will be thinking about how Goodall and Galdikas's animal research is alike and different.

After reading both biographies, explain to students that the topic of these two women's biographies would be "animal behavior researchers." Then show students how you fill in the Venn diagram (Figure 10-6 on p. 113). Explain that one person's name goes on one side and the other person's on the other side. Tell students they write something that was the same for both researchers where the circles overlap. Their Venn diagram will be similar to the figure on page 112 (Figure 10-4).

After completing the Venn diagram, discuss the similarities and differences. Tell students that the researchers were alike in the categories of what they studied, being pioneers, and living status.

Guided Practice
For guided practice, you want to use two short texts as you guide students through discovering similarities and differences. For the purpose of this lesson, we will go to pages 36 and 37 of *Girls Research!* and read the very short biographies of Bonnie Dunbar and Mae Jemison, both female astronauts. Hand out a Venn diagram to each student. Tell them they will need to read both texts before filling in the Venn diagram and that they will have to reread the biographies to make sure they are putting in the correct information. Have students read each selection. Explain that the overarching topic is "researchers," and ask if they can identify a more specific topic as you did with the animal behavior researchers. The answer will be something like "astronaut researchers." Then guide students in filling in their Venn diagrams (Figure 10-6 on p. 113). Begin by having students write how the women are both the same. Then ask how they are different. The Venn diagram will look like Figure 10-5 on page 112.

When reviewing, ask students in what categories the astronauts are alike. They both worked as astronauts and researchers and went up in space.

Figure 10-4: Venn Diagram for Jane Goodall and Biruté Mary Galdikas

Venn Diagram for Jane Goodall and Biruté Mary Galdikas

Topic: Animal Behavior Researchers

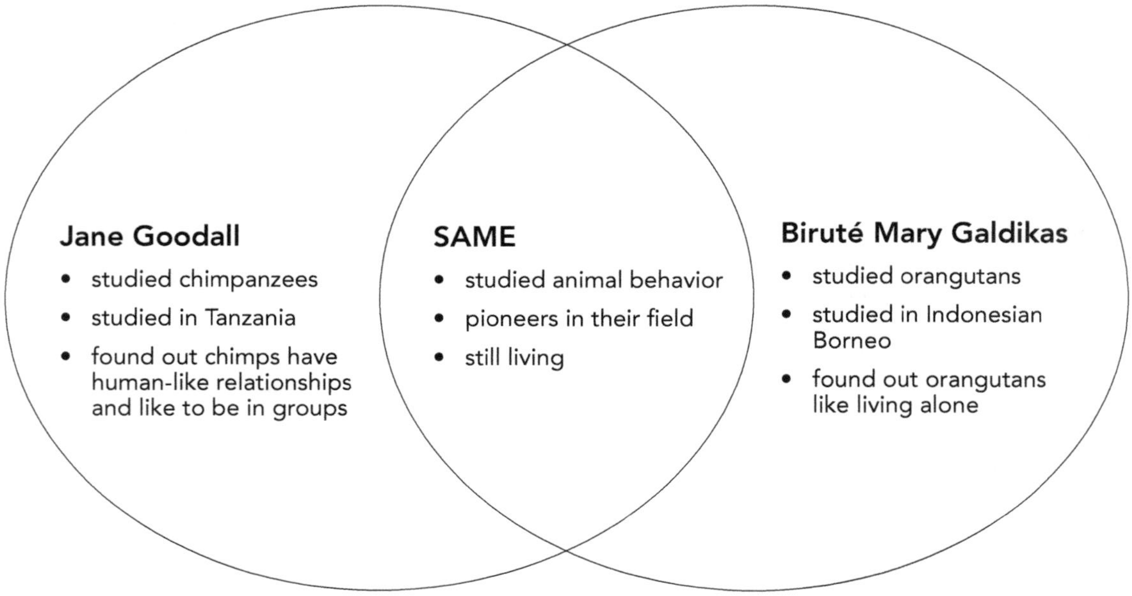

Jane Goodall
- studied chimpanzees
- studied in Tanzania
- found out chimps have human-like relationships and like to be in groups

SAME
- studied animal behavior
- pioneers in their field
- still living

Biruté Mary Galdikas
- studied orangutans
- studied in Indonesian Borneo
- found out orangutans like living alone

Figure 10-5: Venn Diagram for Bonnie Dunbar and Mae Jemison

Venn Diagram for Bonnie Dunbar and Mae Jemison

Topic: Astronaut Researchers

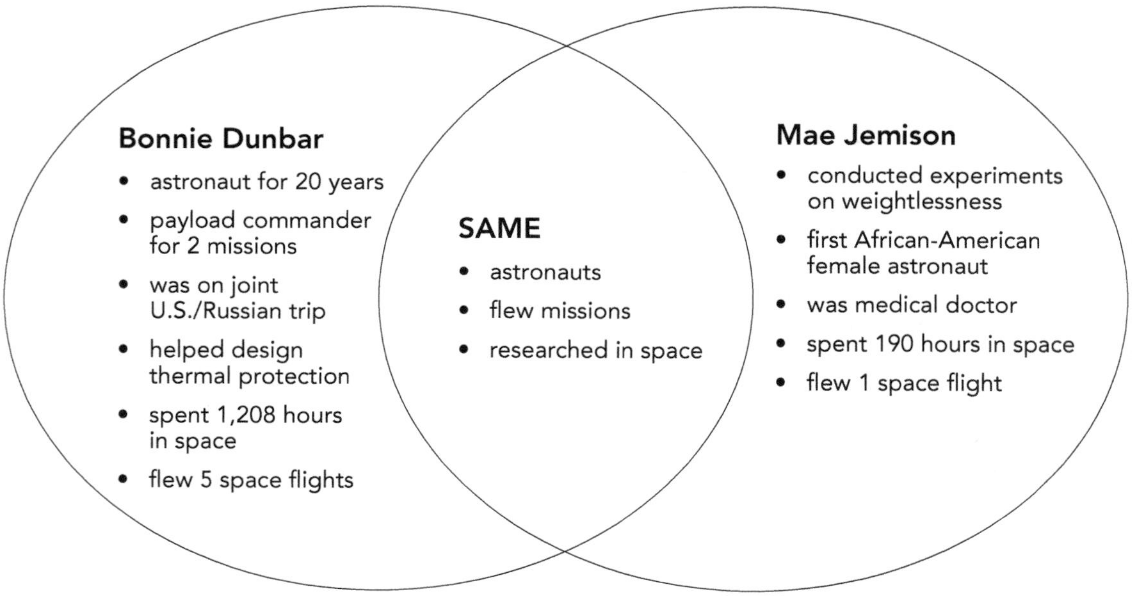

Bonnie Dunbar
- astronaut for 20 years
- payload commander for 2 missions
- was on joint U.S./Russian trip
- helped design thermal protection
- spent 1,208 hours in space
- flew 5 space flights

SAME
- astronauts
- flew missions
- researched in space

Mae Jemison
- conducted experiments on weightlessness
- first African-American female astronaut
- was medical doctor
- spent 190 hours in space
- flew 1 space flight

Figure 10-6: Venn Diagram: Comparing Two Informational Texts

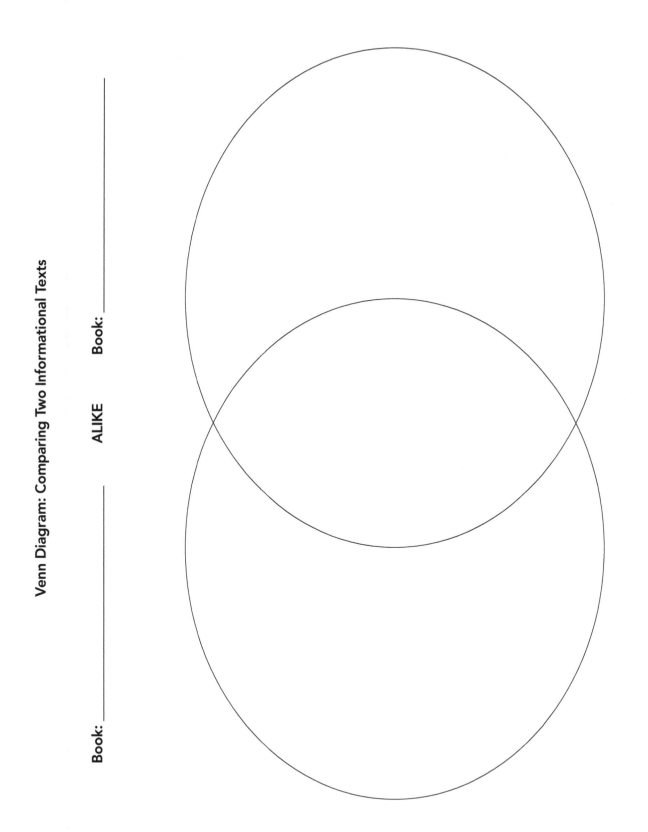

Venn Diagram: Comparing Two Informational Texts

Book: _____

ALIKE

Book: _____

Student Application: Tiered Activities for Differentiation

In order to differentiate instruction with the *Venn Diagram: Comparing Two Informational Texts* (Figure 10-6 on p. 113), think about what your students need to be successful. Will it be better to leave some of the pieces of the Venn diagram blank? Should you tell students how many facts will go into each section? The suggestions below are meant to guide but can be modified for your students.

Initial Level

At this level, give students the *Venn Diagram: Comparing Two Informational Texts* (Figure 10-6 on p. 113) with the similarities filled in. Have them read over the similarities and then refer to both texts to identify the differences.

Teacher action: Fill in the "same" area with facts from the text prior to giving the Venn diagram to students. Tell students the topic.

Transitional Level

At this level, give students the *Venn Diagram: Comparing Two Informational Texts* (Figure 10-6 on p. 113) and tell them the number of facts that should be in each section. For instance, explain that there are three similarities, text one should have three differences, and text two should have four. Have students name the topic.

Teacher action: Tell students the number of facts that should be in each piece of the Venn diagram.

Accomplished Level

At this level, do not provide additional scaffolding. Tell students they are to fill out the *Venn Diagram: Comparing Two Informational Texts* (Figure 10-6 on p. 113). Ask students to try to categorize the similarities of text one and text two. Have students name the topic.

Additional Recommended Books (Sets)
Topic Set: Oil Spills

Benoit, P. (2010). *The BP oil spill*. A True Book. New York: Scholastic.

Berger, M. (1994). *Oil spill!* Let's-Read-and-Find-Out Science. New York: HarperCollins Publishers.

Topic Set: The Art of Painting

Parker, M. B. (2012). *Colorful dreamer: the story of artist Henri Matisse*. New York: Dial Books.

Rosenstock, B. (2014). *The noisy paint box: the colors and sounds of Kandinsky's abstract art*. New York: Alfred A. Knopf.

Topic Set: The Art of Music

Brown, M. (2013). *Tito Puente, mambo king, rey del mambo*. New York: HarperCollins Publishers.

Weatherford, C. B. (2014). *Leontyne Price: voice of a century*. New York: Penguin Random House.

Chapter 11

Determining Point of View

What Is Point of View?

Linder (2012) notes there are two distinct types of point of view (POV) expressed in the CCSS: "One is about the narration and one is about the character" (n.p.). She goes on to explain that when talking about first-person, second-person, or third-person POV, we are really talking about POV of the narration. This type of point of view recognizes "where the narrator appears to stand in relationship to the reader as he tells the story" (Brooks, 2009, p. 75). POV is the vantage point from which the story is told. According to Linder (2012), rather than focusing on "simple narration identification" (n.p.), POV instruction should emphasize the second type of POV, namely, the character's point of view. A character's POV can be analyzed by investigating the character's "experiences, beliefs, attitudes, and values" (Linder, 2012, n.p.). This analysis helps readers understand the character's views of the world. When thinking about POV in informational writing, we need to take into account the author's purpose and his or her beliefs about the topic.

What Does the Literature Say?

We begin by reviewing point of view (POV) of the narration, which is probably what most of us think of when we hear the term *point of view*. In first-person point of view (*I* position), there is no distance between narrator and story because the narrator **is** the focus of the story. In second-person point of view (*you* position), the reader is made to feel as though he or she is a participant **in** the story. In third-person point of view (*he/she/it* position), the narrator stands **outside** the story and observes what's going on (Brooks, 2009, bold added, p. 75). Tapply (2002) cleverly explains that point of view "determines how your readers will experience the story. It gives them eyes, ears, noses, tongues, and fingers, as well as a brain for processing and interpreting the signals their senses send. POV tells readers where to sit, stand, walk, and run as your novel's events unfold. It determines what they will know and what will be withheld from them" (n.p.).

Backes (2001) speaks to the character's point of view by explaining, "The point of view—how you choose to tell your story—determines the voice of your writing. Children's stories are told from the viewpoint of your main character. Who this character is—his or her personality, temperament, strengths and weaknesses—will affect how the story is told" (n.p.).

Oster (1989) suggests that recognizing and understanding a character's (or narrator's) POV is essential for critical reading. She notes, "Before we take a narrator's story completely at face value, we must understand who is speaking and how that speaker is viewing the events or characters; we may have a different view" (p. 90). She suggests we approach POV by asking questions, such as "How would I feel in that person's place? How would others on the scene be reporting the same events?" (p. 90). She goes on to say that by asking these types of questions, readers can be "alert to the various possibilities, opinions, interpretations that an event, relationship, or dialogue—fictional or factual—can yield" (p. 90). Perhaps most striking is the following conclusion: "A story told from one particular point of view allows us, rather forces us, to 'see' the way that person is seeing, to see through the eyes of another" (Oster, 1989, p. 90).

Salvadore (2012) acknowledges that writers of nonfiction reveal their topics and their points of view when they decide what to include and not include, the word choices they use, and sometimes the illustrations they supply.

Increasing Complexity through the Grades

Between third grade and fifth grade, students are expected to delve deeply into POV. They begin by recognizing characters' points of view and comparing them to their own. By fifth grade, students analyze how a character's point of view affects what is told and how information is revealed.

At grade three, according to the CCSS, students are expected to "distinguish their own point of view from that of the narrator or those of the characters" (CCSS.RL.3.6). When reading informational texts, students are expected to "distinguish their own point of view from that of the author of a text" (CCSS.RI.3.6).

At grade four, students should be able to "compare and contrast the point of view from which stories are told, including the differences between first- and third-person narrations" (CCSS.RL.4.6). When reading informational texts, students are expected to "compare and contrast a firsthand and secondhand account of the same event or topic; describe the differences in focus and the information provided" (CCSS.RI.4.6).

At grade five, students should be able "to describe how a narrator's or speaker's point of view influences how events are described" (CCSS.RL.5.6). Students reading informational texts should also be able to "analyze multiple accounts of the same event or topic, noting important similarities and differences in the point of view they represent" (CCSS.RI.5.6).

Model Lesson 1: Point of View

For this lesson, it's best to select a book, preferably a picture book, in which the main character—the character telling the story—has a well-defined POV that evolves throughout the text.

Lesson Objective:
Students will be able to identify shifts in a character's point of view from the beginning to the end of a story.

Teacher Modeling
For this lesson, we'll use *Good-bye, 382 Shin Dan Dong* (Park & Park, 2002), the story of a little girl named Jangmi, her family, and their move from Korea to America. Jangmi, the main character, is anxious about the move and sad to be leaving her family and best friend, Kisuni. Jangmi's point of view is easily identifiable all the way through the book.

Before you read, let students know that when you finish you'll be talking about Jangmi's point of view—how she viewed her life at the start of the story, during the story, at the end of the story. You'll also be talking about how her view changed and why. Explain that good readers try to understand how characters view their situations. They think about the problem the character is facing and how the character might feel in the situation. Readers may put themselves in the shoes of the character and wonder if they would feel and react to the situation as the character did.

Reread *Good-bye, 382 Shin Dan Dong* and have the following seven questions visible for all to see. Hide the answers. As you read each question, think aloud your answer and how you determined it, when necessary.

1. Which character is telling this story? Who is the main character? (Jangmi)

2. What problem is this character facing? (Her family was moving from Korea to America.)

3. At the start of the story, how did this character view her world and what was happening to her? In other words, what was her point of view? (She was sad and nervous about having to move. She didn't like the idea of leaving her best friend Kisuni, and she was scared because there would be many new things in America—for example, different types of food.)

4. Did the main character's point of view change? (It was starting to change.)

5. When did it change? (When Jangmi and her family moved to their new house, neighbors came to welcome them to the neighborhood. A little girl, Mary, was with them. She brought a bowl of watermelon and honeydew melon. Jangmi said that perhaps one day she and Mary would do the same things she did in Korea with Kisuni but not right now.)

6. Why did the character's point of view change? (Jangmi's point of view began to change after she saw where she'd be living and after she met Mary, but she was still thinking about her life in Korea and missing her friend Kisuni.)

7. How do you know? (The book ended with Jangmi writing a letter to her friend Kisuni.)

Finally, share Oster's (1989) quote: "A story told from one particular point of view allows us, rather forces us, to 'see' the way that person is seeing, to see through the eyes of another" (p. 90) and ask students to react to it. How might the statement apply to this story?

Guided Practice

Prepare a role-playing activity. Write a scenario on a card. Sample scenario one: An 11-year-old boy has to play with his 3-year-old cousin while the cousin's mom does laundry. The 11-year-old boy is bored and would rather be playing video games with his friends. Select a student to be the younger child, a student to be his mom, and one student to be the 11-year-old boy. Only these three students will know what you've written on the card. The actors should talk and interact to illustrate their points of view. The students who are watching should try to determine how each actor views the situation. Once students have engaged in the role-playing activity, initiate a discussion: Have students explain how each actor's point of view influenced his or her actions, what was communicated, and how it was communicated.

Repeat this process with scenario two: A middle-school girl dreams of being on the Olympic gymnastics team, but she lacks the confidence she needs to win under pressure. Her coach believes she has the ability to compete.

For this lesson, we use *Thunder Cake* (Polacco, 1990), a delightful picture book told from a young girl's point of view. At the start of the story, the young girl is terrified of thunderstorms. Her loving grandmother taught her how to make thunder cake and, in the process, how to overcome her fear of thunderstorms. Read aloud *Thunder Cake* so students can get the gist and enjoy the story line. Display and read aloud the seven questions you used in the "Teacher Modeling" section of this lesson to remind students about the process they can use to determine POV. Next, display the following three questions:

1. What was the main character's point of view at the start of the story?

2. How do you know?

3. When and why did the main character's point of view change? Provide evidence.

Explain that as you think about the young girl's point of view, you'll be relying on these three questions. Compare and contrast the questions to the original seven questions. Let students know that in order to answer the three new questions, they will need to know who the main character is and what challenge(s) this character faced. By condensing the questions to just three, you are gradually encouraging students to be responsible for understanding the necessary story elements.

Have students work in small heterogeneous groups to discuss the answers to the three questions. As they work, visit each group to evaluate how much support each student will need in order to be successful when working independently.

When all groups have had time to discuss the questions, have a few students explain how they answered them.

Finally, display the following two questions:

1. Explain how the main character's point of view changed throughout the story.
2. What influenced this change or these changes?

Ask students what information they would need to have to answer these two questions. Hopefully, they will say they need to know who the main character is, what problem this character is facing, what his or her point of view was at the start of the story, and what it was at the end of the story.

Conclude the lesson by reminding students that readers comprehend stories more fully when they think about how the main character views the problem and events in the story.

Student Application: Tiered Activities for Differentiation

If thinking about a character's point of view is a new skill for your students, they should begin by reading short texts (picture books or a few short chapters from a chapter book) that contain characters who display clear points of view.

In this part of the lesson, we differentiate based on the number and types of questions students use to identify POV, as modeled in the previous lesson.

Initial Level

Students will provide written answers to the following questions:

1. Which character is telling this story? Who is the main character?
2. What problem is this character facing?
3. At the start of the story, how did this character view her world and what was happening to her? In other words, what was her point of view?
4. Did the main character's point of view change?
5. When did it change?
6. Why did the character's point of view change?
7. How do you know?

Teacher action: Select a text in which the main character's point of view clearly changes from the beginning to the end of the story. Also, distribute the seven questions to each student. You may want to have students work with a partner, if necessary.

Transitional Level

Students will provide written answers to the following questions:

1. What was the main character's point of view at the start of the story?

2. How do you know?

3. When and why did the main character's point of view change? Provide evidence.

Teacher action: Select a text in which the main character's point of view changes from the beginning to the end of the story. Also, distribute the three questions to each student.

Accomplished Level

Students will provide written responses to the following two questions:

1. Explain how the main character's point of view changed throughout the story.

2. What influenced this change or these changes?

Teacher action: Select a text in which the main character's point of view changes from the beginning to the end of the story. Also, distribute the two questions to each student.

Additional Recommended Books

Gardiner, J. R. (1980). *Stone Fox*. New York: The Trumpet Club.

Nodset, J. L. (2010). *Go away, dog*. New York: Sandy Creek.

Rathmann, P. (1995). *Officer Buckle and Gloria*. New York: G.P. Putnam's Sons.

Model Lesson 2: Identifying Point of View in Informational Texts

Looking closely at the facts, statistics, details, and examples writers choose to include in (or leave out of) an informational text can help readers determine an author's point of view.

Lesson Objectives:

Students will be able to identify an author's purposes for writing an article and the author's point of view. Students will also be able to compare and contrast their point of view with that of the author.

Teacher Modeling

On construction paper, trace around a pair of flip-flops, draw a pair, or find a clip art image of a pair online. Make sure your flip-flops include the Y-shaped piece that fits between one's toes. Photocopy for students. Then have students cut out a pair of flip-flops. Each pair should be cut into two individual flip-flops.

Explain that an author's point of view in an informational text can be determined by thinking about the author's reason for writing the text. Once the reason is clear, readers look closely at the information the author shares. The information will reveal what the author believes and what he or she wants us to believe. To illustrate this point, read aloud a short text. We selected *Did Someone Say "Free Land"?* (Miller, 2006). Before reading the article aloud, set a purpose for listening: Let students know that after you read the article, you'll be asking them to show a thumbs-up or thumbs-down to let you know if they would have wanted to take advantage of the Homestead Act of 1862. Read the article and then spend a couple of minutes having students share their reasons. Note that if you cannot find this article, any article on the Homestead Act should work.

Let students know that when you read the short text again, you're going to try to figure out the author's purpose for writing it—was it to inform, to instruct, to persuade, or to entertain? You'll also be thinking about what the author wanted us to learn about the Homestead Act, what she believed, and what she wanted us to believe.

Read the article aloud again, and then display one flip-flop using a documentation camera.

Explain that Melissa Miller wrote this article to give us information about the Homestead Act. On the back of the flip-flop, write the name of the article and "to inform."

Use the top front of the flip-flop—where you put your toes—to write what you think the author believes about this topic, and use the bottom of the flip-flop—where you put the arch and heel of your foot—to list evidence from the article that helped you figure out her beliefs. Explain that readers can often get clues about an author's beliefs from the title of articles, subtitles, topic sentences, and the words writers use to describe the topic.

You might record the following information:
The author believes: The Homestead Act of 1862 was a good opportunity for people who met the requirements. Provide evidence, including the words "Free Land" in the title, the number of acres Americans were promised, and how many people applied. Note that the author didn't share any reasons not to apply for land.

Display the second flip-flop. You'll use this one to compare and contrast your POV with that of the author. Decide if you agree with this author's point of view or not. Write "Yes" or "No" on the top of the second flip-flop (where your toes would go) to let us know if you agree with the author or not. For instance, you might say that based on the information in the article, you would write "Yes" on the flip-flop. In the bottom of the flip-flop (where the arch and heel of your foot would go), explain your thinking. You might write "It seems as though the Homestead Act would be a wonderful opportunity to get free land."

Finally, arrange the flip-flops to show if they are a "matched pair" or not. Put them side by side, facing the same direction, if you and the author share the same point of view about the topic; face the flip-flops in opposite directions if your point of view is completely different from that of the author; or arrange the flip-flops in a way that shows that you fall somewhere in between.

Guided Practice

Begin by reviewing *Did Someone Say "Free Land"?* (Miller, 2006) and the information you wrote on the first flip-flop above. Next, introduce another short article on the Homestead Act, *The Homestead Act Went into Effect May 20, 1862* (written by the staff of the Library of Congress, n.d.). Use the same thumbs-up/thumbs-down prompt as you did in the previous lesson, and allow a few minutes after you finish reading for students to share their thoughts.

Next, display a new, blank pair of flip-flops on your whiteboard or use a documentation camera. On the back of one flip-flop, record the title of the article and the author's purpose. Students should say that the article was written to inform. Have students help you determine the author's purpose, his point of view, and evidence that supports the point of view. As students provide responses, record them on the flip-flop (as you did in the model lesson above). Students may say that the author believes the homesteaders could get free land and be successful, but that it would not be easy. Your notes may include: *Evidence: "Land available! Come and get it!"; took 20 years for Congress to pass the act; unfamiliar territory; isolated; grasshoppers that destroyed corn crops; no schools or social gatherings; railroads made it easier to travel; railroads raised the demand for beef.*

Display the second blank flip-flop. Invite a student to share his or her point of view. Does this student agree with the author? Was the Homestead Act both an opportunity and a gamble for pioneers? Have the student write "Yes" or "No" on the flip-flop and explain his or her reasoning. Have the student arrange the flip-flops to show if they are a "matched pair." If the student and author share the same point of view, both flip-flops should be side by side, facing the same direction. If the student and author disagree, the flip-flops should be side by side but facing opposite directions. If the student and author are somewhat in agreement, one flip-flop may be placed vertically on the desk, while the second flip-flop may be placed horizontally beside the first.

Before concluding the lesson, review the author's point of view from the previous lesson with the author's point of view from this lesson. Did the author of *Did Someone Say "Free Land"?* share the same point of view as the author of *The Homestead Act Went into Effect May 20, 1862*? Look back at the information you recorded on the two flip-flops. Would they be a "matched pair"? Ask a student to arrange the two flip-flops to represent the differences in their points of view. Talk about why the points of view were different and how the points of view influenced what each author included in his or her article.

Student Application: Tiered Activities for Differentiation

We differentiate these activities by having students at the Initial and Transitional Levels read to identify an author's POV and then compare the author's POV with their own. Students at the Initial Level complete part of the task orally, while students at the Transitional Level write notes to record their thinking. Students who are working at the Accomplished Level compare the POV of two authors who have written about the same topic but may or may not share the same POV.

Initial Level

Students will fill out two flip-flops. On the back of the first flip-flop, they'll write the title of the article and author's purpose (inform, explain, persuade, or entertain). On the front, they'll write the author's point of view and include evidence to support this statement. On the second flip-flop, students write "Yes" or "No" to express whether or not the author's point of view and theirs are the same. They should be prepared to orally explain their reasoning. Students arrange the flip-flops on their desk to convey whether or not they are a matched pair.

Teacher action: Select one informational text that presents a clear purpose and author's point of view. The text should be on students' instructional reading level. Have flip-flops ready to distribute.

Transitional Level

Students will fill out two flip-flops. On the back of the first flip-flop, they'll write the title of the article and author's purpose (inform, explain, persuade, or entertain). On the front, they'll write what the author believes and include evidence to support this statement. On the second flip-flop, students write "Yes" or "No" to express whether or not the author and they share the same POV. On the bottom of the second flip-flop, they explain their reasoning. They should arrange the flip-flops on their desk to convey whether or not they are a matched pair.

Teacher action: Select one informational text that is written on students' instructional reading level. Have flip-flops ready to distribute.

Accomplished Level

Students will read two different texts on the same event or topic and fill out two flip-flops. On the back of each, they'll write the title of the article and author's purpose (inform, explain, persuade, or entertain). On the front of each, they'll write each author's point of view and include evidence to support these statements. They should arrange the flip-flops on their desk to convey whether or not they are a matched pair. Students should be prepared to orally report on whether they agree with either author's point of view and why or why not.

Teacher action: Select two informational texts on the same topic. Have flip-flops ready to distribute.

Additional Recommended Articles or Books (Informational Texts)

Floca, B. *Locomotive.* New York: Atheneum Books for Young Readers.

Nyikos, S. A. (2014). "Balancing rocks." *Highlights for Children, 69*(11), 12–13.

Sala, E. (2009). "Ocean alert!" *National Geographic Kids*, 392, 10.

Chapter 12

Getting Started with Arguments: Claims, Reasons, and Evidence

What Are Claims, Reasons, and Evidence?

Unlike persuasion, in which the writer or speaker can use emotions, authority, fear, generalizations, logic, and more to influence someone's beliefs or behavior, arguments are designed to use logic to substantiate that something is true. An argument is based on a claim, or a belief, which is grounded in evidence. In order to have an argument, the claim needs to be debatable—there must be room for disagreement. Think of a court case. The defense attorney claims that his client is innocent and then uses logic and evidence to prove beyond a shadow of a doubt that the claim is true. In the intermediate grades, we don't expect students to analyze complex argument structures, but we can begin to lay the foundation by having them identify how authors "use reasons and evidence to support particular points in a text," which is a career and college readiness standard. *Points* are claims or beliefs the author presents; *reasons* support the points and are used to convince readers that the points are valid; *evidence* includes details, facts, quotes, numbers, and so on that support the reasons.

What Does the Literature Say?

Students are often exposed to beliefs that are supported with reasons and examples, but they may not always realize it. An author, for example, may try to convince readers that a little boy is having a terrible, horrible, no good, very bad day. She defends her belief that this day is horrendous with reasons and evidence. Another author may try to convince readers that traveling along the Oregon Trail was challenging in many ways. She presents logical examples to support her claim. A different writer may claim that wild animals should not live in captivity. This author may include valid reasons to justify his points. These authors aren't necessarily trying to influence the reader's beliefs and behaviors, as we might expect in persuasive advertisement or in propaganda. Instead, they are trying to make a case for their views.

Fulton and Poeltler (2013), an assistant professor and a second-grade teacher, respectively, acknowledge, "Arguing an idea from evidence is not an easy task. We found that our students could make claims about an idea and sometimes provide some sort of an explanation, but they struggled to support their claims with evidence" (p. 30). Yet, generating evidence and comprehending evidence-supported claims are important skills. Ford (2008) reports that the "… language (particularly the construction and critique of evidence-based explanations and arguments) has been identified as an essential aspect of doing science" (Washburn & Cavagnetto, 2013, p. 129). Evidence-based explanations and arguments appear not only in science materials, but across the curriculum and in different genres. Haria (2010) points out that one reason students may find it challenging to construct meaning from arguments is that arguments are often embedded within different text structures. According to Haria (2010), to comprehend arguments, students need to be able to (1) understand that what they are reading is an argument; (2) recognize that argument is often found within a larger text structure, such as narrative or informational texts (in other words, it is not without a context); (3) acknowledge that the reader may come to the text with preconceived beliefs and must keep an open mind; and (4) assess the merit of the argument (pp. 30–31).

In recent years, the emphasis on reading has shifted from asking students to make personal connections to asking them to focus on what is stated directly in the text (Serafini, 2013). This attention to close reading, as described by Fisher and Frey (2014), includes, among other features, text-dependent questions (questions that can be answered only by citing evidence from a text) and "discussion of the text, including argumentation" (p. 369). Furthermore, students throughout the elementary grades are now being assessed on how well they can justify their understanding of texts by supplying evidence from passages. In order for fourth graders to achieve at the "Advanced" level on the National Assessment of Educational Progress (NAEP, 2009), for example, they must demonstrate that they can "make complex inferences and construct and support their inferential understanding of the text. Students should be able to apply their understanding of a text to make and support a judgment" (n.p.). By providing students with opportunities to analyze texts for logical arguments, we are teaching them how to think critically about authors' claims and supporting evidence.

Increasing Complexity through the Grades

As we investigate claims, reasons, and evidence, we focus on Standard 8 of the CCSS: "Delineate and evaluate the argument and specific claims in a text, including the validity of the reasoning as well as the relevance and sufficiency of the evidence" (CCSS.ELA-Literacy.CCRA.R.8). Surprisingly, Standard 8 applies only to informational texts (RI); there is no corresponding standard in the Reading Literature (RL) strand. Since we agree with Haria (2010) that arguments can be embedded in both narrative and informational texts, we'll focus on both genres in this chapter.

At grade three, the CCSS expectation is that students will be able to "describe the logical connection between particular sentences and paragraphs in a text (e.g., comparison, cause/effect, first/second/third in a sequence)" (CCSS.RI.3.8). Students should be familiar with transition words and phrases, such as *after, on Wednesday, soon, before lunch, for example, but, even though, down the street, because, finally, first, second, next,* and *then.* They should also recognize that writers use pronouns to link sentences (e.g., using a proper name in one sentence and a pronoun to represent the person in the next). Writers also repeat key words in sentences and often use synonyms to provide cohesive links between ideas.

At grade four, the CCSS expectation is that students will be able to "Explain how an author uses reasons and evidence to support particular points in a text." (CCSS.RI.4.8). At this level, students analyze texts for authors' beliefs, reasons that explain why authors feel and think the way they do, and evidence—how authors back up their thoughts and feelings with examples, facts, details, etc. Students look at the author's main ideas and details that support them.

At grade five, students continue to build on what they learned in grade four about authors, their beliefs, and how they support their ideas. In addition, at this grade level students should be able to "explain how an author uses reasons and evidence to support particular points in a text, identifying which reasons and evidence support which point(s)" (CCSS.RI.5.8). Students should be able to analyze the text, identifying both explicit and implicit points the author is trying to make, explain why she or he made them, and determine how the information supplied either supports or perhaps doesn't fully support the points.

Model Lesson 1:
Reasons and Evidence to Support Claims

In this lesson, we introduce the idea that *points* are claims or beliefs the author presents; *reasons* support the points and are used to convince readers that the points are valid; *evidence* includes details, facts, quotes, numbers, and so forth.

Lesson Objective:
Students will be able to find reasons and/or evidence to support a claim.

Teacher Modeling
Read aloud *Brave Irene* (Steig, 1988). For this first read, have students listen for the gist of the entire story (who is in the story and what happened). Next, explain that some people may claim Irene is brave—as the title says. If students aren't familiar with the word *brave*, spend time reviewing its meaning (e.g., heroic, courageous, willing to face danger).

Display a blank *Reasons or Evidence* chart (Figure 12-1 below). As you read aloud the first six pages of *Brave Irene*, talk about the reasons or evidence you find that support the idea that Irene is brave. Jot down notes in Figure 12-1. Your completed chart might look like Figure 12-2 below.

Figure 12-1: Reasons or Evidence That Show Irene Is Brave (Blank)

Reasons or Evidence That Show Irene Is Brave
1.
2.
3.
4.

Figure 12-2: Reasons or Evidence That Show Irene Is Brave

Reasons or Evidence That Show Irene Is Brave
1. Irene insisted on going to the palace even though she knew it was snowing and that it would be a long walk.
2. Irene faced a very cold wind that hit her in the face, but she kept going.
3. The weather got worse, but she didn't stop.
4. Even though she stumbled and the box was hard to carry, she walked up the hill to Farmer Bennett's sheep pasture.

Finally, display the *Valuemeter* (Figure 12-3 on the next page), the one without the arrow, and think aloud as you define each category (all terms are real words!): *Fantabulous* = a combination of *fantastic* and *fabulous*; outstanding! *Splendiferous* = splendid, rather impressive. *A-Okay* = all right, not terrific, but no problems. *Not Quite* = could be better.

Figure 12-3: Valuemeter (Blank)

VALUEMETER

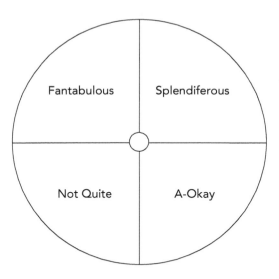

Figure 12-4: Valuemeter

VALUEMETER

Return to the chart and use the *Valuemeter* to rate the reasons and evidence you've found so far. Determining a rating to which everyone can agree isn't as important as providing an opportunity for students to evaluate the quality of the evidence. You may say something like, "I think the author is doing a splendiferous job of providing reasons and evidence to support Irene's bravery. We've only read a few pages, and already he has supported his claim with several effective reasons. After thinking through your rationale, demonstrate how you draw a pointer from the center of the *Valuemeter* to the word *Splendiferous* (Figure 12-4 on p. 126).

Guided Practice

Explain that you already have reasons and evidence showing that Irene is brave. Speculate that some people may think she is stubborn rather than brave. Define *stubborn* if need be ("a quality that makes you continue trying to do or achieve something that is difficult," according to Merriam-Webster's Learner's Dictionary online). Explain that when people are stubborn, they are so determined to do something, they never give up. Spend a couple minutes sharing and having students share examples of stubborn actions to be sure everyone understands this word.

Now let's see if we can find reasons or evidence to show that Irene is stubborn. Display a blank *Reasons or Evidence* chart on which you can record reasons or evidence that support the claim that Irene is stubborn (Figure 12-5 below).

Figure 12-5: Reasons or Evidence That Show Irene Is Stubborn (Blank)

Reasons or Evidence That Show Irene Is Stubborn
1.
2.
3.
4.

Read the next three pages of *Brave Irene* and have students help you fill in the *Reasons or Evidence* chart above. Your completed chart might look like Figure 12-6 below.

Figure 12-6: Reasons or Evidence That Show Irene Is Stubborn

Reasons or Evidence That Show Irene Is Stubborn
1. The snow was so deep that she was having trouble walking.
2. The snow got into her boots and her feet were freezing, but she was determined to keep going.
3. The wind got so bad that it broke branches off the trees and prevented Irene from going ahead. Irene was persistent and walked backward into the wind.
4. Even when the wind told her to go home, she refused.

Finally, display a *Valuemeter* (Figure 12-3 on p. 126). Have students turn and talk, discussing where they think you should point the arrow. After they have had time to formulate their answers, call on a few students to elicit their responses and draw an arrow from the center of the *Valuemeter* to the most appropriate word.

Students may begin to see that many of their reasons and evidence can be used simultaneously to support "brave Irene" and "stubborn Irene." That's fine. You'll come back to this point at the end of the lesson after students have read the entire book to see what they think then. For now, randomly divide the class into two groups. Have half of the class work together to record reasons and evidence that support the claim Irene is brave, while the other half of the class work together to record reasons and evidence that support the claim Irene is stubborn. As students work, circulate to assess which students will be assigned the Initial Level, Transitional Level, and Accomplished Level follow-up activities.

When complete, have students share their reasons and evidence for "brave Irene" and "stubborn Irene." Many of their answers will probably be the same. Invite students to discuss the following questions: Are people who are brave always stubborn? Are people who are stubborn always brave?

Student Application: Tiered Activities for Differentiation

We differentiate these activities by providing the following support: At the Initial and Transitional Levels, identify the claims and students find reasons or evidence to support them. Additionally, at the Initial Level, students work with a partner and at the Transitional Level, students work independently. Students working at the Accomplished Level make a claim and support it with reasons or evidence. At all levels, students use the *Valuemeter* to rate the quality of the reasons or evidence they find.

Initial Level

Working in pairs, students find reasons or evidence to support a teacher-determined claim, draw an arrow on the *Valuemeter*, and explain (orally) why they put the pointer where they did.

Teacher action: Select a text that has a clear claim and several reasons or pieces of evidence to support it. Using the *Reasons or Evidence* chart (Figure 12-7 on p. 129), fill in the claim you want students to support before distributing the chart to students. Pass out a copy of the *Valuemeter* (Figure 12-3 on p. 126) to each pair of students.

Transitional Level

Working individually, students find reasons or evidence to support a teacher-determined claim, draw an arrow on the *Valuemeter*, and provide a written explanation of why they put the pointer where they did.

Teacher action: Select a text that has a clear claim and several reasons or pieces of evidence to support it. Using the *Reasons or Evidence* chart (Figure 12-7 on p. 129), fill in the claim you want students to support before distributing the chart to students or having students create their own. Pass out a copy of the *Valuemeter* (Figure 12-3 on p. 126) to each student.

Accomplished Level

Working individually, students find reasons and evidence to support a claim they make, draw an arrow on the *Valuemeter*, and provide a written explanation of why they put the pointer where they did.

Teacher action: Select a text that has a clear claim and several reasons and pieces of evidence to support it. Have students create a copy of the *Reasons or Evidence* chart (Figure 12-7 below) and pass out the *Valuemeter* (Figure 12-3 on p. 126) to each student.

Figure 12-7: Reasons or Evidence

Reasons or Evidence That Show:
1.
2.
3.
4.

Additional Recommended Books

This lesson could be replicated with any text that provides different perspectives. We recommend the following:

dePaola, T. (2005). *Stagestruck*. New York: Putnam's Sons.

Giff, P. R. (1987). *The secret at the Polk Street School*. The Polk Street Mysteries. New York: Dell Publishing.

MacLachlan, P. (1985). *Sarah, plain and tall*. New York: Trumpet.

Model Lesson 2:
Reasons and Evidence to Support Claims

To investigate claims, reasons, and evidence, we use texts that contain more than one major point. It's best to use a short article or a couple of pages from a book so students aren't overwhelmed when they first begin to identify claims, reasons, and evidence. This lesson should follow the previous lesson.

Lesson Objective:

Students will be able to determine reasons and evidence that support claims.

Teacher Modeling

Begin this lesson by reviewing the following terms: *Points* are claims or beliefs the author presents; *reasons* support the points and are used to convince readers that the points are valid; *evidence* includes details, facts, quotes, numbers, and so on that support the reasons.

For this lesson, we use *Max Hunter Collection: A Local Legacy* (article from the Library of Congress) (Figure 12-9 on p. 130). Have available copies of the article so students can read along with you. Your first read-aloud should enable students to enjoy the text and become familiar with its content.

Display a copy of the *Points and Reasons (Blank)* chart (Figure 12-8). Read aloud the article a second time and stop after the first point (belief or claim) is introduced (*Without people like Max Hunter, important pieces of our nation's history would be lost*). Talk about why this is a *claim* (a point the author is trying to make), and record the claim on the chart. Next, talk about whether or not the point is supported. In this case, the claim is supported. As you think aloud, explain how you know which reasons and pieces of evidence are linked to which claim. Record the reasons and evidence you find to support each claim.

Figure 12-8: Points and Reasons (Blank)

Points (claims)	Are the points supported? (Y/N)	What reasons and evidence support the points?
1.		
2.		

Figure 12-9: *Max Hunter Collection: A Local Legacy*

Max Hunter Collection:

A Local Legacy

Without people like Max Hunter, important pieces of our nation's history would be lost. He alone preserved more than 20 years of music and folk stories from people in the Ozarks. Can you guess how he did it?

Hunter was a traveling salesman from Springfield, Missouri, who went into the hills and backwoods of the Ozark Mountains. He took a reel-to-reel tape recorder with him to record folk songs and stories of the people in this remote area. Thanks to him, 1,600 Ozark Mountain folk songs, recorded between 1956 and 1972, are available for listening at the Springfield-Greene County Library in Springfield, Missouri.

It was a good thing that Hunter recorded these folk tales and songs when he did, because once radio and TV became popular, people in the Ozarks stopped sitting on their porches entertaining themselves with stories and music. Many patterns of Ozark life would have been lost.

Can you imagine what listening to these songs will tell you about life in the Ozarks that you won't find in a history book?

Your completed chart might look something like the following *Points and Reasons—Max Hunter Collection* chart (see Figure 12-10 below). Next, review the quality of the reasons and evidence. Explain that similar to a jury in a court case, you are going to decide if there is enough strong evidence to support the author's point(s) or not. Briefly go back through the points and the reasons/evidence. Make a determination about your "verdict." In this case, you might say that you think there was strong evidence to support the author's points because the author provided reasons (why we need people like Max Hunter) and evidence (number of songs he recorded, what the songs were about, where people can find the collection). The author also presented one more point, which was supported by a reason. In a court case, jurors can decide that there is enough strong evidence to support a case, there is not enough strong evidence, or the jury can be deadlocked—meaning that the jurors can't come to a decision about the evidence. Explain that in the case of *Max Hunter Collection*, your verdict would be that the author provided enough strong evidence to support his or her claims.

To bring closure, as a whole group, have students talk briefly about whether or not they agree with the claims the author made.

Figure 12-10: Points and Reasons—*Max Hunter Collection*

Points (claims)	Are the points supported? (Y/N)	What reasons and evidence support the points?
1. Without people like Max Hunter, important pieces of our nation's history would be lost.	Yes	• He preserved more than 20 years of music and stories from people who lived in areas of the Ozark Mountains where few people visited. • He recorded 1,600 songs between 1956 and 1972. • The songs and stories tell us about life in the Ozarks. (NOTE: Explain that this evidence supports the first point rather than the second point, even though the fact is in the second paragraph.) • The recordings are now in a library in Missouri.
2. It was good that Max Hunter collected the songs when he did.	Yes	• After he recorded the songs and stories, fewer people sat on their porches. Instead, they watched TV or listened to the radio.

Guided Practice

For this activity, we use page 6 of *Your Skeletal System Works!* (Brett, 2015) (Figure 12-11 on p. 132). Have copies of the page available so students can read along with you. The first read-aloud should enable students to enjoy the text and become familiar with its content. Next, reread the page and stop after the first point is introduced. Have students help you identify (1) the point the author is making, (2) whether the point is supported, and (3) the reasons or evidence that support the point. Repeat when you get to the second point the author made. Use the *Points and Reasons (Blank)* chart (Figure 12-8 on the previous page) to record the points as well as the supporting reasons and evidence. When complete, your chart may look something like Figure 12-12 on page 133.

Figure 12-11: *Your Skeletal System Works!*

Jobs of the Skeletal System

Your skeleton supports your body and gives it shape. The rib cage protects your heart, lungs, and liver. The skull is like a helmet. It protects your brain.

Important work also happens inside bones. Bone **marrow** makes blood cells. These cells give your body oxygen and fight germs. Bones also store **calcium** and other **minerals**.

Fact:
Humans have two sets of 12 ribs, for a total of 24 ribs.

marrow—the soft substance inside bones that is used to make blood cells

calcium—a soft, silver-white mineral found in teeth and bones

mineral—a substance found in nature that is not an animal or a plant

6

Figure 12-12: Points and Reasons: *Your Skeletal System Works!*

Points (claims)	Are the points supported? (Y/N)	What reasons and evidence support the points?
1. Skeletons support the body and give it shape.	Yes	Explains what the rib cage and skull do to protect parts of the body.
2. Important things happen inside the bones.	Yes	• Explains how bone marrow makes cells, which help the body fight germs. • Bones contain calcium and other minerals.

Next, pass out three index cards to each student. Have students write "enough strong evidence" on one card, "not enough strong evidence" on the second card, and "deadlocked" on the third. Have students review the information on the chart and then ask them to vote by holding up the card that most closely represents the quality of the reasons and evidence. Ask students to justify their "verdicts."

Student Application: Tiered Activities for Differentiation

Match each student to the activity that provides them with the right amount of support they need to be successful. At the Initial Level, provide students with a preselected text and identify two claims. Students read to identify and evaluate the reasons and/or evidence to support each claim. At the Transitional Level, select the text, but students identify two claims in the text and evaluate their supporting reasons and/or evidence. At the Accomplished Level, identify the text and students identify three claims and evaluate their supporting reasons/evidence.

Initial Level

Students will determine whether or not two teacher-determined points (claims) from a preselected text are supported with evidence. Students record the supporting evidence on the *Points and Reasons (Blank)* chart (Figure 12-8 on p. 130). Below the chart, they should write their "verdict" (*enough strong evidence, not enough strong evidence*, or *deadlocked*) and provide a rationale for the verdict they selected.

Teacher action: Select a text for students to read that has clear, well-supported points. Distribute the version of the *Points and Reasons (Blank)* chart (Figure 12-8) with the "points" column filled in. On a whiteboard, have a list of possible verdicts: *enough strong evidence, not enough strong evidence*, and *deadlocked*. Explain that *deadlock* means "to not have enough information to make a decision."

Transitional Level

Students will identify two important points from a preselected text, record supporting reasons or evidence, write their verdict, and justify it.

Teacher action: Select a text for students to read that has clear, well-supported points. Have students recreate a *Points and Reasons (Blank)* chart (Figure 12-8 on p. 130). On a whiteboard, have a list of possible verdicts: *enough strong evidence, not enough strong evidence*, and *deadlocked*.

Accomplished Level

Students will identify three claims an author makes from a preselected text. They record supporting reasons or evidence, write their verdict, and justify it.

Teacher action: Select a text for students to read that has clear, well-supported points. Have students recreate the *Points and Reasons (Blank)* chart (Figure 12-8 on p. 130). On a whiteboard, have a list of possible verdicts: *enough strong evidence, not enough strong evidence,* and *deadlocked.*

Additional Recommended Books

Bryant, J. (2013). *A splash of red: The life and art of Horace Pippin.* New York: Knopf Books.

Jenkins, S. (2012). *The beetle book.* New York: Houghton Mifflin.

Simons, L. M. B. (2015). *Transportation long ago and today.* Long Ago and Today. North Mankato, MN: Capstone.

Chapter 13

Examining Text Structure: Sequence

What Is Sequence Text Structure?

Sequence, sometimes referred to as chronological order, is defined as things or events occurring in a successive order. In a narrative, the plot is a sequence of events, yet there is usually a smaller sequence within each event. When we focus on sequence within events, we are reading for detail; when focusing on the sequence of events, we are looking at the bigger picture and analyzing the text in a deeper way. Sequencing is usually a straightforward text structure in both narrative and informational text but not always. In narrative, foreshadowing or flashbacks can interrupt the normal flow of events, and the reader must place this information in the proper sequence. In an informational text, the sequence can also be presented out of order. For instance, an author discusses an event that occurred in 2002 but then brings up support/information from an event that occurred in 1998.

What Does the Literature Say?

Students live their school day in sequence, usually beginning with taking attendance and lunch count to gathering their materials as they head for home. In the same way, sequenced narrative text is more likely to be familiar to students, as they have encountered this text structure their entire life from morning cartoons to bedtime story reading. Yet, comprehension gained from watching a sitcom or an animated film does not translate into the same level of comprehension as when reading a book. It has been shown that teaching text structure, with other effective comprehension strategies, does improve comprehension (Reutzel, Read & Fawson, 2009).

Research indicates that more organized texts result in better reader comprehension. In the case of sequence, it is important to note that chronological texts tend to report events in chronological order but do not necessarily specify causal relations between the events (Bohn-Gettler & Kendeou, 2014). According to Bohn-Gettler and Kendeou (2014), in informational texts the chronological texts are often a series of sentences in which a date is provided, followed by a description of an event that occurred on that date. We could also conclude that in narrative texts, the sequential order evolves within the chronological order of the series of events and that students learn early in their education that stories have a beginning, a middle, and an end—usually in that order. Fisher, Frey, and Lapp (2008) concluded that during think-alouds, comprehension improves when teachers regularly comment on text structure and explain how text structure can help the reader. In addition, pointing out signal words indicating the text structure was also helpful.

The goal in the classroom is to help students unpack the text structure of both narrative and informational texts. When we teach students to identify text structure and how to use the structure of text to select information needed to construct meaning, their comprehension will improve. Explicit instruction is important when teaching text structure so this information can be used to increase comprehension. According to Akhondi, Malayeri, and Samad (2011), students need to recognize and use text organization, as this skill is essential to comprehension and retention.

Increasing Complexity through the Grades

We might say the ability to understand and recognize text sequence begins in the younger grades with book handling skills and the ability to find the beginning, middle, and end of a book. When looking at grades three through five of the Common Core State Standards, there are marked differences in expectations. When students can recognize and use the sequence text structure to aid in their comprehension of the text, we have been successful.

At grade three, students are expected to be able to use text features to locate relevant information efficiently (CCSS.RI.5.3). In the case of sequence, this would involve being able to relate the information in the correct order and recall important information. Although this seems straightforward, we all know this can be confusing for some students.

At grade four, students are expected to be able to describe the overall structure in a text or part of a text (CCSS.RI.5.4). This deepens the level of understanding as perceived for grade three. The description would then include all the relevant characteristics, qualities, and events. So in the case of sequence, important details would need to be included in the description of the event or events.

At grade five, the expectation is that students are able to compare and contrast text structures from two or more different texts (CCSS.RI.5.5). At this level, students should be able to explain how two or more texts are different within their text structures. It would be beneficial if the texts were on the same topic, giving students another viewpoint.

Model Lesson 1: Sequential Order in Narrative

Students have been brought up surrounded by narrative text structure—watching cartoons, seeing animated films, playing games that repeat the same sequences, and listening as books were read to them. But having to recall the order of events would not have begun for many until they started school. This lesson teaches the concept of sequential order and aids students in sequential recall.

Lesson Objective:
Students will be able to describe story events in sequential order.

Teacher Modeling
To introduce sequential order in the actions and events in plots, explain to children that events in stories usually happen in sequential order. We suggest you share a small event in your own life or use the event offered below by reading the text and then discussing and noting the sequence of events. This should be written and projected on a screen. Explain that sometimes narrative text has signal words (like *first, next, then*), but often signal words are not in the text. Tell students they need to think how events would happen logically. In front of students, put on a thick pair of gloves and then try to put a ring on your finger. Ask students why the ring doesn't fit. Once they explain it's because you put the glove on first, say, "Yes, just like in a story, things must happen in a logical order." Ask the following: "When getting dressed, what goes on first, shoes or socks?" Be sure students understand the answer is socks because that is the logical order—the order that makes sense.

Show students how you can follow a sequence in a story. For instance, the following can be used:

I stayed up until two last night because I had to prepare a slide show, and I am so tired. I set my alarm for 7:30 a.m. to get into work by 9:00, so I would have time to set everything up for the meeting. But I slept through my alarm and woke up at 8:30! I was very worried because the meeting started at 9:30. I immediately jumped out of bed, brushed my teeth, got dressed, and headed out the door without even any coffee! After that, I hopped in my car and arrived at work with only 15 minutes left until the meeting. Next, I frantically ran up to the meeting room, hooked the laptop up to the projector and was ready to go—with five minutes to spare! When people entered the meeting, I smiled like it was my best day ever. After the meeting started, the slide show went off without a hitch, and my boss complimented my work as we left the room.

After reading the story, discuss signal words (see text box on p. 139). Go through the text and model how you can spot signal words. Circle the signal words. Go back and write a sequence of events. It may look like this:

- I stayed up until 2:00 a.m. and set the alarm for 7:30.
- I woke up at 8:30 and jumped out of bed.
- I got to work fifteen minutes before the meeting was to start.
- I was ready for my meeting on time.
- Everything went well.

Read the sequential list together and point out to students that this is actually a summary of the story. Explain to students that some stories use signal words, but often you have to follow the chain of events. Show the below scenario on a projector or write it on the whiteboard. Have students listen as you read the following and see if they can identify the order of three events.

Tom was late for his doctor's appointment, so he hurried into the doctor's office. Tom smiled and gave the receptionist his name and sat down on the most comfortable chair he saw. Then he had to wait an hour before he saw the doctor!

First, ask students if they see a signal word, then underline "then" and mention we know things happened before that sentence. Next, explain the first thing that happened was (1) Tom hurried into the doctor's office. Discuss what happened next: (2) Tom gave the receptionist his name and sat down. And finally, the last event was (3) he waited an hour before seeing the doctor. Explain that we can tell the order of events without signal words, but signal words do help us identify a sequence of events.

Guided Practice

The *I Survived* series allows readers to "live in" a real event and obtain a clearer view of what happens during a catastrophe while the title itself foreshadows the story's ending. Any of these books could be used to teach sequential order, but for the purpose of this model lesson, we chose *I Survived the Japanese Tsunami, 2011* by Lauren Tarshis. This story deals with two major themes: that of the young male character, Ben, dealing with the death of his father and then suddenly having to survive the Japanese tsunami of 2011. In this story, the teachings of Ben's father help Ben to survive the disaster and get reunited with his mother and brother. Chapter 8 (pp. 42–48) has Ben trapped in an underwater car and opens his thoughts to the readers as he makes his escape. This short scenario is perfect for guided practice.

Initially, have students read the chapter silently or in partners. Prior to reading, tell students to notice the sequence of events in the chapter because you will be working with the sequence after they have finished reading. Ask them to visualize as they read, so they can really "see" what Ben is doing to escape. After discussing the chapter, turn students' attention to page 44, the third paragraph that begins with "The water was past Ben's mouth now, brushing against his nose." Explain that you are going to follow the sequence of Ben escaping from the sunken car. Have them read through the paragraph until they get to the first thing Ben does as he tries to escape. Ask, "What is the first thing

Ben does?" (He takes a deep breath.) Continue asking questions that lead to the next event. Guide students to the following sequence of events:

- Ben takes a deep breath.
- Ben tries to open the window with the electric button, but it doesn't work.
- He grabs the steering wheel and kicks the window. Eventually he breaks it.
- He squirms out the window.
- He pushes himself against the car and rockets to the surface.

Ask students how they know this is the order of events even though the book did not give them one signal word. Explain that they need to think logically when working with sequence just as in real life; you would need to find your shoes first before putting them on!

Student Application: Tiered Activities for Differentiation

In order to differentiate the follow-up activity, provide more information within the sequence for the Initial and Transitional Levels. We suggest that you begin this exercise with a sequence of no more than four events. All students should be told what section of the text is to be sequenced.

Initial Level

At this level, provide a scaffold for students in three ways. First, skim the text with students to see if they can identify any signal words that will help them with the sequence. Second, give the first and last event in the sequence. Third, tell students the number of events that they should identify. Students are to provide the missing events within the sequence.

Teacher action: Guide students in skimming the text. Provide the first and last event and the total number of events.

Transitional Level

At this level, provide the first event and give the number of events that should be included in the sequence. Students are to read and identify the rest of the sequence.

Teacher action: Provide the first event and the total number of events.

Accomplished Level

At this level, only provide the information that tells students what piece of the text they are to sequence.

Teacher action: Check to see that students began with the first event.

Additional Recommended Books

d'Lacey, C. (2009). *Gruffen (The dragons of Wayward Crescent)*. New York: Orchard Books.

Lowry, L. (1989). *Number the stars.* New York: Houghton Mifflin Harcourt Publishing Company.

Tarshis, L. (2010). I survived series. New York: Scholastic.

Model Lesson 2:
Sequence Text Structure in Information Text

Text structure can be difficult to identify because more often than not, one type of text structure is embedded in another. For example, a text could be based on the description text structure but have sentences that focus on compare and contrast or cause and effect. In addition, the majority of texts are not formed around one text structure, but include a variety of text structures within the text. It is important when selecting text to teach sequence, that chronological order is the basis of the text or the part of the text you are planning on using.

For this lesson, we use *Island: A Story of the Galápagos* by Jason Chin (Scholastic, 2012). This book is an excellent choice, as parts of the text are great examples of sequence, and the entire book is based on the sequence of island growth as shown in its five sections titled "Birth," "Childhood," "Adulthood," "Old Age," and "Epilogue."

Signal Words for Sequence

First, second, third, later, next, then, now, initially, before, after, when, since, finally, preceding, again, previously, following, another, additionally, meanwhile, eventually, lastly, momentarily

Sample signal phrases: after time goes by; time passes; days, weeks, or years go by; days, weeks, or years pass by

---

Lesson Objective:
Students will be able to identify chronological text structure.

Teacher Modeling

We need to begin our instruction of sequence or chronological text structure by discussing sequence with students. Begin your lesson by discussing this scenario: Explain that you have an egg and a frying pan or show a plastic egg in a pan. Then ask, "Can I make scrambled eggs this way?" The answer, we hope, will be no. The next question would be, "What do I need to do?" Answers will vary depending upon students' prior knowledge, but all will agree that something needs to happen to the egg before it is placed in the pan. Explain, that yes, certain steps must occur in a sequence before a person can make scrambled eggs. Go through that sequence for students. As you explain the steps of making scrambled eggs, write the directions on the board. Your "recipe" may look like the following:

Break two eggs in a small bowl. Then add a little milk. Next, using a fork, mix the eggs and milk thoroughly. Now, spray oil into the frying pan and heat it up. Next, pour the egg mixture into the frying pan. Then, stir the egg mixture as it cooks. When the mixture is almost dry, shut off the heat. Finally, scoop the cooked eggs onto your plate and eat.

Once again, explain to students that there is a sequence to what happens to make scrambled eggs and this must be done in order. Explain that you could not put the eggs in the pan, cook them, and then add the milk. If the sequence changes, it can change everything. Tell students that some informational texts are written in a sequence, and just like with scrambled eggs, everything must happen or has happened in a particular order. Go back into the text and underline the events (steps). Explain to students that there are signal words with some of the events (steps). Circle the signal words and explain that they help the reader with the order of events. You may want to prepare an anchor chart with common signal words (see text box above). Go back and number the sentences to give students a visual of the order.

Once students understand the importance of sequential order, share the first four pages of *Island: A Story of the Galápagos*. These pages (from the "Birth" chapter) show, in pictures, the initial development of an island from an underwater volcano. In addition, the text uses signal words, such as: *first time, each time, many years pass, eventually, in time*, and *later*. Tell students your purpose for reading is to figure out the order of events that happened to form the island. Start by reading the "Birth" chapter and discussing what is happening. Share the second page (unpaged) as the graphics show seven pictures of the volcano continually erupting and eventually becoming dormant. Talk about how the tiny island volcano continues to grow with each eruption, and how the sequenced pictures show that growth. If possible, have enlarged pictures of these seven scenes piled out of order. Let your students place the pictures in order and tell you how they knew where to put the pictures. They will say something like "from smallest to biggest." Explain that the goal of sequence structure is just that, to begin at the beginning of something and bring it up to the end. After reading the text, go back and point out the signal words that help explain the sequence. Tell students it is these types of words that let the reader know the author is talking about a sequence of events. Show students how you summarize the events by using arrows to show sequence. Go through each page; unpack your own thinking as you decide what information is important enough for the sequenced summary. Explain that you are not copying from the text, but paraphrasing what the author has written. Underline signal words that you use in the writing. Your summary would look like this:

For the **first** time, a volcano rises above the water.

↓

Then each time the lava spews, it cools and hardens and makes the island grow.

↓

Many **years pass** and mangrove trees begin to grow.

↓

Later, birds, iguanas and other animals make the island their home.

Now, tell students you can summarize the events by writing:
First the volcano rises, then the lava spews, making the island grow. Eventually, trees begin to grow.

Guided Practice

Once you are confident students understand that sequencing means placing events in order, guide them through the process by copying the sheet provided on page 142, Figure 13-1, *Guided Practice: Informational Text—"Growing Sunflowers."* First, make a chart of signal words that could be found in the text (see p. 139 *Signal Words for Sequence*). Give each student a copy of the text. Point out words on the chart and explain that there are other words that signal sequence, but the chart gives us a good idea of what to look for when recognizing the sequence text structure. Tell students that you will be reading to them about growing sunflowers and that the text has some signal words to help them, but not all of the steps have signal words. Then do the following:

- Read through the text with students, asking them to notice the order of events and signal words.
- Next, have students read the text with a partner. Have them underline events they see. Suggest that they circle the signal words. Remind them that not all of the events (steps) in this text have signal words.
- Then have students number in order the sentences they have underlined.
- Finally, together as a class or group, have students tell you what to write on the whiteboard to make a summary of the events.

Your sequence of events should look like this:

Go shopping for sunflower seeds that can be planted.

First, put some planting soil in a flower pot.

Place two or three seeds in the pot.

After, put more soil in the flower pot.

Put a saucer under the flower pot.

Then, water the planted seeds.

Place the flower pot in a sunny area.

Eventually, when the plant is four inches tall, plant it outside.

Ask students to help you in summarizing this sequence. Ask what happens first, next, and so forth. Your summary may look like this:

First, put soil in the pot, then put three seeds in, and after that, pour soil on top. Then, water the seeds and put the pot in a sunny area until the plant is four inches high, when it can be planted outside.

When you have finished modeling and practicing the skill of sequencing text events, students should be ready to complete this independently. You will need to match students with one of the activities below, at the level that will make students think yet be successful in completing the activity. Working on the second chapter of *Island: A Story of the Galápagos,* titled "Childhood," or on another book written in sequential order will help you ensure students can read and record important information in sequential order.

Student Application: Tiered Activities for Differentiation

At all levels, signal words may be included. Whether they are given by the teacher, available on an anchor chart, or supplied by students, it is important students understand that signal words give a clue to the different types of text structure. Students are expected to be more independent as they get to the Accomplished Level.

Initial Level

Working in partners, students read the second chapter of *Island: A Story of the Galápagos,* entitled "Childhood." (Or use another book written in sequential order.) Using the signal words you provide on chart paper or a whiteboard, have students copy the sentences from the book that contain these signal words.

Teacher action: If using "Childhood," make a chart or whiteboard list available to students with these words/phrases listed: *After one million years, After two million years, Now, Meanwhile, One day, Eventually.* (The sentences with these signal words will provide a decent summary.)

Transitional Level

Working independently, students read the second chapter of *Island: A Story of the Galápagos*, entitled "Childhood" (or use another book written in sequential order). Using the signal words you provide on chart paper or a whiteboard, students paraphrase the sentences that these signal words occur in.

Teacher action: Make the chart of words in the Initial Level available to students.

Accomplished Level

Working independently, have students read the second chapter of *Island: A Story of the Galápagos*, entitled "Childhood" (or use another book written in sequential order). Without scaffolding, have students paraphrase the sentences that sequence the events and then write a short summary of the sequence.

Teacher action: Remind students to refer to the chart of signal words to aid in their independent work.

Additional Recommended Books

Byrd, R. (2003). *Leonardo: beautiful dreamer*. New York: Penguin Young Readers Group.

Higgins, N. (2015). *Experiment with what a plant needs to grow*. Minneapolis, MN: Lerner Publishing Group.

Taylor, S. S. (2010). *Amelia Earhart: this broad ocean*. White Plains, NY: Disney-Hyperion. (Note: This book is a graphic novel.)

Figure 13-1: Guided Practice: Informational Text—"Growing Sunflowers"

Growing Sunflowers
By Nancy L. Witherell & Mary C. McMackin

Growing sunflowers is actually very easy. In order to make sure your sunflower will grow, you must get sunflower seeds that are for planting, not for eating. You would need to go shopping as sunflower seeds that can be planted are sold in seed packages at a gardening store or center. Once you have your seeds, it is recommended that you start your seed indoors in a small flower pot.

To plant, first, you would put some planting soil in a flower pot until it is about three-fourths full. Place two or three seeds in the pot. This is to make sure at least one of the seeds will grow. After placing the seeds, put more planting soil in the flower pot until the dirt is about one inch from the top. Make sure you have a saucer or flower pot tray under the flower pot, and then water the planted seeds. Place your flower pot in a sunny area. Continue to water when the soil is getting dry, and at least one plant will sprout. Eventually, when the plant is about four inches tall, plant it outside in a sunny area.

Chapter 14

Demystifying Cause and Effect

What Is Cause and Effect?

Cause and effect is a text structure used in both informational and narrative text. In this type of text structure, the author offers either a cause or an effect or both. The causal relationship is a difficult one because cause and effect easily become a series, sometimes consisting of multiple causes and effects. In essence, the cause produces the effect. In simple terms, the *cause* is the action that makes something else happen, and the result is the *effect*. This often results in a chain of events. As readers become accustomed to this text structure, the book, whether informational text or narrative, becomes more predictable to the reader and aids in comprehension as the reader searches for the next piece of information.

What Does the Literature Say?

People live in a continuum of problems to solutions, which, when looked at differently, can be causes and effects. This is basically the text structure of our life. When we are driving a car and get low on gas (an action that causes something else to happen), the effect is that we would run out of gas if we did not fill up the gas tank. If we are thirsty (the action that causes something else to happen), we take a drink (the effect or result), then our body is hydrated and we no longer feel thirsty. If a small child grabs a bowl of cereal off the table (action), the result could be either a child who is no longer hungry or a floor covered with cereal. Unfortunately, this life pattern does not often transfer into reading without some explicit teaching. One of the qualitative factors of text complexity for informational texts is text structure organization, and according to Fisher, Frey, and Lapp (2012), a text is more complex if it does not follow the traditional structures such as cause and effect, making students' understanding of the cause and effect scenario even more important. Although, a preponderance of research does not specifically focus on cause and effect, research does support the teaching of text structure knowledge to increase students' comprehension (Akhonid, Malayen & Samad, 2011). The knowledge of text structure gives readers a plan as they read, which facilitates understanding of the text.

By third grade, students are expected to recognize informational text structures (Akhonid, Malayen & Samad, 2011). Having prior knowledge of text structures as students begin to read more complex texts aids in their comprehension. According to Bohn-Gettler and Kendeou (2014), instructional context, text structure, and working memory influence the processing of informational text. In addition, Bohn-Gettler and Kendeou (2014) found that during reading, the cause and effect text structure elicited the highest degree of knowledge-based inferences. They hypothesize that this text structure allowed students to incorporate additional background knowledge as they attempted to find and assess possible solutions to the problem presented. The goal for teachers is to help readers recognize the text structure to enable interacting more highly with the text to improve comprehension and recall.

Increasing Complexity through the Grades

The ability to recognize text structures enables students to deepen their understanding of the text. The Common Core State Standards expect students to be able to recognize text structures and use this recognition to aid in their understanding of how the structures relate to the text as a whole.

At grade three, for informational texts, students are expected to use text features "to locate information relevant to a given topic efficiently" (CCSS.RI.5.3). In the case of cause and effect, students would be expected to connect the cause to be able to identify the effect. This gives students the ability to be able to recognize types of text structures—in this case, cause and effect. In the case of narrative, students are to be able to refer to parts of the text using the correct term, such a *chapter* or *stanza*.

At grade four, for informational texts, students are expected to "describe the overall structure" of the information provided in the text (CCSS.RI.5.4). Students must be able to distinguish the different types of text structures and, in the case of cause and effect, be able to identify the cause and the effect, recognizing both as part of the text structure. For narrative text, students are to explain major differences by citing structural elements of poems and drama.

At grade five, for informational texts, students are expected to "compare and contrast the overall structure" (CCSS.RI.5.5) of the information presented to at least two other texts. In this case, students will need to be able to identify cause and effect along with other text structures in order to make the necessary comparison. For narrative text, grade five students look at the overall structure of a poem, drama, or story and explain how it fits together.

Model Lesson 1: Describing Cause and Effect

The focus of this lesson is to identify cause and effect text structure. Roald Dahl's *The BFG* (1982) is a delightful story. The first chapter begins with cause and effect, and the causal relationships continue at various places within the book. For those not familiar with this childhood favorite, it involves a young orphan girl, Sophie, who is snatched from her dormitory bed during the "witching hour" by the BFG, the Big Friendly Giant. Although the book starts off a bit scary, it catches the young reader's interest immediately. Through myriad adventures within the story, Sophie and the BFG manage to have nine child-eating giants captured and save the day.

Lesson Objective:
Students will be able to describe the cause and effect text structure as used in this book.

Teacher Modeling

When taking cause and effect into story plot, we once again must remind students that the *cause* is an action that makes something else happen, and the *effect* is the result. We can help students understand this concept as we use well-known fairy tales to teach how cause and effect take place within the actions in a story.

After explaining cause and effect, begin your modeling by discussing the story of Cinderella. Although stories are usually seen in the problem/solution text structure through story mapping, they often contain cause and effect. The main problem with Cinderella is that she is lovely and nice but lives without material goods or love. The solution, of course, is becoming a princess and obtaining wealth and love. But with cause and effect, we look at Cinderella in a different light. Discuss with students the ballroom scene when the clock strikes 12 and Cinderella realizes she must leave immediately as the spell is about to end. Explain that the cause in this case (the action of the clock striking midnight) brings about the effect (Cinderella realizing she must leave quickly). Next in the story, Cinderella runs from the palace to her coach (cause, as this is an action that causes something else to happen) but loses her glass slipper (effect, as this is a result of her running). Again discuss this as cause and effect. As the fairy tale continues, the prince searches for the foot that fits the glass slipper (cause, as this is an action that causes something else to happen). At this time explain to students that searching for Cinderella is the cause, and see if they can identify the effect (finding Cinderella). And in true fairy tale style, you can bring this to conclusion: The prince marries Cinderella (cause), and she lives happily ever after (effect).

Snow White also involves a number of causal relationships. When looking at this fairy tale from the problem/solution standpoint, the main problem is a young princess who cannot wake up and the solution is a kiss from a prince. Yet, the story contains a number of causal relationships that eventually help Snow White get her "happily ever after" ending. Talk to students about the story of Snow White, and ask if they remember the part in which the mirror tells the queen (Snow White's mean stepmother) that she is no longer the fairest in the land. Help students identify the cause (the action of the mirror talking to the queen) and the effect (the queen becomes jealous and spiteful; a second effect is that the queen decides to kill Snow White). Use a box figure (as shown on Figure 14-1: *Cause and Effect* graphic organizer on p. 147) and fill in the first box with "mirror tells queen she is no longer the prettiest in the land." Then follow that arrow and fill in the second box with "the queen becomes jealous." Explain to students that the first box contains the cause, and the arrow points to the box that has the effect (result). Continue to model this throughout the retelling of Snow White. Continue on with the story—the queen orders the huntsman to kill Snow White (cause), but instead he lets her go in the woods (effect), where Snow White finds a home with the dwarfs (second effect). Snow White agrees to live with the dwarfs and keep their house clean (cause), and the effect is that the dwarfs have a clean house; a second effect is that they begin to care for Snow White. Eventually, the queen finds and poisons Snow White (cause) and she cannot wake up (effect). The prince finds her and kisses her (action), and she once again wakes up (result).

Guided Practice

Draw two rows of the cause and effect to boxes (with arrows) on the board or continue to use the *Cause and Effect* graphic organizer (Figure 14-1 on the next page). Hand out graphic organizers to either individual students or partners. Together with students, begin to read *The BFG*, explaining that everyone should be trying to identify cause and effect as you read the first chapter, "The Witching Hour." Remind students that the *cause* is an action that causes something else to happen, and the *effect* is the result. Explain that everyone will be writing the cause in the first box and following the arrow to write the effect in the second box. This story begins with the effect, and then explains the cause, so students will need to be guided through the first causal relationship. The book begins with the line, "Sophie couldn't sleep" (p. 9). As you read on, the author states, "The moonbeam was like a silver blade slicing through the room on to her face" (p. 9). Discuss how moonlight in your face could cause a person not to sleep. Ask students to tell you what the cause is and then what the effect is. Pointing to the first box on the board, explain that the cause goes in the first box and the arrow points to the effect, which is written in the second box. Have students write on their paper as you do this on the board, and check to see that they understand the procedure.

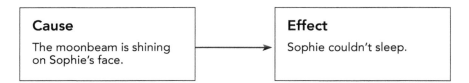

Cause
The moonbeam is shining on Sophie's face.

Effect
Sophie couldn't sleep.

Continue to read as Sophie looks out the window and sees something scary coming down the road. Have students identify the cause and the effect. Have students write this on their paper. Volunteers can fill in the boxes on the board or projected chart. The result should be:

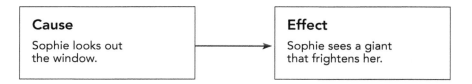

Cause
Sophie looks out the window.

Effect
Sophie sees a giant that frightens her.

Student Application

In order to tier instruction, use the *Cause and Effect* graphic organizer (Figure 14-1 on p. 147). Scaffolding is suggested starting on page 148.

Figure 14-1: Cause and Effect

Cause and Effect   **Name:** _____

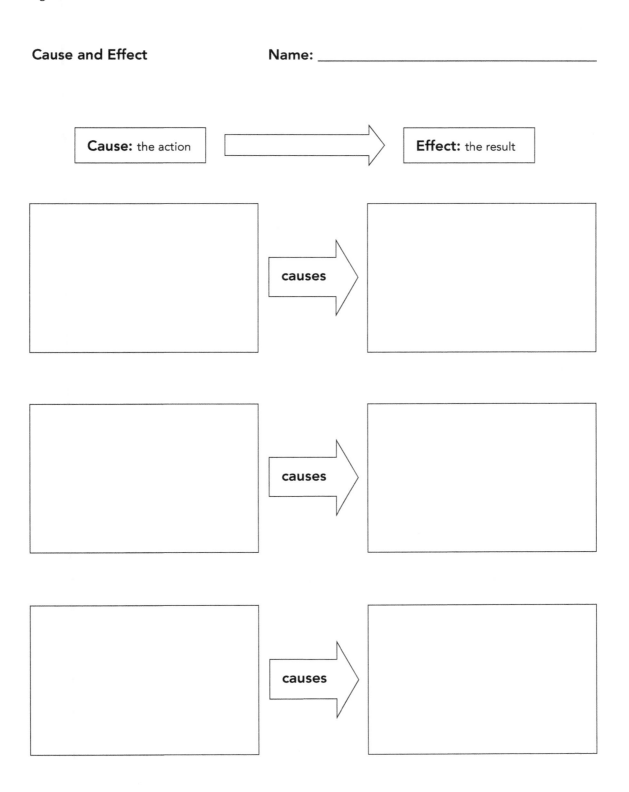

Initial Level

Because cause and effect can be so confusing at this level, this should be a matching activity for students who need the most support. Students can work in pairs and match the cause to the effect.

Teacher action: Fill in the *Cause and Effect* graphic organizer (Figure 14-1 on p. 147) and copy for students. Cut the graphic organizer into small squares around the answers, and put the cut squares into envelopes. In pairs, have students match the causes and effects after reading the designated text.

Transitional Level

Use the *Cause and Effect* graphic organizer (Figure 14-1 on p. 147) with the causes already filled in the sheet. Students fill in the effects.

Teacher action: Fill in the "Cause" boxes. (To save time, fill in the effects and then make copies for students at the Transitional Level).

Accomplished Level

At this level, do not provide additional support.

Teacher action: The *Cause and Effect* graphic organizer (Figure 14-1 on p. 147) will be blank, though you may consider writing in the first cause.

Additional Recommended Books

O'Dell, S. (1987). *Island of the blue dolphins*. New York: Yearling Books.

Sachar, L. (2000). *Holes*. New York: Scholastic.

Smith, R. K. (1984). *The war with grandpa*. New York: Bantam Doubleday Bell Books for Young Readers.

Model Lesson 2: Describing Cause and Effect

The focus of this lesson is to identify cause and effect. *Polar Bears' Search for Ice: A Cause and Effect Investigation* (Olson, 2011) is an informational text that explains how important icebergs and large iceberg chunks are to polar bears' survival.

Lesson Objective:

Students will be able to describe the cause and effect text structure as used in this book.

Teacher Modeling

The concept of cause and effect needs to be modeled concretely to ensure all students understand. Since cause and effect can be one event or a series of events, and it is not always linear, the explanation needs to encompass these facets. Begin by explaining the *cause* is an action that makes something else happen and the result from that action is the *effect*. For example, if I put too much ketchup on my hot dog (the action that causes something else to happen), the result (effect) of this action might be ketchup on my top, on my face, on the floor, and on the counter—or all of these.

Put a paper towel on a desk and pour water on it. Have students identify the cause (poured water) and effect (wet paper towel). Now, using the wet paper towel, wipe the desk. Have students identify the cause (wiping the desk) and the effect (a clean desk, we hope).

With the secretary in on the scene, forget to send down attendance and then have him or her ask for the attendance over the intercom. Talk about this with your students. Why did the secretary have to ask for the attendance? (You forgot to send it down.) Identify this as the cause. What was the effect? That the secretary had to use his or her time to ask for the attendance, and a second effect would be that the class was interrupted. Then ask students what you were talking about before the interruption. Discuss how this was a cause and effect: The interruption (cause) made you to forget what you were speaking about (effect).

Then discuss with students the following scenario: A water bottling company puts water with bacteria in their bottles. The bottles were sold and the water made people sick. This is a cause and effect: The company bottled the contaminated water (cause) and made several people sick (effect). Ask, "What do you think the water bottling company did?" Answers will vary, but we can imagine such answers as "getting the water back, doing a recall." This, in essence, would be a second effect from the contaminated water. Then go on to say that because it cost so much for the water bottling company to recall the water, the company had to go out of business. Explain that there is now another cause and effect, the recall (cause) and the company going out of business (effect). Ask students if they can think of what happens to workers when a company goes out of business (the loss of jobs, which becomes another effect).

As you can tell by the previous examples, this gets complicated. To begin your modeling of cause and effect, it is best to use concrete examples and keep the scenarios simple. Once your students understand the concept of cause and effect, and that it can be a series or there can be multiple causes and effects, it is time to take this skill into the text. You may choose a book that you are using in class. The book, *Polar Bears' Search for Ice: A Cause and Effect Investigation* by Gillia M. Olson (2011) has a series of causes and effects and works well for a model lesson. This book was chosen because the vocabulary is strong but not confusing, and the causes and effects are easy to follow. The author's message focuses on our need to take care of the earth.

Guided Practice

To begin this lesson, read the title and ask students why a polar bear might be searching for ice. The book begins with polar bears on a small piece of ice (the effect). After reading the first page and showing the picture, ask students why they think the author is pointing out that the polar bears are floating "on melting chunks of ice" (p. 4). Answers may vary, but the bears are obviously in trouble as they are standing close together surrounded by melting ice and water. Continue reading with students as you guide them to causes and effects through the first paragraph on page 6, where the author states that polar bears are weighing less and fewer cubs are surviving. Ask students if "polar bears are weighing less and fewer cubs are living" is a cause or an effect. Guide them with this question: "Are either of these an action that causes something else to happen?" After students say no, explain that as we read on, we will discover the cause or causes of these effects. Begin a visual to help:

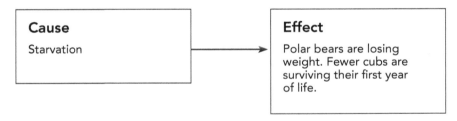

Cause	**Effect**
Starvation	Polar bears are losing weight. Fewer cubs are surviving their first year of life.

In this case, the author chooses to mention the effects prior to the cause. In the next sentence, the author states that polar bears may be facing starvation. Ask students, "Is starving an action that causes something else to happen?" You can now fill in the cause box to show starvation is the cause.

As you read further, the author states that polar bears' search for food has caused more attacks on campsites and homes. So we have another event in the chain. Again, ask students if they can tell you the cause of bears attacking campsites and homes. This causal relationship is straightforward, and students should be able to then identify the effect. You can have students draw and complete a visual as you did. The results should be:

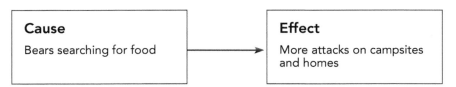

Student Application: Tiered Activities for Differentiation

We suggest you have students begin this skill in partners. As mentioned previously, cause and effect can be very complicated, and working in teams at this point will help students be successful.

In order to differentiate the activity, use the *Cause and Effect* graphic organizer (Figure 14-1 on p. 147). If the informational text you select has several cause-effect relationships, you may need to have a second copy of the graphic organizer in order to have enough boxes. If you need more than two copies, most likely the text would be too confusing and you should select a less complicated text for this lesson.

The arrow and box must be big enough for young children to write in. You may consider starting the cause and effect when there are only three causal relationships left within the text. If there are not three, have students cross out the extra arrow and box to minimize confusion.

Initial Level

At this level, provide a *Cause and Effect* graphic organizer (Figure 14-1 on p. 147) that has the causes filled in, and students complete the results.

Teacher action: Fill in causes, and remind students that *causes* are actions that make something else happen, and *effects* are the results.

Transitional Level

At this level, fill in alternating causes and effects using the *Cause and Effect* graphic organizer (Figure 14-1 on p. 147). Filling in the first cause starts students off on the correct path. After that, they alternately apply their knowledge of cause or effect.

Teacher action: Fill in the cause for one causal relationship and the effect for the next until all causal relationships have been included.

Accomplished Level

At this level, do not provide additional support. Give students the *Cause and Effect* graphic organizer (Figure 14-1 on p. 147).

Teacher action: The graphic organizer will be blank, though you may consider writing in the first cause or checking to see that students have started off correctly.

Additional Recommended Books

Donald, R. L. (2001). *Water pollution*. A True Book. New York: Children's Press.

Rice, W. (2013). *Endangered animals of the jungle*. Time for Kids. Westminster, CA: Teacher Created Materials.

Yoo, P. (1995). *Sixteen years in sixteen seconds: the Sammy Lee story*. New York: Lee & Low Books.

Chapter 15

Reading Within and Across Texts

What Is Reading Within and Across Texts?

Students are being asked to interact with texts in a variety of ways. They engage in close readings of individual texts, read texts on the same topic while focusing on *intertextuality*—the relationship and influence that one text has on another—and analyze and integrate information from multiple sources. In other words, they read within and across texts to construct meaning and to build content knowledge. In this chapter, we first concentrate on mysteries, exploring how they are written so readers can use knowledge of text structure to comprehend texts within this subgenre of narration. We also look across texts as we help students integrate ideas from two texts on the same topic.

What Does the Literature Say?

Merriam-Webster defines *genre* as "a category of artistic, musical, or literary composition characterized by a particular style, form, or content." This definition has been recognized for centuries and, as many of us were taught, each genre has its own set of defining characteristics. Today, however, many researchers no longer define *genre* by a set of governing rules or characteristics, but rather by the function or the purpose the text serves (Duke, Caughlan, Juzwick & Martin, 2012; Kamberelis, 2005/2010). Genres have changed as social needs have shifted, and the lines between genres have become blurred (e.g., *Magic School Bus* series that blends narration and science information). Subgenres that didn't exist at the turn of the 21st century now allow readers and writers to communicate through social media. Kamberelis (2005/2010) suggests that when we teach elementary students about genres, we should emphasize how subgenres of each genre are related, so students understand how texts are written to serve different purposes and to communicate different types of information.

In this chapter, we explore mysteries, a subgenre of narration. Mysteries contain many of the same features we see in other narratives with slight variations. There is a main character, a setting, a problem that usually is an intriguing puzzle to solve, some tension that adds to the suspense, thrilling cliffhangers to enhance the uncertainty of the resolution, and a solution that ties everything together (Warner, n.d.). As Wilhelm and Otto (2001) point out, the main character is usually the person who is trying to solve the problem. They go on to say that in most mysteries, the suspects and their motives must be evaluated, and "hidden evidence"—clues that often seem unimportant—become critical in the case. Readers must use inferences to connect the dots and construct meaning. Readers must be willing to endure ambiguity and suspense until the problem is solved, and "red herrings"—clues that look plausible but are distracters—may lead readers to false conclusions (p. 142).

When students read, they use their schemata—or cognitive networks—to help them make connections among new information, information they've read in texts, and past experiences. The similarities in how mysteries are constructed provide a structure or framework for comprehension. Likewise, when students read multiple informational texts on a single topic, they consider similarities and differences in the information and points of view presented. Britt and Sommer (2004) explain that reading two texts requires the same processes as single-text readings, with additional demands on making intertext links between the texts. Readers must be able to identify truths, discrepancies, and so forth in the multiple texts.

According to Spivey and King (1989), "Constructivism portrays readers as making meaning by integrating content from source texts with previously acquired knowledge in a process that involves the operations of *selecting, organizing,* and *connecting*. Readers select content on the basis of some criterion, organize the content by applying their knowledge of text structure and connecting related ideas by discovering and generating links" (p. 9).

Kamberelis (2005/2010), who studied narrative, scientific, and poetic genre knowledge of kindergarteners, first graders, and second graders recommends, "The more different kinds of genres that children learn to deploy, analyze, and synthesize, the deeper and broader their potential for cognitive, communicative, critical, and creative growth is likely to be" (Kamberelis, 1999, p. 453).

Increasing Complexity through the Grades

Students begin to read across texts by reading books that have a great deal in common. They may read books by the same author, books that contain the same characters, or books that are about the same topic. As students progress, they are asked to "select, organize, and connect" (Spivey & King, 1989, p. 11) ideas, themes, and concepts in texts that have less obvious similarities. Students may read and compare books within the same genre, texts on the same content topic, or texts from different genres that have similar themes (e.g., a poem and a short story that center on a theme of *loyalty*).

At grade three, according to the CCSS, students are expected to "compare and contrast the themes, settings, and plots of stories written by the same author about the same or similar characters (e.g., in books from a series)" (CCSS.RL.3.9). Teachers often create author studies to investigate how famous children's authors, such as Roald Dahl, Sharon Creech, Patricia Polacco, Kevin Henkes, and Matt Christopher, construct their narratives. When reading informational texts, students are expected to "compare and contrast the most important points and key details presented in two texts on the same topic" (CCSS.RI.3.9). Doing so allows students to investigate what information is included, what is omitted, and why authors make decisions about content and style.

At grade four, students are expected to "compare and contrast the treatment of similar themes and topics (e.g., opposition of good and evil) and patterns of events (e.g., the quest) in stories, myths, and traditional literature from different cultures" (CCSS.RL.4.9). At this grade level, students need to think critically across multiple texts. They need to focus on *intertextuality*—relationship and influence that one text has on another—also evident in CCSS.RI.4.9, which requires students to "integrate information from two texts on the same topic in order to write or speak about the subject knowledgeably" (CCSS.RI.4.9).

At grade five, students are expected to "compare and contrast stories in the same genre (e.g., mysteries and adventure stories) on their approaches to similar themes and topics" (CCSS.RL.5.9). At this grade level, students focus on *intertextuality* within a genre. Genre studies, which focus on both the characteristics of the genre and the purposes the genre serves, can be an effective way to delve deeply into themes and topics. When reading informational texts, students should be able to "integrate information from several texts on the same topic in order to write or speak about the subject knowledgeably" (CCSS.RI.5.9). Students *select, organize,* and *connect* (Spivey & King, 1989, p. 11) information across texts to build new knowledge.

Model Lesson 1: How Are Mysteries Constructed?

If you are looking for short, easy mysteries for your students to read, you might want to search online for "MysteryNet's Kids Mysteries."

Lesson Objective:
Students will be able to distinguish the elements of mysteries in order to enhance comprehension.

Teacher Modeling

Begin by recalling some mysteries with which your students may already be familiar. You might mention the popular children's TV cartoon *Scooby-Doo*. Scooby, along with his sidekicks Shaggy Rogers, Daphne Blake, Velma Dinkley, and Fred Jones, solved many mysteries with the help of their Mystery Machine. Students may also be familiar with *Miss Nelson Is Missing!* (Allard), *Holes* (Sachar), and the *Cam Jansen* series (Adler). Think aloud as you ponder why mysteries are such a popular genre, and then share a short mystery with students. For this lesson, we'll use *The Case of the Ruined Roses (Solve-it 28)* (Wheeler, 1998–2001), available on MysteryNet's Kids Mysteries website. The short text will enable us, in one lesson, to focus on the elements mystery writers use to create their stories.

Begin by explaining that mysteries are a special type of narrative. Show the *Narrative vs. Mystery* chart (Figure 15-1), and talk about the similarities and differences between narratives and mysteries.

Figure 15-1: Narrative vs. Mystery

Elements	Narrative	Mystery
Character	Character(s)	Character and sometimes sidekicks—friends who help solve a problem/case
Setting	Setting—sometimes described through the five senses	Setting—sometimes described through the five senses
Problem	Character is facing some kind of a conflict, struggle, or challenge	Character knows something is wrong and looks for clues to figure out what's going on (e.g., something is missing, you witness a crime, a pet is stolen)
Plot/Suspects	Series of events that lead to the conclusion	Series of suspects who are likely to have committed a crime and events that focus on suspects
Red herrings	(Not usually in narratives)	Clues that seem as if they'll lead to the solution but are really there to throw off the reader (e.g., someone is acting strangely, someone unexpected arrives, a note appears)
Resolution	The story comes to a satisfying conclusion.	The problem (mystery) has been solved. We know who did it!

Display or distribute copies of *The Case of the Ruined Roses (Solve-it 28)*, along with the *Accomplished Level Mystery Elements* chart (Figure 15-2 on the next page). Read through the story so students can get the gist. When reading the story for the second time, complete the *Accomplished Level Mystery Elements* chart. Your chart might look something like Figure 15-3 on page 156. Review the elements of mystery (e.g., tension, red herring) as you complete the graphic organizer.

Figure 15-2: Accomplished Level Mystery Elements

Accomplished Level Mystery Elements			
Name of mystery:			
Character(s)/Sidekick(s):			
Setting (five senses):			
Problem:			
Suspects:			
Suspect			
What we know about this suspect			
How did the character(s) solve the problem?			
Red herring:			
Who did it?			

Figure 15-3: Accomplished Level Mystery Elements: *The Case of the Ruined Roses (Solve-it 28)*

Accomplished Level Mystery Elements *The Case of the Ruined Roses (Solve-it 28)*				
Name of mystery: *The Case of the Ruined Roses (Solve-it 28)*				
Character(s)/Sidekick(s): Nina and her cousin Max				
Setting (five senses): Coach Thornton's yard (Note: The author didn't use the five senses to describe the setting.)				
Problem: Ten rose bushes had been pulled from the ground.				
Suspects: Alex Avery, Sam Cartland, and Mike Brooks				
Suspect	Alex Avery	Sam Cartland	Mike Brooks	
What we know about this suspect	At Dairy Bar all morning. Amy confirmed this. Wasn't mad at the coach but didn't want to visit him either.	Was home watching football tapes. Before that, he watched the same UFO TV show that Nina watched. He said UFOs had been reported since 1947.	At the gym all morning. He signed in the log book at 8:55 a.m.	
How did the character(s) solve the problem? Nina said she watched a TV show about UFOs, which were first reported in 1800. Sam said he was home watching the show about UFOs. He said they were first reported in 1947, which was not true. He was caught in a lie.				
Red herring: The children went on to talk to Mike after Sam revealed what he knew about UFOs, even though Max knew Sam had lied.				
Who did it? Sam Cartland!				

If possible, return to MysteryNet's Kids Mysteries website and select "Sam" as the person Max suspected of ruining the roses. You will see the percentage of readers who thought Sam committed the crime and can read a short paragraph that explains how Max figured out the mystery.

Guided Practice

For this part of the lesson, we use *Ballpark Mysteries #1: The Fenway Foul-up* (Kelly, 2011), a mystery for second- to fourth-grade readers that would take about an hour for you to read aloud. It's short enough to be read aloud in a couple of sessions yet developed enough to contain all the elements of mysteries. Before beginning to read aloud, remind students that they will be listening to determine the problem and the person they think committed the crime.

Stop reading at the end of Chapter 8 (so the story's resolution isn't yet revealed). Have students jot down on a piece of paper the name of the person they think stole Big D's baseball bat. Have students hold up their papers so you can see which students identified the correct suspect. Read Chapter 9 to confirm that the photographer stole the bat. Next, display the *Accomplished Level Mystery Elements* chart (Figure 15-2 on p. 155). Have students help you fill in the organizer. Return to the text to verify answers when necessary. Your completed chart may look like Figure 15-4 on page 158. Conclude by initiating a brief discussion about the similarities and differences students found between *The Case of the Ruined Roses* and *The Fenway Foul-up*. Did the same elements appear in both stories? Explain.

Student Application: Tiered Activities for Differentiation

In the following activities, we differentiate by having students think more deeply at each level about the elements of mysteries.

Initial Level

Students will identify the character and sidekicks, if there are any; the setting; the problem to be solved; how the character solved the case; and who did it.

Teacher action: Select a mystery that's written at students' independent reading level and contains all elements in Figure 15-5 on page 160. Distribute a copy of Figure 15-5 to each student.

Transitional Level

Students will identify elements specified in the Initial Level and information about the suspects.

Teacher action: Select a mystery that's written at students' independent reading level. The mystery should contain all the elements found in Figure 15-6: *Transitional Level Mystery Elements* on page 161. Distribute a copy of Figure 15-6 to each student.

Accomplished Level

Students will identify the elements specified in the Transitional Level as well as red herrings.

Teacher action: Select a mystery that's written on students' independent reading level. The mystery should contain all the elements found in Figure 15-2: *Accomplished Level Mystery Elements* on page 155. Distribute a copy of Figure 15-2 to each student.

Once students have completed their charts, have them form small groups so they can compare and contrast the elements of this genre across the mysteries they read.

Figure 15-4: Accomplished Level Mystery Elements: *Ballpark Mysteries #1: The Fenway Foul-up*

Accomplished Level Mystery Elements *Ballpark Mysteries #1: The Fenway Foul-up*				
Name of mystery: *Ballpark Mysteries #1: The Fenway Foul-up*				
Character(s)/Sidekick(s): Kate and Mike				
Setting (five senses): Fenway Park—talked about the Green Monster				
Problem: Big D's favorite baseball bat was stolen				
Suspects: Bobby the batboy, the photographer, a man wearing a Yankees' cap, a lady working in the souvenir shop.				

Suspect	Bobby the batboy	The photographer	A man wearing a Yankees' cap	A lady working in the souvenir shop
What we know about this suspect	Was older, looked suspicious, had access to the bats.	Took Big D's photos, was near the bats before Big D's went missing, had camera bag and tripod case, said it would be nice to be rich, was near batting practice and in the souvenir shop.	Ate sunflower seeds, had long white poster tube that he protected carefully, tube was big enough for a baseball bat, upset because tube was knocked over.	Worked in souvenir shop, could be an accomplice.

How did the character(s) solve the problem? When Kate learned that pine tar makes things sticky, she remembered feeling a sticky bat in the souvenir shop. She knew the photographer had been in the shop and had been near the bats during batting practice. She thought that like the Morse Code on the scoreboard, clues could be hidden in plain sight. The photographer said it would be nice to be rich. All the clues pointed to him.

Red herring: the batboy, who had access to the bats; Kevin, the man with the Yankees' cap and poster tube; the lady in the souvenir shop, who could have been an accomplice

Who did it? The photographer

Additional Recommended Books

Brezenoff, S. (2011). *The ghost who haunted the capitol*. Field Trip Mysteries. North Mankato, MN: Capstone.

Dearl, E. (1998–2000). *The case of the disappearing dimes (Solve-it 27)*. Retrieved on October 10, 2015, from http://kids.mysterynet.com/solveit/solveit027/.

Konigsburg, E. L. (2007). *From the mixed-up files of Mrs. Basil E. Frankweiler*. New York: Atheneum.

Figure 15-5: Initial Level Mystery Elements

Initial Level Mystery Elements
Name of mystery:
Character(s)/Sidekick(s):
Setting (five senses):
Problem:
How did the character(s) solve the problem?
Who did it?

Figure 15-6: Transitional Level Mystery Elements

Transitional Level Mystery Elements				
Name of mystery:				
Character(s)/Sidekick(s):				
Setting (five senses):				
Problem:				
Suspects:				
Suspect				
What we know about this suspect				
How did the character(s) solve the problem?				
Who did it?				

Model Lesson 2: Integrating Information from Two Informational Texts

In this lesson, we'll be modeling how to take notes from two texts to gather information about a topic. We'll also engage in a variation of Kagan's *Give One, Get One* (n.d.) activity, as described below.

Lesson Objective:
Students will be able to "integrate information from two texts on the same topic in order to speak about the subject knowledgeably" (CCSS.RI.5.9).

Teacher Modeling

For this lesson, we'll use two informational texts about Amelia Earhart: *Amelia Earhart* (Mara, 2002), a 30-page Rookie Biography that includes many primary source photos, and *You Can't Do That, Amelia!* (Klier, 2008), an engaging picture book that depicts Earhart's accomplishments. Before reading, set a purpose for listening. Let students know that after you read the texts, you'll be asking them the following question: "If you lived when Amelia Earhart lived, would you want to hang out with her?" Have students be ready to justify their answers.

Read each book through first for enjoyment and to show the illustrations. Then return to the question you posed. Would students want to hang out with Amelia Earhart? Why or why not? Use this open-ended question to discuss the content of the books.

Next, display a blank copy of a *Give One, Get One (Blank)* chart (Figure 15-7).

Figure 15-7: Give One, Get One (Blank)

Text A:	
Give One	Get One

Explain that as you reread *Amelia Earhart*, you will be looking for **important** ideas about this famous pilot. We've listed four pieces of information as examples in the "Give One" column of Figure 15-8 *Give One, Get One—Amelia Earhart* on the next page, but you should aim to record five to eight pieces of information. Let students know that you are taking notes, not copying sentences from the book. Think aloud as you record your notes and explain the decisions you're making.

Repeat this same process using *You Can't Do That, Amelia!* on the second *Give One, Get One* chart. (see Figure 15-9: *Give One, Get One*—You Can't Do That, Amelia! on the next page).

Figure 15-8: Give One, Get One—*Amelia Earhart*

Text A: Amelia Earhart	
Give One	Get One
Always dreamed of flying a plane	
Studied to be a nurse	
Took flying lessons	
Set a record by flying up to 14,000 feet	

Figure 15-9: Give One, Get One—*You Can't Do That, Amelia!*

Text A: You Can't Do That, Amelia!	
Give One	Get One
As a child, built a roller coaster in her backyard	
Roller coaster went from rooftop to ground	
Took flying lessons	
Set a record by flying 14,000 feet high	

To model how you'll fill in the "Get One" column, keep Figure 15-8 for yourself (notes from *Amelia Earhart*) and give Figure 15-9 (notes from *You Can't Do That, Amelia!*) to a student volunteer. Look over your "Give One" column and give one of your ideas to your student volunteer. He writes the idea you gave him in his "Get One" column. The volunteer then gives you one of his ideas, and you write it in the "Get One" column on your sheet. Explain that when students engage in their own *Give One, Get One* activity in the "Guided Practice" section of this lesson, they'll be giving and getting ideas from their classmates. You are demonstrating how the process works with just your one volunteer.

Point out that both texts may contain some of the same information. Furthermore, let students know that it's fine to give and get information that you already have on your sheet. Information that is repeated across texts is often important information.

Conclusion: Spend a few minutes reviewing what you learned about Amelia Earhart: What about her life was most impressive? Why is she such a famous American? What surprised you? What new questions do you have? In addition, emphasize that you were able to learn a great deal about Amelia Earhart because the information came from more than one book.

Guided Practice

For this practice, it's best to use relatively short texts or short sections from longer texts. We'll use *Rachel Carson and Her Book That Changed the World* (Lawlor, 2012), a picture book of Rachel Carson's life, and *Writing about the Ocean*, a short article about Rachel Carson from the America's Story collection on the Library of Congress website.

After you've read the two texts with your students, have students create a T-chart with "Give One" in the left-hand column and "Get One" in the right-hand column. Half the students should title the chart Text A: *Rachel Carson and Her Book That Changed the World*, and the other half should title it Text B: *Writing about the Ocean* for the other half. Have students using Text A help you determine information to record in the "Give One" column of their charts. Students who have this chart should record the information as you go along. Once you have five to eight pieces of information recorded, repeat the process with Text B. Here are possible notes students may record from each text:

Rachel Carson and Her Book That Changed the World

1. grew up in a house near lots of woods, orchards, and fields
2. a story she wrote at age 11 was published in a magazine
3. mom sacrificed to send Rachel to college
4. concerned about environment
5. graduate school—Johns Hopkins University, biology
6. few women biologists—nobody would hire her
7. began writing and publishing
8. best seller—*The Sea Around Us*
9. concerned about insecticides and other chemicals
10. *Silent Spring* helped change laws to protect the environment

Writing about the Ocean

1. First book, *Under the Sea-Wind*, didn't sell well at first
2. Second book, *The Sea Around Us*, on best-seller list for 39 weeks
3. *Sea Around Us*—about what lives in the ocean, written poetically
4. *Sea Around Us*—translated into 30 languages
5. Ecology = study of all living things that exist in the ecosystem
6. Helped people think about the environment in new ways
7. Worried about ocean pollutants
8. Got people to think about how to protect the environment

Once all students have information in their "Get One" columns, it's time for them to give some ideas away and get some new information from their classmates. To do this, have students holding the chart for Text A: *Rachel Carson and Her Book That Changed the World* find and share information with classmates who have notes from Text B: *Writing about the Ocean* and vice versa.

Conclude: Have students form small groups and discuss what they learned about Rachel Carson. What surprised them? What about her life was most impressive? Why is she such a famous American? What new questions do students have?

Student Application: Tiered Activities for Differentiation

Students will be differentiated for this activity by the level of the text they are assigned. All students should be reading texts on the same topic so they can share ideas in the *Give One, Get One* activity.

After students have read the text that is best for them, have them meet in small groups with others who read the same text. Allow a few minutes for students to discuss the content of the text. This should take place before students begin to record information on the *Give One, Get One* sheets. This step will allow each student to review the important ideas in the text before completing the chart. Once students have reviewed the content of the texts, have them fill in five to eight pieces of information. Depending on the amount of support students need, they may work with you, with a partner, or independently to complete the sheet. When everyone has at least five pieces of information on his or her sheet, have students move around. Allow enough time for students to give and get information from a few classmates.

Conclusion: Divide students into small heterogeneous groups, and have them share what they learned about the topic. What surprised them? What new questions do they have?

Additional Recommended Books

Penguins

Bone, E. (2009). *Penguins*. London, England: Usborne Publishing.

Tatham, B. (2002). *Penguin chick*. Let's-Read-and-Find-Out Science. New York: HarperCollins.

Whitfield, D. (2009). *Penguins*. Amazing Animals. New York: Weigl Publishers.

Underground Railroad

Evans, S. W. (2011). *Underground: finding the light to freedom*. New York: Roaring Brook Press.

Levine, E. (2007). *Henry's freedom box: a true story from the Underground Railroad*. New York: Scholastic.

Williams, C. (2009). *The Underground Railroad: journey to freedom*. Mankato, MN: The Child's World.

Magnets

Boothroyd, J. (2011). *Attract and repel: a look at magnets*. Lightning Bold Books. Minneapolis, MN: Lerner Publications Company.

Branley, F. M. (1996). *What makes a magnet?* Let's-Read-and-Find-Out Science. New York: HarperCollins.

Vogel, J. (2011). *Push and pull! Learn about magnets*. Mankato, MN: The Child's World.

Chapter 16

Understanding Structural Elements of Drama

What Is a Drama?

A drama is a performance by actors whose words and actions work in tandem to tell a story. Donovan and Pascale (2012) make a distinction between theater and drama: Unlike theater, which often includes lights, costumes, sets and lines to memorize, and elaborate final products, drama is more about the "process of exploration—on the growth and imagination of its participants" (p. 105).

What Does the Literature Say?

According to Wilhelm (1999), "all drama, like the most interesting times in anyone's life, is about important conflicts and the characters' successful or unsuccessful approach to and resolution of these conflicts" (p. 45). Wilhelm goes on to say, "The basic problem-solving pattern in a drama is conflict + consequences = tension + suspense" (p. 45).

Sometimes teachers, administrators, and parents overlook drama and the arts, considering them add-ons rather than an integral part of an instructional program, but there is growing evidence that suggests the arts can play a pivotal role in strengthening academic achievement. Donovan and Pascale (2012), for instance, report, "Drama can bolster comprehension of a story by allowing students to explore the story from inside and by physically embodying the story and its characters" (p. 113).

The following two studies with elementary and middle school students support the integration of arts into the curriculum. The first, research conducted with middle school students in a low-performing Maryland school (Snyder, Klos & Grey-Hawkins, 2014), showed that students achieved a 20 percent growth on the Maryland State Assessment and a 77 percent decline in discipline referrals during a four-year period in which the school community designed and implemented an arts integration model. The authors note, "The integration of art into the academic content curricula provides a logical approach to address the variety of students' intelligences that are reflected in their different learning styles" (p. 3).

In the second study, researchers worked with eight fourth-grade classrooms to determine whether a drama-based reading comprehension program would improve reading scores on the comprehension subtest of the Iowa Test of Basic Skills. Four randomly selected classes were taught using *Reading Comprehension through Drama (RCD)*, a specially-designed, drama-based program; the four other classes (the control group) received instruction through their traditional text-based programs. The results showed that students who participated in the drama-based program "improved an average of three months more than students who did not participate" (Rose, Parks, Androes & McMahon, 2000, p. 60).

Young children, too, benefit from reading and acting out texts. Flynn (2004/2005), for example, points out that the act of rereading passages in preparation for reader's theater promotes retention of the passages' content and enhances fluency, which is an essential component of comprehension. And Adomat (2012), in a seven-month study with first graders who were receiving reading support, found that using a dramatic approach to literacy instruction enabled children to move around, be actively immersed in the story for extended periods of time, develop inferential comprehension skills, and investigate themes (p. 349). The inclusion of dramatic elements in the literacy curriculum provides motivation for students who may not otherwise have the stamina to sustain their reading for an entire text. Whether working with early childhood, upper elementary, or middle school students, the integration of drama into the curriculum seems to provide rewarding and beneficial results for students.

Increasing Complexity through the Grades

In this chapter, we focus only on the Reading Literature component of Standard 5 (CCSS), since the Reading Information components of Standard 5 (CCSS) address many of the text structures we explore in other chapters (e.g., chronological order, cause and effect).

At grade three, according to the CCSS, students are expected to "refer to parts of stories, dramas, and poems when writing or speaking about a text, using terms such as *chapter*, *scene*, and *stanza*; describe how each successive part builds on earlier sections" (CCSS.RL.3.5).

At grade four, students should be able to "explain major differences between poems, drama, and prose, and refer to the structural elements of poems (e.g., verse, rhythm, meter) and drama (e.g., casts of characters, settings, descriptions, dialogue, stage directions) when writing or speaking about a text" (CCSS.RL.4.5).

At grade five, students should be able "to explain how a series of chapters, scenes, or stanzas fits together to provide the overall structure of a particular story, drama, or poem" (CCSS.RL.5.5).

Model Lesson 1: Structural Elements of Drama

For this lesson, we use the book *Take a Walk in Their Shoes: Biographies of 14 Outstanding African Americans* (Turner, 1989). Each chapter in this book presents a short biography of a famous African-American and a follow-up skit about the person. In the "Teacher Model" part of the lesson, we'll use the chapter on Leroy "Satchel" Paige, one of the greatest pitchers to play baseball. We chose *The Rediscovery of "Satchel" Paige* not only because it is about an important American, but also because this relatively short play contains the following elements of a drama script: a specified setting, a cast of characters, scenes, and stage directions (i.e., comments that provide readers/actors with information about how to say their lines, how to look or move, how to act, etc.). This script does not include the role of a narrator—a role that is often found in scripts—but the play we'll use in the guided practice section, *The Douglass "Station" of the Underground Railroad*, does include narrators.

Lesson Objective:
Students will be able to demonstrate their comprehension of a drama by focusing on the setting, cast of characters, and stage directions.

Teacher Modeling

To prepare for *The Rediscovery of "Satchel" Paige,* make name cards for the following characters: Daddy, Daughter, Son, and Grandpa. Write each name on a separate piece of heavy paper, punch two holes in the top of each card, and attach a ribbon or piece of yarn so students can wear their name tags around their necks. Also, have a box ready that can serve as a treasure trunk and a few baseball cards or index cards that can represent baseball cards.

Begin the lesson by reading aloud Paige's biography (pp. 149–155, sharing the illustrations on pp. 150 and 152) to familiarize students with this important American. Set a purpose for listening by letting students know that you'll be asking them the following question after you read aloud the story: "What did Leroy 'Satchel' Paige do that showed 'he loved baseball and life'?"

Next, have a copy of the skit on pp. 156–160 available for each student. Think aloud as you proceed on a "play walk"—just as you might do on a book walk. (Note: If your students are already familiar with the structure of plays, feel free to skip this part of the lesson and pick up the lesson where you'll read the play, as listed below by the *.) Read aloud the title, *The Rediscovery of "Satchel" Paige,* and talk through what you're thinking: "*Rediscovery* is an interesting word. I wonder who 'Satchel' Paige is and who will discover him again?" Next, point to the word "CAST" and explain that a cast is the list of the characters who will be in the play. In this play, there are four actors: Daddy, Daughter, Son, and Grandpa. Next, point to "SCENE I" and explain that each scene is a separate part of the play. Usually a new scene signifies that something is going to change (Lisle, 2015). Make note of the first stage direction, which lets the actors know where they are (in the attic) and what they are doing (tidying up the attic) when the play opens. This stage direction is the setting for Scene I.

Next, explain that in narratives (stories), when a character speaks, his or her words are written in quotation marks. In plays, however, actors read the words that follow their names. Write the following example on the whiteboard: CONNOR: Declan, where did you put my sneakers? Say, "If I were CONNOR, I would read aloud 'Declan, where did you put my sneakers?'" Explain that actors never read the names that are written in capital letters. If need be, demonstrate again using an example or two from *The Rediscovery of "Satchel" Paige.*

Continue on your "play walk," stopping at the top of page 157. Point to the first line. Daddy is speaking. Call attention to the italicized words in parentheses that follow Daddy's name. Let students know that these words are stage directions that give actors information about how they should read or act out their lines. In this case, the person who wrote this script wants Daddy to chuckle a little bit as he reads his lines. Direct students' attention to the other two stage directions on this page, and explain why the scriptwriter included them in the play.

Move on to page 158 and stop at Scene II. Explain that, similar to the stage direction at the beginning of Scene I, the italicized words under "Scene II" let the actors know the setting for this scene. The setting has changed from the attic to the supper table.

* Now it's time to read the play. To model how the play works, you should take on the role of Daddy and invite three students to take on the roles of the other characters. Pass out the name tags. You may want to have other students be children in the family (standing or sitting with the cast). Remaining students may serve as the audience.

After reading the play, talk about the settings and the characters. If possible, display a clip art image of a trophy or have a real trophy available. Explain that this will be the coveted trophy for the BC (Best Character) Award, which will be presented to the character who has played an important part in developing the story. Explain that you would like the award to go to Daddy because he was the character who introduced the children to Satchel Paige. Without him, the children wouldn't have known that Satchel contributed so much to the game of baseball. Print "Daddy" on the trophy. Explain that not everyone needs to agree that Daddy was the BC; others might want the award to go to Grandpa, for instance, because he was the one who knew all about Satchel; Grandpa saw Satchel play ball and could explain what made Satchel so exceptional. Let students know that it's fine to nominate any one of the characters for the BC Award as long as they can justify their nomination with evidence from the play.

Before concluding the lesson, return to the stage directions on page 157. Remind students that the first direction provided Daddy with instructions on how to speak. The writer wanted the actor who is playing Daddy to chuckle a bit. Then, look at the next direction. This direction lets Daddy know that he should pick up some cards and act as though he's hunting for a particular one. These two stage directions let the actors know exactly what to do. In some cases, however, the directions aren't as specific. Point out the direction for Daddy in the middle of page 158, for instance. Daddy has to show that he's thinking about what happened in the past. It's up to the actor to determine how to show what's going on inside him. Perhaps the actor could look off into the distance and shake his head slightly as he reads his line. Similarly, look at the stage direction for Son on page 159 and exhibit a facial expression that lets the audience know Son feels knowledgeable!

Finally, pretend you are the director. Let students know that you'll add another stage direction. Turn to the top of page 158 and read the question that Son asks. Son wants to know if Daddy ever went to a game in which Satchel Paige pitched. Explain that as the director of the play, you think it would catch the audience's attention if Son stood up and pretended he was pitching a ball as he asks his question. Add this new stage direction to the script. [e.g., SON (*standing and pretending to pitch a ball*) ...]

To conclude the lesson, recap that actors perform plays using scenes and stage directions to help present the story.

Guided Practice

To prepare for this activity, have available name tags for the following characters in *The Douglass "Station" of the Underground Railroad* (Turner, 1989): First Narrator, Second Narrator, Harriet Tubman, First Son, Second Son, Frederick Douglass, Anna Douglass, and eight slaves. (Note: The slaves do not have speaking parts.) Also, prepare a chart with the names of the characters (see Figure 16-1: *The Douglass "Station" of the Underground Railroad Character Chart* on p. 171). Students will use this chart to "vote" for characters they believe are worthy of the BC Award.

Begin by reviewing the following terms: *setting*, *cast of characters*, and *stage directions*. Ask students what each term means and why each part is important in a script. Next, share *Oh My, What a Drama!* (Figure 16-2 on p. 172). Let students know that they will be helping you fill it in after reading *The Douglass "Station" of the Underground Railroad*. Remind them that each of them will be nominating a character for the BC Award. To be nominated, a character should have played an important part in developing the story.

Explain that seven characters will perform *The Douglass "Station" of the Underground Railroad*. Two of these characters are narrators. Narrators are characters who speak directly to the audience and provide comments that help the audience know what's going on in the scene. Go on a brief "play walk" of *The Douglass "Station" of the Underground Railroad*. Next, assign students to read the parts of the characters in this play. Allow time for them to practice reading their parts silently before you have them read aloud the text. After performing the play, have students help you fill in the setting information on the *Oh My, What a Drama!* sheet (Figure 16-2 on p. 172). Where did this play take place? Then give each student a sticker (colored dot or star). On the character chart (Figure 16-1 on p. 171), have each student place a sticker under the name of the character he or she would nominate for the coveted BC Award. Tally the scores and briefly have students defend their choices. Record the name of the award recipient on the *Oh My, What a Drama!* sheet (on p. 172). Go back through the script, having students identify a stage direction that provides an actor with instructions for speaking (e.g., the direction for First Son on page 114) and one that provides information about what an actor should do while reading his or her lines (e.g., the direction for Anna Douglass on page 114). Next, have students become the directors. Have them suggest a place where they could add another stage direction. Then complete the last two sections of *Oh My, What a Drama!* by adding two more stage directions: one stage direction that will provide an actor with instructions for speaking and one stage direction that will provide information about what an actor should do while reading his or her line.

Conclude this guided practice by asking students if they liked performing this story as a play or if they would have preferred reading it as a traditional story. Have them use terminology such as *cast of characters*, *narrator*, *setting*, and *stage directions* in their discussion.

Student Application: Tiered Activities for Differentiation

We differentiate the products in these graphic organizers; yet, all three graphic organizers look very similar. The Initial Level organizer, for instance, doesn't give students the impression that it's easier than the Transitional Level or the Accomplished Level organizers. Nor does it appear that students at one level are doing less (or more) work than students at the other levels.

Initial Level

Students will use a sentence frame to identify the story setting(s), select one character to receive the coveted BC Award, and justify the choice. Finally, they will be the director by adding one stage direction. They should use the sentence frame on the sheet to guide them.

Teacher action: Select a play that students can read independently. The play should include a specified setting or one that can be easily inferred and several stage directions for children to use as models when they write their own stage directions. Distribute a copy of the *Be the Director* sheet to each student (Figure 16-3 on p. 173).

Transitional Level

Students will describe the setting of the story, select one character to receive the coveted BC Award, and justify the choice. Students will be the director and add one stage direction.

Teacher action: Select a play that students can read independently. The play may include more than one setting and several stage directions for children to use as models when they write their own stage directions. Distribute a copy of the *Action, Please* sheet to each student (Figure 16-4 on p. 174).

Accomplished Level

Students will describe the setting of the story, select one character to receive the coveted BC Award, and justify the choice. They will add one stage direction that will provide an actor with instructions for speaking and one stage direction telling what an actor should do while reading his or her lines.

Teacher action: Select a play that students can read independently. The play may include more than one setting and several stage directions for children to use as models when writing stage directions. Distribute a copy of the *Oh My, What a Drama!* sheet to each student (Figure 16-2 on p. 172).

Figure 16-1: *The Douglass "Station" of the Underground Railroad* Character Chart

First Narrator	Second Narrator	Harriet Tubman	Frederick Douglass	Anna Douglass	First Son	Second Son

Figure 16-2: Oh My, What a Drama!

Oh My, What a Drama!
Name:
Title of play:
(1) Settings:
(2) Who should receive the BC Award?
What did this character do to deserve this award?
(3) Go back to the script to add a stage direction that will provide information about how an actor should speak while reading his or her lines. Write the name of the character, the stage direction, and what the character will say in this space.
(4) Go back to the script to add a stage direction that will provide information about what an actor should do while reading his or her lines. Write the name of the character, the stage direction, and what the character will say in this space.

Figure 16-3: Be the Director

Be the Director
Name:
Title of play:
(1) Settings: This play took place _____ and _____
(2) Who should receive the BC Award?   What did this character do to deserve this award?
(3) Go back to the script and decide where you could add a stage direction. In the space below, write the character's name, the stage direction, and what the character will say. Character's name: Stage direction: Words the character will say:

Figure 16-4: Action, Please

Action, Please
Name:
Title of play:
(1) Settings:
(2) Who should receive the BC Award?
What did this character do to deserve this award?
(3) Go back to the script and add a stage direction. Write the name of the character, the stage direction, and what the character will say in this space.

Additional Recommended Books (Plays)

Lewis, L. (n.d.). *The incredible animal race*. Retrieved on October 10, 2015, from http://www. educationworld.com/a_curr/reading/ReadersTheater/pdfs/ReadersTheater014-download.pdf.

Rebman, R. C. (1996). "Elizabeth Blackwell: The First Woman Physician." *Plays—The Drama Magazine for Young People, 55* (7), 53–58.

Turner, G. T. (1989*). Take a walk in their shoes: biographies of 14 outstanding African Americans*. New York: Dutton. (See *The Beauty of Being Free*, pp. 122–127.).

Model Lesson 2: Building from Scene to Scene

This lesson should follow the previous lesson, "Structural Elements of Drama."

Lesson Objective:

Students will be able to identify changes in scenes that help move the story from the beginning to the middle and to the end.

Teacher Modeling

For this lesson, we'll use *How Coyote Stole Fire* (2013), the adaptation of a Native American myth by Spencer Kayden.

To prepare for this lesson, make a name card for each of the 13 characters in this play and have two dry sticks available.

Pass out a copy of the *How Coyote Stole Fire* script to each student. Go on a "play walk," as you did in the prior lesson, to familiarize students with the structure and overall gist of the play. Point out the cast of characters, scenes and where they take place, and stage directions.

Assign students (or ask for volunteers) to take on the roles in the play. Provide time for them to practice reading their parts silently before asking them to read them aloud. You should become one of the characters, so you can model your reading.

After you and your students have performed the play, explain the scenes in a play follow a logical order and that each scene usually includes a change that helps move the story forward. For example, if you used *The Rediscovery of "Satchel" Paige* (Turner, 1989) in your previous lesson, recall that in Scene I, the characters learn about Satchel Paige. The scene ends with Daddy suggesting that the children ask their grandfather about Satchel Paige because Grandpa knew more about Satchel. In Scene II, there is a change: Grandpa enters the play. He recalls what he remembers about seeing Satchel play and why baseball players who batted against Satchel started to wear batting helmets. Good readers keep an eye out for these changes because the changes move the story along. Say, "Let's test this out with *How Coyote Stole Fire*." Display the *Scene-by-Scene Replay* (Figure 16-5 on p. 178).

Thinking aloud, recall that in Scene 1, Coyote thinks he can help his animal friends stay warm. Record this in the first box of Figure 16-5 on page 178. Go through each scene, identifying what changed in each one and jotting down the information in the graphic. In Scene 2, Coyote had a plan. In Scene 3, Coyote reveals his plan and asks for help. In Scene 4, Coyote steals fire, and in Scene 5 he escapes with the help of his friends Squirrel and Frog. It's in Scene 6 that Fire Beings try to get fire back from Wood, are unsuccessful, and fly back up the mountain. In the final scene, Scene 7, Coyote rubs two sticks together and fire reappears.

Before concluding the lesson, review in which scenes the major elements of the story occurred: The problem occurred in Scene 1—Coyote decides to try to help his friends stay warm. The problem was resolved in Scene 7, when Coyote shows his friends how to get fire out of wood. The most suspenseful scene was Scene 5. Coyote escaped with fire, but just barely. In the process, his tail was burned and turned white, which is why coyotes now have white tips on their tails. His friend Squirrel touched the hot fire and her tail began to curl. One of the Fire Beings caught Frog's tail. Frog escaped, but his tail was pulled off. Even today, squirrels have curled tails and frogs no longer have tails.

Guided Practice

For this lesson, we'll use *The Moment* (*Know Your World Extra*, n.d.), a seven-scene play about Kacie, a girl who is too nervous to audition for a play.

To prepare for this lesson, make a name card for each of the nine characters in this play and have on hand a large bowl—one that won't break when it's dropped.

Have a copy of the *The Moment* script available for each student. Go on a "play walk," as you did above, to familiarize students with the structure and overall gist of the play.

Assign students (or ask for volunteers) to take on the roles in the play. Be sure to let students practice reading their parts silently prior to performing. Once the performance is complete, display the *Scene-by-Scene Replay* sheet (Figure 16-5 on p. 178) and have students help you fill it in. Next, ask a couple of students which scene was their favorite and why. Ask another student to recall the story's problem and in which scene he or she learned about the problem. Turn to another student and ask in which scene the problem was solved and how. Finally, initiate a discussion about the scene that was the most suspenseful. Which one was it and what made it so suspenseful?

Student Application: Tiered Activities for Differentiation

Students will be using tiered graphic organizers in these activities. Each organizer has enough space to use with plays containing five scenes. However, if the plays your students are reading contain fewer than five scenes, have students cross out the extra scene boxes on the sheet before they begin to fill them out. If they are reading plays that contain more than five scenes, have students add the appropriate number of boxes on the back of the graphic organizer so they have a box for each scene.

Initial Level

Students will identify the changes that helped move the story line along, cite their favorite scene, and explain why it was their favorite. They will record their thoughts on the *Scrolling through Scenes* sheet (Figure 16-6 on p. 179).

Teacher action: Select a play that students can read independently and that contains only a few scenes. Distribute a copy of the *Scrolling through Scenes* sheet to each student.

Transitional Level

Using the *Changing Scenes* sheet (Figure 16-7 on p. 180), students will identify the changes that create the forward-moving structure of the play, identify the scene in which they learned about the problem, cite the problem, identify the scene in which the problem was resolved, and explain how it was resolved.

Teacher action: Select a play that students can read independently and that contains multiple scenes. Distribute a copy of the *Changing the Scenes* sheet to each student.

Accomplished Level

Using the *Scene Scenario* sheet (Figure 16-8 on p. 181), students will identify the changes that create the forward-moving structure of the play, identify the scene that was most suspenseful because it contained a turning point in the play, and explain what made this scene so suspenseful.

Teacher action: Select a play that has a suspenseful scene that marks a turning point in the story. Distribute a copy of the *Scene Scenario* sheet to each student.

Additional Recommended Books (Plays)

"The Salem Witch Trials." (Oct. 28, 2013). *Scholastic Action*, 12–17.

Turner, G. T. (1989). *Take a walk in their shoes: biographies of 14 outstanding African Americans.* New York: Dutton. (See *In the Footsteps of Dr. King*, pp. 20–24).

"The Watsons go to Birmingham." (Sept. 16, 2013). *Scholastic Action*, 12–17.

Figure 16-5: Scene-by-Scene Replay

Scene-by-Scene Replay
SCENE 1
WHAT HAPPENED?
SCENE 2
WHAT CHANGED?
SCENE 3
WHAT CHANGED?
SCENE 4
WHAT CHANGED?
SCENE 5
WHAT CHANGED?
SCENE 6
WHAT CHANGED?
FINAL SCENE (SCENE 7)
WHAT HAPPENED?

Figure 16-6: Scrolling through Scenes

Scrolling through Scenes
SCENE 1
WHAT HAPPENED?
SCENE 2
WHAT CHANGED?
SCENE 3
WHAT CHANGED?
SCENE 4
WHAT CHANGED?
FINAL SCENE
WHAT HAPPENED?
Which scene was your favorite? Scene _____   Why?

Figure 16-7: Changing Scenes

Changing Scenes
SCENE 1
WHAT HAPPENED?
SCENE 2
WHAT CHANGED?
SCENE 3
WHAT CHANGED?
SCENE 4
WHAT CHANGED?
FINAL SCENE
WHAT HAPPENED?
In which scene did you learn about the problem in the story?
What was the problem?
In which scene did someone solve the problem?
How was the problem solved?

Figure 16-8: Scene Scenario

Scene Scenario
SCENE 1
WHAT HAPPENED?
SCENE 2
WHAT CHANGED?
SCENE 3
WHAT CHANGED?
SCENE 4
WHAT CHANGED?
FINAL SCENE
WHAT HAPPENED?
Which scene was the most suspenseful because it included a turning point in the story?
Explain what made this scene so suspenseful.

References

Adomat, D. S. (2012). Drama's potential for deepening young children's understandings of stories. *Early Childhood Education Journal, 40*, 343–350.

Akhondi M., Malayeri F. A. & Samad A. A. (2011). How to teach expository structure to facilitate reading comprehension. *The Reading Teacher, 64*(5), 366–372.

Auld, M. (adapted by LaBella, S.) (n.d.). *Anansi and the yam hill*. Retrieved on October 10, 2015, from *http://www.educationworld.com/a_curr/reading/ReadersTheater/pdfs/ReadersTheater029-download.pdf*.

Backes, L. (2001). Characters and point of view. Retrieved on October 10, 2015, from *http://www.fictionfactor.com/children/viewpoint.html*.

Bates, D. (2014–2015). Songs, interviews, and visual images: Primary source texts to invigorate and enhance Common Core Standards-based learning. *Illinois Reading Council Journal, 43*(1), 30–39.

Beers, K. (2003). *When kids can't read: What teachers can do*. Portsmouth, NH: Heinemann.

Bidner, J. (2006). *Is my dog a wolf? How your pet compares to its wild cousin*. New York: Lark Books.

Bjorklund, R. (2014). *Blue whales*. Nature's Children. New York: Children's Press.

Bluestein, N. A. (2010). Unlocking text features for determining importance in expository text: A strategy for struggling readers. *The Reading Teacher, 63*(7), 597–600.

Bohn-Gettler, C. & Kendeou, P. (2014). The interplay of reader goals, working memory, and text structure during reading, *Contemporary Educational Psychology, 39*(3), 206–219.

Britt, M. A. & Sommer, J. (2004). Facilitating textual integration with macro-structure focusing tasks. *Reading Psychology, 25*, 313–339.

Brooks, R. (2009). *Writing great books for young adults*. Naperville, IL: Sourcebooks, Inc.

Brown, A. L., Campione, J.C. & Day, J. (1981). Learning to learn: On training students to learn from texts. *Educational Researcher, 10*(2), 14–24.

Brown, A. L., Day, J. & Jones, R. (1983). The development of plans for summarizing texts. *Child Development, 54*(4), 968–979.

Bunyi, A. (2011). Finding the message: Grasping themes in literature. Retrieved on October 10, 2015, from *http://www.scholastic.com/teachers/top-teaching/2011/02/helping-students-grasp-themes-literature*.

Burke, J. (2000). *Reading reminders: Tools, tips, and techniques*. Portsmouth, NH: Boynton Cook Publishers.

Calkins, L., Ehrenworth, M. & Lehman, C. (2012). *Pathways to the Common Core*. Portsmouth, NH: Heinemann.

Carlisle, J. E. (2010). Effects of instruction in morphological awareness on literacy achievement: An integrative review. *Reading Research Quarterly 45*(4), 464–487.

Caskey, M. M. (2007). Improving classroom instruction: Understanding the developmental nature of analyzing primary sources. *Research in Middle Level Education Online, 30*(6), 1–20.

Catling, P. (1952). *The chocolate touch*. New York: Scholastic.

Chin, Jason. (2012). *Island: a story of the Galápagos*. New York: Scholastic.

Coleman, J. M., Bradley, L. G. & Donovan, C. A. (2012). Visual representations in second graders information book compositions. *The Reading Teacher, 66*(1), 31–45.

Cooney, B. (1982). *Miss Rumphius*. New York: Puffins.

Crabtree. T., Alber-Morgan, S. & Konrad, M. (2010). The effects of self-monitoring of story elements on the reading comprehension of high school seniors with learning disabilities. *Education & Treatment of Children. 33*(2), 187–203.

Dahl, R. (1982). *The BFG*. New York: Scholastic.

Davis, K. (2014). *Mr. Ferris and his wheel*. New York: Houghton Mifflin Publishing Company.

del Pino, M. del Carmen Gil, García, V. J. L., Millán, J. C. V. (2013). Study of recall in reading skill with relationship of prior knowledge-researching significative intergrupal differences. *International Education Studies, 6*(12), 15–24.

Donovan, L. & Pascale, L. (2012). *Integrating the arts across the content areas*. Huntington Beach, CA: Shell Education.

Duke, N. K., Caughlan, S., Juzwick, M. M. & Martin, N. M. (2012). Teaching genre with purpose. *Educational Leadership, 69*(6), 34–39.

Fagella-Luby, M., Schumaker, S. J. & Deshler, D. D. (2007). Embedded learning strategy instruction: Story-structure pedagogy in heterogeneous secondary literature classes. *Learning Disability Quarterly, 30*(2), 131–147.

Fertig, G. (2005). Teaching elementary students how to interpret the past. *Social Studies, 96*(1), 2–8.

Fisher, D. & Frey, N. (2014). Close reading as an intervention for struggling middle school readers. *Journal of Adolescent and Adult Literacy, 57*(5), 367–376.

Fisher, D., Frey, N. & Lapp, D. (2008). Shared readings: Modeling comprehension, vocabulary, text structures, and text features for older readers. *The Reading Teacher, 61*(7), 548–556. DOI:10.1598/RT.61.7.4.

Fisher, D., Frey N. & Lapp, D. (2012). *Text complexity: Raising rigor in reading*. Newark, DE: International Reading Association.

Fitzgerald, J. & Spiegel, D. L. (1983). Enhancing children's reading comprehension through instruction in narrative structure. *Journal of Reading Behavior, 15*(2), 1–17.

Fluck, M. J. (1978). Comprehension of relative clauses by children ages five to nine years. *Language and Speech, 21*(2), 190–201.

Flynn, E. A. (2007). Reconsiderations: Louise Rosenblatt and the ethical turn in literary theory. *College English, 70*(1), 52–69.

Flynn, R. M. (2004/2005). Curriculum-based Reader's Theatre: Setting the stage for reading and retention. *The Reading Teacher, 58*(4), 360–365.

Fox, B. (2008). *100 Activities for developing fluent readers*. New York: Pearson Allyn Bacon Prentice Hall.

Fulton, L. & Poeltler, E. (2013). Developing a scientific argument. *Science and Children*, 50(9), 30–35.

Gardill, M. C. and Jitendra, A. (1999). Advanced story map instruction: Effects on the reading comprehension of students with learning disabilities. *The Journal of Special Education. 33*(1), 2–17.

Gelzheiser, L. (2005). Maximizing student progress in one-to-one programs. *Exceptionality,* *13*(4), 229–243.

Gelzheiser, L., Hallgren-Flynn, L., Connors, M. & Scanlon, D. (2014). Reading thematically related texts to develop knowledge and comprehension. *The Reading Teacher, 68*(1), 53–63. Doi:10.1002/trtr.1271.

Gerstein, M. (2003). *The man who walked between the towers.* Brookfield, CT: Roaring Brook Press.

Gibson, E., Desmet, T., Grodner, D., Watson, D. & Ko, K. (2005). Reading relative clauses in English. *Cognitive Linguistics,16*(2), 313–353.

Graham, S. & Herbert, M. (2011). Writing to read: A meta-analysis of the impact of writing and writing instruction on reading. *Harvard Educational Review, 81*(4), 710–744.

Grünke, M., Wilbert, J. & Stegemann, K. (2013). Analyzing the effects of story mapping on the reading comprehension of children with low intellectual abilities. *Learning Disabilities-A Contemporary Journal, 11*(2), 51–66.

Hamilton, V. (1997). *A ring of tricksters: Animal tales from America, the West Indies, and Africa.* New York: Scholastic.

Haria, P. D. (2010). *The effects of teaching a genre-specific reading comprehension strategy on struggling fifth grader students' ability to summarize and analyze argumentative texts.* (Doctoral dissertation). Retrieved from ProQuest Dissertation and Theses (Accession Order No. 3423407).

Harris, T. L. and Hodges, R. E. (1995). *The literacy dictionary, the vocabulary of reading and writing.* Newark, DE: The International Reading Association.

Hedin, L. R. & Conderman, G. (2010). Teaching students to comprehend informational text through rereading. *The Reading Teacher, 63*(7), 556–565.

Helen Keller Biography for Kids. (n.d.) Retrieved on October 10, 2015, from http://mrnussbaum.com/helen-keller/.

Jellyfish or Plastic Bag? (2015). *Scholastic News Edition 2, 71*(7), 1–4.

Jitendra, A.K., Hoppes, M.K. & Xin, Y.P. (2000). Enhancing main idea comprehension for students with learning problems: The role of a summarization strategy and self-monitoring instruction. *Journal of Special Education, 34*(3), 127–139. DOI:10.1177/002246690003400302.

Johnson, J., Reid, R. & Mason. L. (2010). Improving the reading recall of high school students with ADHD. *Remedial and Special Education, 33*(4), 258–268. DOI: 10.1177/07441932511403502.

Kagan strategy: Give one, get one. (n.d.). Retrieved on October 10, 2015, from http://www.pendercountyschools.net/UserFiles/Servers/Server_3727387/File/Give_One_Get_One.pdf.

Kamberelis, G. (1999). Genre development and learning: Children writing stories, science reports, and poems. *Research in the Teaching of English, 33*(4), 403–459.

Kamberelis, G. (2005/2010). *Writing and/in genres and/in fourth and fifth grade.* Retrieved on October 10, 2015 from *http://www.reading.org/Libraries/book-supplements/bk767Supp-Kamberelis.pdf.*

Kayden, S. (Nov./Dec. 2013). *How coyote stole fire, (adaptation).* Retrieved on October 10, 2015, from www.Scholastic.com/storyworks.

Keats, E. J. (1965). *Whistle for Willie*. New York: Viking Press.

Keene, E. O. & Zimmerman, S. (1997). *Mosaic of thought: Teaching comprehension in a reader's workshop*. Portsmouth, NH: Heinemann.

Kelly, D. A. (2011). *Ballpark mysteries #1: Fenway foul-up*. A Stepping Stone Book. New York: Random House.

Kendeou, P., van den Broek, P., Helder, A. & Karlsson, J. (2014). A cognitive view of reading comprehension: Implications for reading difficulites. *Learning Disabilities Research and Practice, 29*(1), 10–16.

Kieffer, M. J. & Lesaux, N. K. (2008). The role of derivational morphology in the reading comprehension of Spanish-speaking English language learners. *Reading and Writing: An Interdisciplinary Journal, 16*(5), 399–422.

Klier, K. W. (2008). *You can't do that, Amelia!* Honesdale, PA: Calkins Creek.

Lawlor, L. (2012). *Rachel Carson and her book that changed the world*. New York: Holiday House.

Lightning chaser. (2013). *Scholastic News Edition 2, 69*(6), 1–4.

Linder, R. (2012). *Common Core and point of view*. Retrieved on October 10, 2015, from *http://ontheweb.rozlinder.com/common-core-and-point-of-view/*.

Lisle, H. (2015). Scene-creation workshop: Writing scenes that move your story forward. Retrieved on October 10, 2015, from *http://hollylisle.com/scene-creation-workshop-writing-scenes-that-move-your-story-forward/*.

Liu, C. C., Chen, S. L., Shih, J. L., Huang, G. T. & Liu, B. J. (2011). An enhanced concept map approach to improving children's storytelling ability. *Computers and Education, 56*, 873–884.

Mara, W. (2002). *Amelia Earhart*. Rookie Biographies. New York: Children's Press.

Marsh, L. (2012). *National Geographic Kids: Caterpillar to butterfly*, Washington, D.C.: National Geographic Society.

Martin, R. (1992). *The rough-faced girl*. New York: Penguin Putnam Books for Young Readers.

Max Hunter Collection. (n.d.). Library of Congress. Retrieved on October 10, 2015, from http://www.americaslibrary.gov/es/mo/es_mo_hunter_1.html.

McTigue, E. M. & Flowers, A. C. (2011). Science visual literacy: Learners' perceptions and knowledge of diagrams. *The Reading Teacher, 64*(8), 578–589.

Merriam-Webster Dictionary. (2015). Retrieved on October 10, 2015, from *http://www.merriam-webster.com/dictionary/theme*.

Miller, M. (2006). Did someone say "free land"? *Appleseeds, 8*(9), 17.

Mitchell, M. K. (1995). *Uncle Jed's Barbershop*. New York: Simon and Schuster.

Moore-Russo, D. & Shanahan, L. E. (2014). A broader vision of literacy: Including the visual with the linguistic. *Journal of Adolescent and Adult Literacy, 57*(7), 527–532.

Morgan, D. N. & Rasinski, T. V. (2012). The power and potential of primary sources. *The Reading Teacher, 65*(8), 584–594.

Morrow, L. M. (1985). Retelling stories: A strategy for improving young children's comprehension, concept of story structure, and oral language complexity. *The Elementary School Journal, 85*(5), 646–661.

National Assessment Governing Board. (2008). *Reading framework for the 2009 National Assessment of Educational Progress.* Retrieved on October 10, 2015, from *http://www.nagb.org/content/ nagb/assets/documents/publications/frameworks/reading/2009-reading-framework.pdf.*

National Assessment of Educational Progress (NAEP, 2009). *The NAEP reading achievement levels by grade.* Retrieved on October 10, 2015, from *https://nces.ed.gov/nationsreportcard/reading/ achieve.aspx#2009ald.*

National Reading Panel (2000). *Teaching children to read: An evidence-based assessment of the scientific research literature on reading and its implications for reading instruction.* Washington, D.C.: National Institute of Child Health and Human Development and U.S. Department of Education.

Nelson, C. S. (1994). Historical literacy: A journey of discovery. *The Reading Teacher, 47*(7), 552–556.

Newkirk, T. (2012). How we really comprehend nonfiction. *Educational Leadership, 69*(6), pp. 29–32.

O'Brien, E. (n.d.). What is an appositive? Grammar Revolution: Grammar the Easy Way. Retrieved on June 28, 2015, from *http://www.english-grammar-revolution.com/appositive.html.*

Oster, J. (1989). Seeing with different eyes: Another view of literature in the ESL classroom. *TESOL Quarterly, 23*(1), 85–103.

Paris, S. G., Wasik, B. A. & Turner, J. C. (1991). The development of strategic readers. In R. Barr, M. L. Kamil, P. Mosenthal, and P. D. Pearson (Eds.), *Handbook of Reading Research (Vol. 2)* (pp. 609–640). New York: Longman.

Park, F. & Park, G. (2002). *Good-bye, 382 Shin Dang Dong.* Washington, D.C.: National Geographic Society.

Paulsen, G. (1999). *Hatchet.* New York: Simon & Schuster.

Pearson, P. D. & Gallagher, M. (1983). The Instruction of Reading Comprehension. *Contemporary Educational Psychology, 8*(3), (317–344).

Peha, S. (n.d.). *Themes and variations.* Retrieved on October 10, 2015, from_ *http://www.ttms.org/say_about_a_book/themes_and_variations.htm.*

Philbrick, R. (2014). *Zane and the hurricane: A story of Katrina.* New York: Scholastic.

Pilkey, D. (1996). *The Paperboy.* New York: Orchard Books.

Polacco, P. (1990). *Thunder cake.* New York: Scholastic.

Pony Express. (n.d.). Library of Congress. Retrieved on October 10, 2015, from *http://www.americaslibrary.gov/es/mo/es_mo_pony_1.html.*

Primary Source Analysis Tool. (n.d.). Library of Congress. Retrieved on October 10, 2015, from *http://www.loc.gov/teachers/usingprimarysources/guides.html.*

Raphael, T. E. & Au, K. H. (2005). QAR: Enhancing comprehension and test taking across grades and content areas. *The Reading Teacher, 59*(3), 206–221.

Reutzel, R., Read, S. & Fawson, P. C. (2009). Using information trade books as models for teaching expository text structure improve children's reading comprehension: An action research project. *Journal Of Reading Education, 35*(1), 31–38.

Robertson, D. A., Dougherty, S., Ford-Connors, E. & Paratore, J. R. (2014). Re-envisioning instruction: Mediating complex texts for older readers. *The Reading Teacher, 67*(7), 547–559.

Roe, B. & Ross, E. (2006). *Integrating language arts through literature & thematic units.* New York: Pearson.

Rohmann, E. (2002). *My friend rabbit.* New York: Scholastic.

Roop, C. & Roop, R. (2001). *Escape from the ice: Shackleton and the Endurance.* Hello Reader. New York: Scholastic.

Rose, D. S., Parks, M., Androes, K. & McMahon, S. D. (2000). Imagery-based learning: Improving elementary students' reading comprehension with drama techniques. *Journal of Educational Research, 94*(1), 55–63.

Rumelhart, D. (1980) On evaluating story grammars. *Cognitive Science*, (4), 313–316. Retrieved on October 10, 2015, from http://csjarchive.cogsci.rpi.edu/1980v04/i03/p0313p0316/main.pdf.

Salvadore, M. (2012). Point of view in nonfiction picture books. Reading Rainbow. Retrieved on October 10, 2015, from http://www.readingrockets.org/blogs/pagebypage/54490.

Schnotz, W., Ludewig, U., Ullrich, M., Horz, H., McElvany, N. & Baumert, J. (2014). Strategy shifts during learning from texts and pictures. *Journal of Educational Psychology, 106*(4), 974–989.

Scott, C. M. (2009). A case for the sentence in reading comprehension. *Language, Speech, and Hearing Services in Schools, 40*(2), 184–191.

Serafini, F. (2013). Close reading and children's literature. *The Reading Teacher, 67*(4), 32–37.

Smeaton, P. S. & Waters, F. H. (2013). What happens when first year teachers close their classroom doors? An investigation into the instructional practices of beginning teachers. *American Secondary Education, 41*(2), 71–93.

Smithsonian National Museum of American History. (n.d.). *Engaging Students with Primary Sources.* Retrieved on October 10, 2015, from *http://historyexplorer.si.edu/PrimarySources.pdf.*

Smolen, L. A., Collins L. J. & Still, K. L. (2008). Enhancing cultural understanding and respect with multicultural tet sets in the K–2 classroom. *Ohio Journal of English Language Arts. 48*(2) 18–19.

Snyder, L., Klos, P. & Grey-Hawkins, L. (2014). Transforming teaching through arts integration. *Journal for Learning Through the Arts,* 10(1). Retrieved on October 10, 2015, from *http://escholarship.org/uc/item/67d5s216.*

Soto, G. (1993). *Too many tamales.* New York: Putnam & Grossett Group.

Spivey, N. N. & King, J. R. (1989). Readers as writers composing from sources. *Reading Research Quarterly, 24*(1), 7–26.

Steig, W. (1988). *Brave Irene.* New York: Farrar, Straus and Giroux.

Tapply, W. G. (2002). Point of view. *The Writer,* 115(8), 26–28.

Tarshis, L. (2013). *I survived the Japanese tsunami, 2011.* I Survived. New York: Scholastic.

The Homestead Act went into effect May 20, 1862. (n.d.). Retrieved on October 10, 2015, from *http://www.americaslibrary.gov/jb/civil/jb_civil_homested_1.html.*

The moment. (October 13, 2006). *Know Your World Extra,* 10–13.

Tomlinson, C. A. & Allan, S. D. (2000). *Leadership for differentiating schools & classrooms.* Alexandria, VA: ASCD.

Tompkins, G. (2010). *Literacy for the 21st Century: A balanced approach*. New York: Allyn & Bacon.

Turner, G. T. (1989). *Take a walk in their shoes: Biographies of 14 Outstanding African Americans*. New York: Dutton.

Twohy, M. (2013). *Outfoxed*. New York: Simon & Schuster.

Wagner, R. K., Muse, A. E. & Tannenbaum, K. R. (2007). Promising avenues for better understanding implications of vocabulary development for reading comprehension. In *Vocabulary acquisition: Implications for reading comprehension* (pp. 276–291). New York: Guilford.

Walmsley, S. (2006). Getting the big idea: A neglected goal for reading comprehension. *The Reading Teacher, 60*(3), 281–285. DOI: 10. 1598RT 60.3.9.

Walther, M. & Fuhler, C. (2008). Pairing fiction and nonfiction books. *Book Links, 18*(2), 22–23.

Warner, P. (n.d.). *How to write a mini-mystery*. FictionTeachers.com. Retrieved on October 10, 2015, from *http://www.fictionteachers.com/fictionclass/mystery.html*.

Washburn, E. & Cavagnetto, A. (2013). Using argument as a tool for integrating science and literacy. *The Reading Teacher, 67*(2), 127–136.

Wells, R. A. & Shaughnessy, M. F. (2009). An Interview with Carol Ann Tomlinson. *North American Journal of Psychology*, 11(3), 643–648.

Wheeler, E. B. (1998-2001). *The case of the ruined roses (Solve-It 28)*. MysteryNet's Kids Mysteries. Retrieved on October 10, 2015, from http://kids.mysterynet.com/solveit/.

Wilawan, S. (2011). Effects of lexical cohesion and macrorules on EFL students' main idea comprehension. *Reading Improvement, 48*(2) 71–87.

Wilhelm, J. D. (1999). Focus on drama. *Instructor,* 109(4), 45–48.

Wilhelm, J. & Otto, W. (2001). *Improving comprehension with think-aloud strategies*. New York: Scholastic. Retrieved on October 10, 2015, from *http://teacher.scholastic.com/reading/ bestpractices/comprehension/genrechart.pdf*.

Willems, M. (2004). *Knuffle bunny: A cautionary tale*. New York: Scholastic.

Witherell, N. & McMackin, M. C. (2002). *Graphic organizers and activities for differentiating instruction in reading*. New York: Scholastic.

Writing about the ocean. (n.d.). Washington, D.C.: Library of Congress. Retrieved on October 10, 2015, from *http://www.americaslibrary.gov/aa/carson/aa_carson_ocean_1.html*.

Zingher, G. (2011). Up and down tales: The theme of elevators. *School Library Monthly, 27*(8), 27–28.

Capstone / Heinemann-Library Resources

Brett, F. (2015). *Your skeletal system works!* Your Body Systems. North Mankato, MN: Capstone.

Burgan, M. (2016). *Daring Play: How a Courageous Jackie Robinson Transformed Baseball.* Captured History Sports. North Mankato, MN: Capstone.

Dahl, M. (2013). *The return of Abracadabra.* Hocus Pocus Hotel. North Mankato, MN: Capstone.

Dowdeswell, E., Dowdeswell, J. & Seddon, A. (2015). *Ernest Shackleton: Polar explorer.* Heinemann First Library. Chicago, IL: Heinemann Library.

Iyer, R. (2015). *Endangered rain forests: Investigating rain forests in crisis.* Endangered Earth North Mankato, MN: Capstone.

Maddox, J. (2015). *Outfield outcast.* Jake Maddox JV. North Mankato, MN: Capstone.

Olson, G. M. (2011). *Polar bears' search for ice: A Cause and Effect Investigation.* Fact Finders. North Mankato: MN: Capstone.

Peschke, M. (2013). *Cupcake queen.* Kylie Jean. North Mankato, MN: Capstone.

Phillips, J. (2014). *Girls research! Amazing tales of female scientists.* North Mankato: MN: Capstone.

Shores, L. (2011). *How to make a liquid rainbow.* Hands-On Science Fun. North Mankato, MN: Capstone.

Additional Resources

List of primary source resources from the Library of Congress (LOC), retrieved October 10, 2015:

http://www.loc.gov/teachers/additionalresources/relatedresources/world/primary.html

http://www.loc.gov/teachers/usingprimarysources/finding.html

Maupin House
capstone

At Maupin House by Capstone Professional, we continue to look for professional development resources that support grades K–8 classroom teachers in areas, such as these:

• Literacy

• Language Arts

• Content-Area Literacy

• Research-Based Practices

• Assessment

• Inquiry

• Technology

• Differentiation

• Standards-Based Instruction

• School Safety

• Classroom Management

• School Community

If you have an idea for a professional development resource, visit our Become an Author website at: *http://www.capstonepub.com/classroom/professional-development/become-an-author/*

There are two ways to submit questions and proposals.

You may send them electronically to: proposals@capstonepd.com

You may send them via postal mail. Please be sure to include a self-addressed stamped envelope for us to return materials.

Acquisitions Editor
Capstone Professional
1 N. LaSalle Street, Suite 1800
Chicago, IL 60602